GANG WARS OF LONDON

GANG WARS OF LONDON

HOW THE STREETS OF THE CAPITAL BECAME A BATTLEGROUND

WENSLEY CLARKSON

JOHN BLAKE

Published by John Blake Publishing Ltd,
3 Bramber Court, 2 Bramber Road,
London W14 9PB, England

www.johnblakepublishing.co.uk

First published in hardback in 2005
Paperback edition published 2009

ISBN: 978 1 84454 831 6

British Library Cataloguing-in-Publication Data:

A catalogue record for this book is available from the British Library.

Design by www.envydesign.co.uk

Printed in the UK by CPI William Clowes Beccles NR34 7TL

1 3 5 7 9 10 8 6 4 2

Papers used by John Blake Publishing are natural, recyclable products made from
wood grown in sustainable forests. The manufacturing processes conform to the
environmental regulations of the country of origin.

To Jimmy, Charlie, Johnny, Tony and all the other old faces who'd turn in their graves if they could see their beloved London today

'He is an outsider and a rebel, a poor man who refuses to accept the normal rules of poverty and establishes his freedom by means of the only resources within the reach of the poor, strength, bravery, cunning and determination.'

E.J. HOBSBAWM, BANDITS

ACKNOWLEDGEMENTS

I WISH TO EXTEND MY GRATITUDE to the following individuals, without whose kind support this book would not have been possible: Freddie Foreman, Jamie Foreman, Piers Thompson, Peter Wilson, Dogan Arif, Jimmy Payne, Josh Feltham, Bob Downside, Billy McGuigan, Adam Bennet, Ronnie Shadwell, Bill Brown, Bernie the Bolt, Paddy Turnbill, Nigel Goldman, Tony Cashman, Bennie Dudman, Geoff Garvey, John McShane, Malcolm World, James Freyne, Cracker Jack, the Moody family, Bernie Khan, Bill Forman, John Aitkens, Roy Dennis, Fred Hayes, Joey Pyle, Mona Stanton, Tony Wiseman, the Edmunds clan, the families of three of the biggest 'families' in London, and everyone else who's helped out on this and all my True Crime books down the years.

Also, my thanks should go to the wonderful sources of Google and MSN, which have helped me with numerous leads about today's Ganglands of London.

Quotations from written material appear, with few exceptions, without the editorial '*sic*'. When it seems that a word was inadvertently missing, it has been added for the sake of clarity. Mistakes in punctuation, grammar and spelling have been corrected in certain instances, but in others it was felt that retaining an error helped convey the flavour of a document and the style of the person being quoted. Some names have been changed, because many of those linked to the most dangerous gangsters still fear their retribution. Many scenes have been constructed through available documents and allegations provided to the author.

CONTENTS

AUTHOR'S NOTE

In *Gang Wars of London*, my aim has been to chart the development of crime in the capital since the end of the last war right up until today's cold-blooded invasion by criminals from all over the globe. It's inevitable that I've missed out a few of the characters who've helped create the villainous fabric of our capital city. So, to those individuals I say sorry, although I'm not sure if any of them will mind!

The intention of *Gang Wars of London* is to chronicle not only the history of London's underworld but also reveal for the first time the chilling activities of the latest, new breed of gangsters who are turning our historic streets into the crime capital of the world.

Overall, the most important result this book can achieve is to expose London as a hotbed of gangsterdom, where crime continues to thrive amid great wealth and civility. It's a unique combination you won't find anywhere else in the world, and I hope you enjoy reading this book as much as I have enjoyed writing it.

Wensley Clarkson, London, 2010

GLOSSARY

BLAGGER   Robber

BOAT   Face

BIRD   Prison sentence

BRIEF   Solicitor

CHARLIE   Cocaine

CLOCK   Notice

COZZERS   Police officers

FACE   Top criminal

FLOPHOUSE   Hideout after robbery

MONKEY   £500

NCIS   National Criminal Intelligence Service

NONCE   Sex molester

OLD LAG   Long-term prisoner

ON THE KNOCK   Credit

ON THE LAM   On the run

PAVEMENT ARTIST   Robber

PONY   £50

STRETCH   Stay in prison

TEAM   Gang of robbers

VERBALLING   Framed by police

INTRODUCTION

CRIME IS LONDON'S BIGGEST SINGLE INDUSTRY. That's not an easy statistic to handle, is it? Britain under New Labour turned into a gold rush for the country's underworld. And when gangsters spend their millions they even help keep legitimate businesses afloat, especially in London's tough inner-city areas.

Ever-shrinking police recruitment combined with officers assigned away from the usual criminal haunts has left the way clear for the underworld to thrive. And the spiralling cost of living under Labour has helped those same villains charge more for drugs in London than anywhere else in Britain, giving them even fatter profits.

The city's criminals make more than £2 billion a year. New Labour came into power promising that crime bosses would have all their assets frozen, and any companies helping known villains would face multi-million-pound fines. But like so many politicians' promises, it's become a matter of easier said than done. To date, only a small percentage of criminals have had their ill-gotten gains confiscated. The rest of them continue to thrive.

A succession of Home Secretaries have insisted that targeting businesses and individuals linked to these so-called 'Super gangsters' will eventually smoke them out. But one former South London drugs baron, now living in a £5 million villa on the Costa del Sol, tells me that, 'They're living in cloud-cuckoo-land. No one's gonna stop these characters making millions every year off crime in London.'

Back in 1998 Jack Straw, New Labour's first Home Secretary, vowed that the police would seize assets if they could prove 'on the balance of probability' that gangsters were living off the proceeds

of their crimes. The police pushed for this power so they could grab 'dirty money' from the bank accounts of major criminals involved with drugs, money laundering, counterfeiting, smuggling and computer fraud. At the time Roy Penrose, head of the Yard's 'elite' National Crime Squad (NCS), insisted that, 'The people involved often don't hide their wealth under a bushel. The natural thing to do is flaunt it – especially the ladies of the family. Profit is the only thing that drives these people. But we'll get them in the end.'

Investigators at The Assets Recovery Agency (ARA), as it was called, had been tearing their hair out trying to confiscate cash from gangsters ever since legislation was introduced in 2002, but found it virtually impossible to prove anything 'beyond reasonable doubt'. Then in January 2007 it was announced that the ARA would be abolished and merged with the Serious Organised Crime Agency (SOCA), because it had become an enormous white elephant, costing the taxpayer almost £100 million while seizing only £13.7 million in the previous year.

A National Criminal Intelligence Service (NCIS) study into London's gangsters showed that of hundreds of criminal drug gangs examined, more than 60 per cent dealt in cannabis, half in cocaine and a similar number in heroin, and about 40 per cent in so-called synthetic drugs such as ecstasy. But because cocaine costs 10 to 20 per cent more in London than anywhere else in Britain the big firms have been doing most of their business in the capital, some of them making millions of pounds *every week*.

The big boys decided long ago that it's much smarter to put money into a drugs deal than dirty your hands by 'going across the pavement', as they used to call robbery back in the 1970s and early '80s when John Thaw and Dennis Waterman, of ITV's *The Sweeney*, were screeching around London in their Ford Granada emulating real-life gun battles with armed blaggers. Drugs money

is laundered through reinvestment in pubs, restaurants, clubs and even 'car fronts', otherwise known as open-air used-car lots. Criminals also dip in and out of property deals, often working with 'legit' nominees. One well-known London property dealer, who was greedy enough to go into 'partnership' with a notorious west London villain, was shot dead after failing to come up with £600,000 owed on a deal.

Another not so well-known source of income for big-name gangsters is the trade in counterfeit currency. A lot of villains have been swift to pick up on this. Barclays Bank recently intercepted £1.7 million-worth of fake money, and it is thought that more than £200 million in forged notes is floating around at any one time.

Today many in the Metropolitan Police (the Met) are pushing to introduce New York-style, so-called 'Zero Tolerance' on the streets of the capital. Ironically, several notorious criminals have been driven over here from the US in recent years because of that very same policy. It's believed that more than a dozen of New York and LA's most fearsome street-gang members are now operating in Britain.

But what of the future of London's underworld? Will all the 'old-school' gangsters survive as numerous others – most of whom are foreign – try to muscle in on the capital's criminal potential?

London has become a key staging post for teams of smugglers dealing in everything from people to drugs. HM Revenue and Customs and the NCIS have set up specialist squads to monitor and infiltrate organised-crime gangs operating in the British capital. But it seems highly unlikely that these steps will prevent the continued emergence of criminals from all over the world. Some foreign gangsters even use more junior London born-and-bred 'faces' to front their operations in the capital. 'That way, no one really knows what they're up to,' explained one British hood.

3

So, ironically, these sinister – often nameless – foreign gangsters are helping the lower-end local London criminals survive. 'No one dares cross these foreign gangs because most of them are much colder than us,' explained ex-bank robber and south London face, Gordon McShane. 'One wrong move and you're dead. It's as simple as that.' As one senior Scotland Yard detective recently explained, 'The UK is full of rich pickings for foreign criminals, and it's going to take more than a few brave words from a couple of politicians to clean out the vermin.'

According to Metropolitan Police sources it's now estimated that at least 300 organised criminal gangs are operating in London and the Southeast of England, generating tens of millions of pounds in illegal profits. The startling scale of crime in the capital is revealed in the most comprehensive analysis yet by the NCIS, which carried out exhaustive surveillance of the biggest and most deadly criminal organisations.

Many London-based gangs now have full-time operatives in the Netherlands, the key point of distribution for cocaine, heroin, cannabis and ecstasy in Europe. But London-based gangsters are also increasingly diversifying into crimes such as fraud, cigarette smuggling and illegal immigration in an effort to boost profits. In an emerging trend, many gangs are also forming new alliances with other groups to try to exploit different illegal activities.

The NCIS report says that 80 per cent of gangs forging alliances are engaged in drug trafficking, mostly in Class A drugs such as heroin, cocaine and ecstasy. But crime groups are diversifying, with 20 per cent of drugs gangs now also operating excise frauds by either smuggling cigarettes or engaging in VAT fraud. Cigarette smuggling is currently one of the so-called boom crimes, costing the exchequer an estimated £3.8 billion a year in lost revenue. Gangs often use the same routes for smuggling drugs and cigarettes

4

that they do for illegal human traffic, one of the biggest growth areas in London crime in recent years.

The Met believes it has identified most of the crime gangs in London, which use at least 24 different languages. Almost half (47 per cent) are classed as 'cultural networks' whose members are bound by a common language or homeland. And these gangs are responsible for a third of today's murders in London. By contrast, only 9 per cent of the gangs are centred on one family. Forty-two per cent are neighbourhood-based or headed by gangsters who met in jail. The remaining two per cent met via the internet to commit fraud or exchange paedophilia images. If a group of people works together to commit crimes, that makes it a gang.

Two-thirds of gangs are involved in Britain's massive £7 billion-a-year drugs trade, and many operate across international borders. But many gangs are highly adaptable, switching between drug dealing, prostitution, fraud or people-smuggling as opportunities arise.

Drugs have caused the biggest change in the capital's underworld over the past 35 years. Taking narcotics is now an established practice in today's society, almost as natural as drinking a pint of beer. A staggering 97 per cent of London clubbers have taken drugs and 57 per cent do so regularly. In the middle-class dinner parties of the suburbs a line of 'Charlie' with your coffee is almost as natural as an after-dinner mint, and the under-thirties spend more on ecstasy than the entire country spends on tea and coffee.

According to a Home Office study, 'Tackling Local Drug Markets', there are 50 million drug deals each year in London. Drug-related stories in national newspapers refer to a vast range of drug-takers across all of our society: plumbers, photographers, psychiatrists, doctors, journalists, receptionists, accountants, actors, dancers, chefs, waiters, investment bankers, TV executives, models, airline cabin crew, solicitors, barristers and even police officers. The British Medical Association says that 13,000 doctors have a drugs problem.

It is no longer possible to claim that adolescent drug-takers come from socially deprived families. In Notting Hill, west London, heroin, cannabis, cocaine and ecstasy are as readily available as antiques are from little shops and street markets. Wealthy, often millionaire, residents say they like getting their drugs at the same time as their weekly shopping.

To meet this demand world production of cocaine has more than doubled in the past ten years and that of heroin has tripled, as drugs have been established as an integral part of London's economic system. Meanwhile, the capital's drug barons are happy to pay customs officers a lot of cash for each truck or aircraft 'mule' waved through. But those payments consist of nothing more than a tiny slice of the tens of millions of pounds profit many drug barons earn each year.

So, many of London's citizens must wonder if it is beyond the enterprise, skill, devotion and undoubted bravery of the Met Police to stop gangsters from flooding the streets of the capital with narcotics. To understand why they have failed we have to look at who the new drug barons are and the role they play in London's economy.

So there we have it: hidden beneath its glamorous façade as one of the world's most fashionable cities is a 'netherland' of criminality. London truly is a place where crime pays.

PROLOGUE

MORE THAN 500 YEARS AGO THE Bishops of Rochester and Winchester bought properties along the edge of the River Thames between Lambeth, Southwark and Wandsworth, which their successors leased out. In the reign of Henry VIII, the Bishop of Rochester's cook, Richard Ross, poisoned the soup at a banquet and became the sole victim of Henry's new penalty for poisoners when he was boiled alive. Meanwhile, the Bishop of Winchester's Thameside territory became notorious for its brothels and carnival atmosphere, which was further enhanced by bear-baiting rings, theatres and the first of the South Bank pleasure gardens. All these attractions encouraged the criminals of the day to mingle in the crowds to pick pockets and scavenge off the rich visitors, before heading back to their homes in the dreadful slum areas close to the river.

Then came the railways: Waterloo Station influenced the banks of the Thames to such a degree that it dragged the residential neighbourhood down even further. The riverside turned into a dismal region of filthy, run-down and overcrowded properties – dominated by violence and deprivation. The area never properly shook off the stench of real poverty until more than 100 years later when the combined efforts of Hitler's bombing raids and the economic realities of life in post-war Britain provided fresh hope for the inhabitants of the Thames-side slums. The descendants of those disease-ridden ghetto victims were encouraged to turn their backs on the cobbled streets and start afresh in the suburbs, although old habits die hard and many of them couldn't shake off their criminal instincts.

It was in the years during and just prior to the Second World War that many of the most notorious outlaws in recent British criminal history were born and raised. Unemployment and the Depression had already swept the nation in the 1930s, with firms laying off their workforces virtually every week. As queues outside labour exchanges grew, clothes became threadbare and food scarce. Across the Atlantic the Depression hit even harder and provoked bloody riots in many US cities. In Europe there was also the sound of Nazi jackboots, sparking a flood of Jewish refugees to flee from Germany.

With money so scarce, it was hardly surprising that so many London children were up to no good from a very early age. Many quickly grew up to appreciate the thrill of grabbing a bar of chocolate from the corner-shop counter and dashing out the door. It was a buzz some of them would spend the rest of their lives trying to replicate.

When the Second World War broke out, rationing was soon put in place in London and throughout the nation, so few luxuries were available, and with most men away fighting on two fronts, crime rapidly increased. The blitzed streets of London were like one big adventure playground for gangs of young tearaways.

During those war years policemen and local youths were regularly involved in clashes, and the long arm of the law knew few restraints. Many kids had their collars felt for the first time by the local constabulary before they were even ten years old. Their personalities developed reflecting the behaviour, attitude, interests, motives and feelings about the world at that difficult time, all of which especially influenced the way they related to other people, with many instantly distrusting strangers.

London's post-war youths emerged as a restless, rebellious generation, determined to make a mark for themselves in the world. But while many of them committed numerous petty crimes, they still retained certain standards and even had codes they abided by. Targeting a man walking along the street and stealing his watch was frowned upon, while raiding cigarette wholesalers or shops was totally legitimate.

Every youngster out on London's streets back then was fascinated by guns. Most had their own toy popguns, and a few had even managed to find real weapons through fathers or grandfathers fighting in Europe or further afield. Not surprisingly, many children longed to know what it was like to fire a gun, so kept their eyes and ears peeled for an opportunity to steal one when the moment was right.

By the age of 13 most of these street-savvy kids had little need for any further education. Many were bright, quick-witted teenagers with an eye for the main chance, and they'd already started earning a crust through crime and by lugging crates around various markets. To the adults who employed them these types of street urchins seemed a humorous, happy-go-lucky bunch, and they were surprisingly hard workers.

Usually, these newly formed gangs of youths met at least twice a week in one particular place, either a café or a youth club. Certain characters emerged as the leaders of these tearaways who were soon specialising in smash-and-grab raids on phone boxes and snatching handbags from unattended cars.

On Saturdays many of these street kids went shoplifting to the big department stores in wealthy areas such as Knightsbridge and Kensington. As legendary criminal Freddie Foreman later explained, 'We all wanted to nick from people who had the money in the first place. I'd snatch at cash registers and grab cash from places like Dorothy Perkins, which was one of my favourites. You could get fistfuls of money out of the cash dropped by the changing rooms. Then you'd have a taxi waiting for you just round the corner.'

Another popular chain was Stone's Electrical Supplies, where washing machines and fridges were displayed on the pavement outside shops. One gang member would go inside and chat to the storekeeper and keep them occupied while his mates made off with the goods.

The Second World War was supposed to have brought out the best in the majority of Londoners. True, there were acts of heroism and sacrifice on foreign fields and seas, as well as on a Home Front battered by Luftwaffe bombs. But for some, the onset of war brought new opportunities and profits. Crime in the capital flourished like never before. Many of those working the 'black market' were often deserting British, American or Canadian servicemen.

One of the biggest headaches for a government desperate to maintain the discipline of rationing and the supply of scarce goods and foodstuffs were the London docks – a magnet for theft, betting and gaming (then illegal), prostitution, and violent robberies, even rapes. But the major problem was looting. During wartime the offence carried the death penalty under the Defence of the Realm Act, but in practice the guilty offenders tended to get no more than five years.

While Home Guard soldiers protected bombsites, undamaged factories and warehouses were left unwatched – and were easy pickings for thieves, and breaking and entering increased dramatically during the war. The cold, hard face of organised crime would eventually emerge from the bombed-out ruins of London. Years later notorious criminal 'Mad' Frankie Fraser reminisced that the war was a great time to make money – as long as you weren't in the services. Avoiding the call-up was crucial, of course, and a lucrative business sprang up in fake certificates, instantly turning 30-year-olds into 40- year-olds, and giving healthy young men dodgy hearts and flat feet.

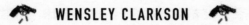

The rosy, retrospective view of London as relatively crime-free during the war has long since been demolished, notably by Edward Smithies in *Crime in Wartime* (1982), and it is now recognised that many criminals continued their normal careers, seizing the fresh opportunities presented by emergency wartime conditions. The blackout in particular provided useful cover for criminal activities of many kinds. Theft and prostitution rackets flourished. Confidence tricksters found new victims among the many servicemen and other visitors briefly passing through London. Rationing 'fiddles' and pilfering offered easy profits, and most Londoners took advantage of the black market in scarce goods at some point or other. In fact, the depleted Metropolitan Police Force and the courts were busy throughout the war, and their records reflect the continuing problem.

Some thieves didn't even hesitate to rob the dead and the injured. As one woman lay injured in the bombed-out rubble of the Café de Paris in Piccadilly, a man came past and leaned down, she thought to feel her pulse. He was actually stealing a ring from her finger.

In the first eight weeks of the London Blitz a total of 390 cases of looting were reported to the police. The Lord Mayor of London suggested that notices should be posted throughout the city, reminding the population that looting was punishable by hanging or shooting. However, the courts continued to treat the crime leniently. When a gang of army deserters were convicted of looting in Kent the judge handed down sentences ranging from five years' penal servitude to eight years' hard labour. Some critics pointed out that Nazi Germany suffered less from this type of crime because looters were routinely executed there.

Widespread fraud was another consequence of the Blitz. Homeowners who had lost their properties during air raids had to wait until after the war to receive full compensation from the

Government, but they could claim an advance of £500 (approximately £20,000 in today's money) with £50 (£2,000) for furniture and £20 (£800) for clothes. So many people lost their homes in London during 1940 that officials of the local National Assistance Office did not have enough time to check people's claims. This was further complicated by people claiming their identity cards and ration books had also been destroyed during an air raid. It wasn't until 1941 that the government realised they were paying out more than they should, and extra staff were brought in to make more detailed checks on the claims being made, effectively filling that fraudulent hole.

It was during the war that selling goods in violation of official regulations became known as the black market. Parliament passed legislation enabling the courts to fine up to £500, with or without two years' imprisonment, plus three times the total capital involved in the transaction. Eventually, around 900 inspectors were employed to ensure that the Ministry of Food rules were obeyed by customers, retailers and wholesalers. Investigators discovered that farmers and smallholders provided most of the black-market food.

Juvenile delinquents were blamed for a high rate of crime in crowded Tube shelters. Often a thief would quietly carry off someone's bags as they slept. Teenage pickpockets also kept busy in public air-raid shelters while others burgled the houses of those who'd gone to seek safety.

Raids on Home Guard armaments stores were a regular occurrence during the war. In February 1943 seven teenage boys stole 2,000 rounds of Sten gun ammunition. The following month three 17-year-olds held up the cashier at the Ambassador cinema in Hayes, on the outskirts of London, with three of those same Sten guns. After they were arrested they admitted that they'd taken part in 43 similar raids in London.

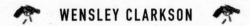

By the middle of the war London was suffering from an acute shortage of alcohol. This was solved by the illegal production of what became known as 'hooch'. Organised gangs set up all over the capital, mixing pure alcohol with juniper and almond essences. Others used industrial alcohol and methylated spirits. However, people were soon dying of acute alcoholic poisoning as a result of drinking hooch. As many of the victims were soldiers, the commanders of many American camps in Britain eventually issued a free bottle of gin or whisky from camp stores to each man going on leave, in an effort to protect them from the evils of hooch.

But much of the crime during the war came from the desperation of people who'd seen the horrors of the First World War, followed by years of the Depression, only to be followed by more sacrifice. Many of the men involved in the black market had never worked, and they were handling exotic goods rarely, if ever, seen before. In the 1940s it was oranges and bananas but by the 1950s and '60s the stakes were much higher than just a bit of ducking and diving on the black market. So it was no surprise that the crooks who'd cut their teeth in wartime crime went on to dominate the ganglands of London in the years following the end of the Second World War.

PART 1
1945–60: WAR-DAMAGED GOODS

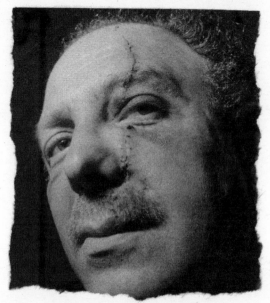

Jack Spot, one of the era's most
powerful gang leaders.

'There wasn't any politeness. They knew what I'd come for.
And I sailed right in.'

NOTORIOUS POST-WAR GANGSTER JACK SPOT

VE DAY, MAY 1945. HUNDREDS OF thousands of people swarmed onto the streets of London, many in a frenzy preparing street parties, dragging out timber they'd been saving for a huge bonfire, and climbing up ladders to hang out bunting and Union Flags. Pianos were pushed out in front of terraced houses and low-rise red-brick blocks of flats. Bells rang out, and as it got dark the streetlights came on for the first time since the beginning of the Blitz five years earlier. At local town halls, fireworks exploded in the sky above as searchlights danced in the moonlight. People sat in the street or stood over bonfires as effigies of Hitler roasted. The war was over... and new opportunities now beckoned for the smartest operators.

Crime had been bred for post-war London, and the underworld was about to take over in the long term. The number of murders in England and Wales rose from 115 in 1940 to 141 in 1945 – an increase of 22 per cent. During the same period there was a 44 per cent increase in wounding incidents and 65 per cent in grievous wounding. The whole ethos of living and surviving in places like London was to change forever. Some of the capital's residents had discovered that the way to thrive was to completely ignore the law, and, for the most part, it would then ignore their transgressions.

With new weapons, and their old, ruthless methods, the pre-war gangs quickly re-established a grip on the newly reopened racecourses after 1945. The war had even encouraged the introduction of the Italian 'springer' knife in place of the open razor. The springer knife was a blade concealed in a metal or leather handle which was released by the touch of a knob – a thin, double-edged stiletto blade then sprang out.

In Soho, protection rackets flourished. Soldiers of all nations crowded into the capital after VE Day with money to spend. Over at Cable Street, in the East End, the area became known as the 'coloured man's village', where African, West Indian, Asian and Indian seamen were the most regular customers in the pubs and clubs. Many tried to get work ashore but there was a severe shortage of rooms. Few landladies would take them in, and the hostels were all overcrowded. Local residents even put together a petition demanding that the area be cleaned up.

So it was inevitable that after the war, gangsters such as the up-and-coming Jack Spot (real name Jack Comer) would emerge in the debris of London. 'Spot' was a small-time crook until he hooked up with a bunch of Italians called the Carlino Gang who'd devised an ingenious way of stealing cars. One of the Carlino mob had seduced a pretty blonde clerk at the Petroleum Office in London. When car owners sent in petrol coupons, she managed to 'mislay' their log books – for which the Carlinos paid her £20 apiece. They then stole cars that closely matched the descriptions in the logbooks, fixed false number plates, and suitably bleached and overprinted the logbook entry before openly selling the cars at market price.

Eastender Jack Spot helped finance their work and quickly made up to £250 a week – big money in those days. But then the Carlino gang were arrested by the police after the tax disc details on one car didn't match up to its logbook. Spot, as the 'financier', was so far removed from the actual crimes he got away without any problems. Avoiding direct involvement in crime was paramount for characters like Spot if they were to build an empire.

After the war many London crooks returned to their former trades, such as smash-and-grab robberies, safe-breaking, stealing cars and just about every petty crime imaginable. Violent armed robberies soon began occurring on a regular basis. Criminals started using loaded weapons, and the police genuinely feared London was turning into something akin to Chicago in the 1930s.

In December 1945, 2,000 Met police officers swamped Soho, checking the papers of everyone they came across in pubs, cafés, dance halls and gambling clubs. The following month, checkpoints were set up on all major roads leading in and out of London and all the Thames crossings between Tower Bridge and Hammersmith. Police hoped to round up some of the 20,000 deserters reckoned to still be on the run. All it really did was flush out a few small-timers, while the bigger fish continued climbing the ranks of the underworld.

Jack Spot quickly got to know his regulars at the illegal gambling dens – 'speilers' – that he had begun opening in the capital. Many of those punters were genuine big-time villains who thought nothing of nicking a large consignment of rationed goods that needed half-a-dozen lorries to shift them. Spot also encountered fences, men who amassed a fortune by handling and then selling-on stolen goods. In Spot's eyes, they had the most important job of all.

Back then in the post-war era practically every commodity was still in short supply. Printing paper, pepper, ice-cream powder, paraffin, meat, textiles, cigarettes, petrol – you name it. But food yielded the highest profit. After the war the government's rationing system still restricted the use of certain food in the home, but not in restaurants, which was virtually a licence to print money, if you could get the meat.

Black marketeers scoured the countryside buying broken-down horses, which would later be served up as choice rump steaks in high-class establishments. As one old lag explained, 'Even the toughest of meat, if pounded long enough by a hefty table-tennis bat studded with gramophone needles, could be served up tender as lamb.'

Jack Spot and his pals soon conceived what they believed would be a real money-spinner. Employing two or three cronies, they clinched a deal with a black marketeer to supply ponies from the

New Forest in Hampshire and invested in vast consignments of cigarettes. They bought two vans, employed their own labour, and bribed truck drivers to look the other way, supping a cup of tea in a pre-agreed café while their vehicles were stolen. Then the load would be transferred to one of Spot's vehicles. Later, the trucks would be found abandoned and empty.

Up-and-coming young criminals emerged from a period during which they'd been steeped in terror, complete with unpleasant memories and fears that were now permanently stored in their minds. And virtually all of them promised themselves that they'd never struggle financially in the way their fathers had done.

By the early 1950s many of the capital's young criminals were being called up for National Service, which came as quite a shock to them, since most were already earning a decent wedge ducking and diving around the streets of London. The army taught them the importance of being fit, although many of them had problems obeying orders. So it was no surprise that after these characters emerged from the army they immediately linked up once again with all their dodgy old London pals.

But these hoodlums knew the rules of the game on their manor. Not grassing-up your mates was taken for granted. But to become a real outlaw you had to do everything your way. Nobody and nothing else mattered – apart from your family and your fellow gang members, of course – and that made you more feared and respected. Some people saw these young villains as budding Robin Hoods, striking blows against the traditional enemy, the police – known as 'the filth', 'the cozzers', 'plod' and all those other derogatory names. Even back then some of the smallest crimes were celebrated and talked about in local pubs, because these 'capers' represented getting one over on the 'Establishment'.

Many played up to their growing reputations. When they walked into certain taverns, the place really did go quiet, like it does in the movies. But some of these characters wanted to be more than just a bit of local muscle; they saw themselves as leaders of men, artful gangsters capable of taking on and beating anyone. Their criminal ascendancy owed much to the transitional period that Britain was going through during the 1940s and '50s. This was a time when spivs were still the people to talk to if you wanted a piece of decent meat for tea. Wartime rationing had continued for years after the end of hostilities in Europe, so people – especially the poor – were forced to go out and find those little luxuries for themselves.

This new breed of young criminal reflected an attitude that prevailed at that time. They wanted money – something their poverty-stricken, and often absent, fathers had never managed to bring to the table in any quantity – and believed that it would create happiness. And, above all, many of them were quick learners and observers. They'd watch their contemporaries getting out and about, wheeling and dealing in everything from coffee to nylons. This new breed of criminal understood the potency of money and had decided from a very young age that they would be rich, come what may.

While most of these characters were, in many ways, cold-blooded thugs, they also had a sense of social conscience and showed great loyalty to those they liked. They knew when to help rather than hinder. They were shrewd and arrogant but wanted wealth so badly that they were prepared to milk their own popularity. They were, in the words of one who knew them back then, 'a strange combination of hard heart and soft mind, capable of beating a man but also just as likely to help an old lady cross the street'. These new young criminals were genuine creatures of circumstance – complex, contradictory and ultimately very dangerous – mainly because they did not know where the traditional lines or boundaries in life existed.

And in the 1940s and '50s they were fast becoming addicted to crime. After initially burgling and carrying out raids on London's docks, it was inevitable they'd graduate to armed robberies. A classic blagging would be on a man collecting takings from a speiler. But these gangs soon moved on to bigger jobs, such as blowing safes and jumping over counters in banks to grab handfuls of cash. They also hit Post Offices, where security was rubbish, and some companies left wages in the safe overnight (there were no cheques or monthly salary slips back then).

The London underworld in those post-war days was an ever-shifting nucleus of people moving backwards and forwards across the capital. The West End thrived because there was a need for people to enjoy themselves, but now drugs, blackmail and 'long firms' – fake businesses that villains persuaded gullible people, and sometimes even High-Street banks, to invest in – could be added to an already potent mix.

In the late 1940s Jack Spot decided that he wanted to make a push back into the racetrack business. Spot knew that in certain parts of England local mobsters ran the reopened courses at a profit, similarly to how the Sicilian razor gang, Sabini's, had before the war. Even track officials themselves were dishing out pitches to bookies. Spot and his pals eventually focused on the royal race meeting at Ascot, just west of London, where Little Jimmy, one of his most hated enemies, and his Islington gang were trying to take over the hallowed turf. They'd already grabbed all the best pitches on the free side of Ascot, and threatened to repel Spot and his team if they made any attempt to move in.

Spot eventually saw off Little Jimmy and his Islington Boys with

ease. Then, with his own followers and the considerable support of his allies in the Upton Park and Ilford gangs of East London, Spot widened his power base by spreading his net across the entire nation's racecourses.

Spot also had to deal with the King's Cross gang, led by bookie Harry White, a curious round-faced fellow who sent his two daughters to Roedean, England's most expensive and exclusive school for girls, yet was renowned for cutting anyone who dared get in his way. Besides being a big presence at the races, White and his mob were also trying to move into the West End club scene.

Initially, Spot sent a couple of scouts to King's Cross to see what White was up to. They reported back that he had surrounded himself with even more minders than usual and was heading that very day into the West End. Spot, accompanied by his senior gang members, Sonny, Moisha and Little Hymie, headed west in his newly acquired white Cadillac. They eventually found White in a club in Sackville Street, off Piccadilly, standing at the bar drinking with racehorse trainer Tim O'Sullivan and White's mouthy minder, Big Bill.

As Spot later recalled, 'There wasn't any politeness. They knew what I'd come for. And I sailed right in.' Spot lashed out at White and hit him over the head with a bottle. White collapsed into a fireplace, and the seat of his trousers caught fire. Spot later said, 'He hollered, but though he was burned, he wasn't badly hurt.'

One of Spot's men then attacked O'Sullivan, who was beaten unconscious. Big Bill was slashed with razors and stabbed in the stomach. Spot recalled, 'They all ran – except Big Bill. He had guts, and he made a fight of it. Unluckily, that meant he got the worst of it.' By the end of the fracas, Big Bill was lying on the floor bleeding profusely from a deep knife wound. Spot got the barman to phone for an ambulance before he and his mob disappeared.

Within days, Harry White let it be known that he was planning a return battle and began assembling troops in King's Cross. White reckoned he'd wipe Spot off the map for good. Spot got together his own private army of at least 1,000 men. They were armed with Sten guns, hand grenades, service revolvers and German automatic Luger pistols. And they had plenty of ammo to spare. Tension built up across Soho, the East End and North London. Business in the dives and the speilers dipped, because people didn't want to get caught in the crossfire. Even the police were on the alert.

But no one knew when or where the battle would commence. Each side continued to dispatch scouts and put out cautious feelers to determine the strength and whereabouts of their opponents. Then Jack Spot took the initiative and phoned Harry White to find out where the battle would take place. White – suspecting Spot was trying to set him up – slammed the phone down and vanished within hours, even clearing his family out of their home. He left behind his gang, ready for battle, under the command of a character called Terrible Mike.

When Spot got back to Aldgate he called together his heavy mob and told them to 'pack it up and get rid of the ironmongery'. So they collected all the Stens, the grenades, revolvers, pistols and ammunition, loaded them into a lorry after dark, and dumped the whole lot in the Thames.

Spot's 'victory' over Harry White meant he believed he could now claim the title of 'King of the Underworld'. He immediately expected utter loyalty and respect from other villains. Instead, he got a ticking-off from the businessmen and bookies he was associated with, who were angry with him for taking on the Whites in the first place. Spot was even persuaded to go to the Essex seaside resort of Southend to cool his heels for a while and to let the dust settle. Later, Harry White recalled, 'He had done what no other man had ever been able to do in 20 years racing – he'd frightened me to death.'

In the summer of 1948, as Heathrow was being constructed to replace Croydon as London's main airport, London crime-boss Jack Spot masterminded a robbery that he believed would confirm his status as King of the Underworld. Sammy Josephs (aka Sammy Ross), a well-connected Jewish thief, told Spot that extremely valuable cargoes were kept at the airport overnight. Josephs had an inside contact prepared to let them know when the next big shipment of valuables was en route.

Spot and Ross had worked together on a series of lorry hijacks over the previous few months. Spot believed meticulous preparation was essential, so his boys joined guided tours of the airport to case the joint. Then, bulky parcels were sent from Ireland to test the lorry delivery system. Sammy Ross and another member of the team, Franny Daniels – both licensed truck drivers – found they were allowed into the area around the main customs building to pick up the parcels without an official pass.

Word then came through that a bonded warehouse inside the airport perimeter was taking delivery of £380,000-worth of diamonds and a further £280,000 of cash on the night of 24 July. Spot's team devised a plan to dope security guards with sedatives in their coffee. Then ten raiders – all wearing nylon stockings over their faces – would follow a single torch light to the customs shed where all the loot was stored. But someone on Spot's team grassed them up. By 11 p.m. all roads leading to the airport were under surveillance, 13 Flying Squad detectives lay in wait in the customs shed, and ten more were hiding in a van round the back. As Spot's team crashed in, a bloody battle ensued. Two of Spot's mob – Billy Benstead and Franny Daniels – turned round and scarpered.

Another gang member, Teddy Machin, escaped by jumping on the back of a moving truck that was on its way out of the airport compound.

The rest of the battered robbers were dragged off in waiting Black Marias. They were all convicted and received up to 12 years imprisonment. Many observers on the underworld grapevine were saying that information on the airport job had been leaked by one of Spot's own henchmen, annoyed that he hadn't been properly paid for a previous robbery.

In the winter of 1948 a pair of young tearaways known as the Kray twins, aged just 15, were getting lots of local press coverage in the East End. Reggie Kray won the London Schoolboy Boxing Championships after having been champion of Hackney. The following year he became the Southeastern Divisional Youth Club champion and the London ATC champion. His brother Ron won the Hackney schoolboy and London junior championships, and a London ATC title.

Ron and Reg also had their own gang of young hoodlums, and had been barred from most of the cinemas and dance halls in the East End. They let it be known that they kept choppers, machetes, knives, swords and a variety of other weapons beneath the bed they both slept in at their parents' home in Vallance Road, Bethnal Green.

By the age of 16 the twins had been nicked for grievous bodily harm (GBH) on three people during a teenage gang fight involving bike chains and coshes outside a dance hall in Mare Street, Hackney. The Krays were later acquitted of the charges at the Old Bailey. Ronnie boasted that he'd purchased his first gun before he'd turned 17 and that he fully expected to shoot someone 'sooner rather than later'.

The Kray twins had been brought up on a staple diet of violence. When they slept, they always placed newspapers on the floor so that they'd hear them rustle if an intruder entered the bedroom of the family home – known as 'Fort Vallance'. They let it be known on the manor that they had a pair of strong right arms and were available to the highest bidder as minders. Ronnie – the more outrageous of the two brothers – liked sharpening his cutlass on oil he spread across the doorstep of Fort Vallance. He'd often swish the blade through the air in an arc, his face contorted with venom and the anticipation of pleasure in combat. Once, he turned to his brother and said, 'Can't you see how that would stop them? Half-a-dozen blokes come at you and then *bingo*! The first one gets his head cut clean off his shoulders and it rolls on the floor. Wouldn't that make 'em run!'

Across London during the late 1940s other criminal mobs were flexing their muscles. In a club in Brixton two gangs had it out with razors and glasses hastily broken on the bar counter. It was a test of strength 'to see who was boss' and afterwards some of them shook hands. But it took four buckets of water to clear the blood from the floor.

A lot of old-time villains, plus young tearaways like the Krays and others, frequented Ziggy's Café in Cobb Street, just off Petticoat Lane in the East End. Ziggy was a smart-looking middle-aged man with a stout gut; a fat cigar was always hanging out of his mouth. His wife served the teas and lunches, and there was a police truncheon on show behind the bar. Ziggy's regulars included characters such as Sammy Wilde, a boxer from the Gold Coast of Africa. He had tribal marks cut down the side of each cheekbone and always carried a knife in a sheath attached to his waistband and often wore a small woollen beret with a coloured tassel on top. At night he made appearances on stage as a fire-eater.

A crew of teenage hoodlums often congregated by a record stall outside Ziggy's 'caff', mingling with dozens of youths from other parts of London. Amongst them were characters named Curly King, Norman Hall, Terry O'Brien, Checker Berry and Flash Ronnie. On one Sunday in 1948, Jack Spot strolled into Ziggy's followed by his henchmen, 'Little' Hymie Rosen and Moisha Blueball, all wearing beige Stetson hats. Everyone moved aside, giving them plenty of space.

Amongst the group of youths outside that day was Ronnie Kray. As Spot and his team disappeared, Ronnie turned round and asked one of the other kids, 'I wonder what would happen if I shot him?' For the first time, Ronnie was aware of the potential power wielded by the big-time gangsters.

Just after the Kray twins turned 20 in the autumn of 1953 they met Jack Spot and members of his firm in the Vienna Rooms, just off the Edgware Road, a second-floor restaurant catering for businessmen, criminals and prostitutes, which also happened to be directly opposite Edgware Road Police Station. The flamboyant Ronnie Kray had already got together a small entourage of good-looking young men to form a spy network in Soho, so he knew who all the main players were. The twins were introduced to Spot by his sidekick, Moisha Blueball, who shared their keen interest in wrestling. Moisha was a smart dresser, but what had impressed the Kray twins were his rarely shown skills as a crooked card player.

Spot and Moisha were sitting at a table alongside the twins when they were introduced to a well-spoken man called Jeff Allen. Moisha took Allen for a couple of grand in a fixed card game later that night. Allen told Moisha and the Krays to meet him in a local

pub an hour later when he'd settle his losses. Allen failed to show up, so Moisha got him on the phone. Allen told him, 'I knew all along I was being conned, and if you come near my home, you'll find me waiting with a shotgun.' Moisha was lost for words and made no attempt at collection. But the twins never forgot Jeff Allen, and he later became one of their closest friends. Anyone who had that sort of bottle was worth having on their team.

Other regulars at the Vienna Rooms at that time included Spitzel Goodman, a dapper little character with thick, black wavy hair, who at one time had been manager of Primo Carnera, the Italian heavyweight champion of the world. Then there was a West Indian called Bar, most of whose right ear was missing. He'd served seven years for shooting and wounding a club owner who owed him money. No one gave Bar any aggro.

But it was Jack Spot's old pal Jack Pokla – a respected money fiddler – whom the Kray twins were particularly keen to meet. Pokla bought stolen property from just about anyone and went on to teach the twins how a good fence operated. Another member of Spot's gang who impressed the Krays was Teddy Machin, who'd been born in Upton Park, close to the West Ham football ground. He had jet-black hair and film-star looks. He'd had a run-in with Jackie Reynolds, another Spot gang member, at the Queen's pub in Upton Park and smashed a broken glass into Reynolds's face, disfiguring him. Reynolds claimed that dozens of villains called him up to offer to help get revenge on Machin. But Reynolds refused, insisting he was still friends with Machin and that it had just been a drunken brawl which went one step too far. The Krays were impressed with such loyalty.

Initially, Jack Spot made the biggest impression on the twins. 'He was the centre of attraction wherever he went. He seemed to control London as boss of the underworld,' Reg later explained.

'Spot dressed like a screen gangster. Ron remembered him as one of the smartest men we ever met, with lovely overcoats, shirts and ties.'

In 1952 the Kray twins were called up for National Service, which led to violence, serious trouble with the military authorities, and periods in custody. After being discharged, they commenced a period of increasing control over criminals, pubs and clubs in the East End. A few years later – on 5 November 1956 – Ronnie Kray was jailed for three years for assaulting Terence Martin in a gang-related incident.

Four years later, in February 1960, Reggie Kray was imprisoned for 18 months for protection-related threats, and whilst he was in prison, Peter Rachman, the head of a violent landlord racketeering operation, gave Ronnie Kray the Esmeralda's Barn night club in Knightsbridge, which served to increase the twins' influence in the West End. They even started being seen with 'celebrities', rather than East-End criminals. And they were also secretly assisted by a wealthy banker called Alan Cooper, who needed protection from the rival Richardson gang from South London.

The Krays tested Alan Cooper by suggesting that he carry out a murder, and Cooper in turn recruited a criminal called Paul Elvey to do the work for him. Elvey was arrested after a tip-off to police, and Detective Superintendent Leonard 'Nipper' Read's team interviewed him. Elvey eventually confessed and Cooper was implicated in three attempted murders. It was Cooper who'd eventually provide much of the evidence against the Krays.

Although **Brighton Rock**, based on the book by Graham Greene, emerged as a legendary film portraying the English ganglands in the late 1940s, it seems to have been less of a favourite with the Kray twins than the Warner Brothers mobster movies of

the 1930s. Reg idolised George Raft, whose real-life connections to US mobsters later made him *persona non grata* in 1960s London, while Ron's style and mannerisms at first owed much to pre-war Hollywood. Ronnie Kray had a penchant for big American cars and by this time dressed like a 1930s Chicago gangster, with a long cashmere coat, tied in a loose belt at the waist, that reached down to his ankles. Ronnie's hair was greased and parted and he usually wore glasses. One cop at the time commented, 'He looked like Al Capone without his fedora.'

However, Ronnie Kray's style became far more Anglicised as the twins climbed the underworld ladder. Savile Row tailoring and the iconic photography of David Bailey eventually contrived to produce an image of sharp-suited menace, a mixture of businessman and boxer, which terrified rivals yet allowed the twins to move easily between gangland and the more conventional world of commerce. At times, the behaviour of the Krays suggested that they'd ceased to believe in the reality of their circumstances; it was almost as if they were appearing in a gangster film of their own creation.

The lucrative money-making schemes of many criminals had been doomed as soon as rationing finally began to ease in the early 1950s. Most simply presumed that they'd have to work a little harder to make the same money. Many scams dried up, and that's when Jack Spot linked up with a well-known Jewish 'businessman' who backed him to be the 'front man' at the Buttolph Club in Aldgate. As Spot later explained, 'It was a private club open for drinking, talking and gambling.' Spot hoped the Buttolph would be his springboard to a new level of criminality. For while speilers outside the capital were dropping like stones, London remained a boom town.

Soon the club was taking in at least £3,000 a week tax-free, and Spot now considered himself a Jewish 'Godfather'. He recalled, 'I didn't have to buy nothing. Every Jewish businessman in London made me clothes, gave me money, food, drink, everything. I was what they called a legend to the Jews. Some crook goes into a Jewish shop, says gimme clothes and a few quid; the local rabbis say, "Go and find Jack Spot. Get Jack, he'll know what to do." So they did, and I'd end up chinning a few bastards. The Robin Hood of the East End, a couple of taxi drivers once told me. "You helped everyone," they said.'

At the Buttolph Club, Jack Spot met up with some classic post-war villains, such as Rube Tarson the counterfeiter, Johnnie Zind the confidence man, Soapy Brucker the expert safe breaker, and dozens of others. The Aldgate club rapidly became a favourite rendezvous for professional criminals. Spot and his pals served drinks over the counter to an assortment of cat burglars, pickpockets, car thieves and hold-up men. And Spot told them how much easier things would be if they were properly organised.

In 1950 Spot's gang of hoods entered a bank through the front door, thanks to the expertise of a cat burglar who'd made wax impressions of all the locks and keys on a previous visit through a high window. The robbers knew all about the alarm system because of inside information supplied by someone who worked there, enabling an alarms specialist to disconnect everything. The safe was opened quickly and expertly, thanks to three safe breakers.

The getaway was equally well planned. Three new, fast cars had been stolen simultaneously the previous night. One was abandoned just 500 yards from the bank; the other two were change-over vehicles found by police two days later. The gang's haul was £5,000 in small currency, which would be worth about £150,000 by today's standards.

Two weeks later Spot's men pulled off another daring raid. This time a consignment of fur coats was driven away from a warehouse in East London at eleven o'clock at night. It wasn't until five hours later that the alarm was raised. After a couple of days the police swooped on every known suspect, looking for the fur coats, but they found nothing.

Meanwhile, Spot's Buttolph Club was being run with military precision: at five o'clock each afternoon the clerks of the Aldgate Fruit Exchange left their office and Jack Spot's so-called 'scene shifters' walked in. The blinds were pulled down and the desks dragged across the room into a side area. Long tables were then set up and chairs placed around the room. In the corner, the snack bar was set up. The Aldgate Fruit Exchange had, in minutes, been turned into the biggest gambling club in London.

The Buttolph was soon being frequented by villains from places across the river, such as Walworth and the Old Kent Road, Kennington, Lambeth, Waterloo, Blackfriars, Peckham, Camberwell and Borough. Now and again, cheapskates would be 'rowed' out of a game and not asked back – a severe black mark against any face. Spot also made a tidy profit from drinks and sandwiches.

But most important of all, the Buttolph had become a vital staging post for Spot to recruit new talent. When he heard that legendary razor man Johnny Carter was about to be released from a five-year stretch for cutting up a rival, Spot picked him up in a limo at the prison gates and gave him full-time membership of his firm, dealing out broken arms and decorating faces to order. Carter was a legendary expert with the chiv (knife), who'd literally carved up a bunch of so-called hard men in a battle over illegal bookie pitches. Carter was held in such high esteem that he was even given his own share of lucrative protection rackets, soaking up money from scores of Soho clubs, boozers and clip joints.

Jack Spot's favourite regular customer at the Buttolph was a cat burglar known as the Shepherd's Bush Kid. 'Climb! Talk about Mount Everest – that's nothing to what the Kid can do on a drainpipe,' Spot explained. 'He's a big built fellow, too, but as fit as any athlete, and in his crêpe-soled shoes he can go up the side of a house like a fly.'

The Kid concentrated on big jobs, which yielded a high return – nicking minks, diamonds and other such valuables to the tune of £500,000 during his career. But the Kid could never hold onto his money. Some nights he'd visit Spot's speiler and blow £5,000 in one session. As Spot later recalled, 'Sometimes the crowd round the faro table was so big the Kid couldn't get near it to see the play or place his bets. So he'd roll up a bunch of fivers and throw 'em over players' heads, and wherever the money landed on the layout would be the card he'd back.'

Another regular in the Buttolph was 'Tall Mick', one of the best pickpockets in London. He worked alone and was always immaculately dressed like the perfect gentleman. Mick's speciality was the so-called 'coat-and-newspaper lark'. He'd stand on a Tube train with a coat over his arm reading a newspaper, looking as if both his hands were occupied. In fact, one was exploring the hip pocket of the person next to him. Mick was also renowned for pushing through the crush in busy theatre crowds. Women's diamond brooches would disappear from the front of their dresses in a split second.

The *Sunday People* columnist Arthur Helliwell summed up the type of London speiler Jack Spot was running:

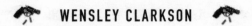

I watched gin rummy being played for £1 a point. I saw a Slippery
Sam school where the kitty averaged between £200 and £250 a hand.
I drank a glass of champagne with a suave, silver-haired, slickly
tailored character who takes a rake-off on a £15,000 to £20,000
turnover every time he runs a chemmy party. I visited a poker game
where you couldn't see the green baize for fivers, and I rounded off my
tour watching a Negro dice game that shifts its rendezvous and
changes its entrance password every night. "I'm driving a Ford V8" was
the open sesame the night I called. There were three other white men
in the dingy, smoke-filled room. The rest were zoot-suited, sombrero-
hatted, jazzily necktied coloured boys. A chocolate-coloured dandy in
a long, black overcoat with an astrakhan collar had the dice.

Jack Spot's biggest rival for the title of King of the Underworld at
this time was classic one-time smash 'n' grab merchant, Billy Hill.
He was a real West Ender, born in 1911 at Seven Dials on the
Holborn side of Leicester Square, which back then was a
Dickensian-type area filled with poverty and street beggars and just
a stone's throw from the vice dens of Soho.

Hill's mother was a 'buyer of bent gear', and his father had
multiple convictions for 'belting cozzers'. His first job as a grocer's
delivery boy came with an attractive sideline feeding his brother-
in-law information about likely targets for burglaries. Then he did
his own break-ins and quickly became an expert at 'drumming', the
speedy ransacking of a house in the owner's absence. Hill then
turned to more lucrative targets, such as the vaults and safes of
banks, building societies, cinemas and restaurants.

Hill later recalled that he got out of borstal (youth prison) at the
age of 19 as 'a tough and bitter young thug, ready to do anything
except go straight'. He added: 'The first thing I did was to buy a
couple of smart new suits and a first-class set of burglar's tools.

Then I got together my first gang. Not that I wanted to stay an ordinary screwsman for long.'

During the war, Hill had been notorious for his smash 'n' grab raids – specialising in throwing bricks into jewellery shop windows and grabbing everything in sight. Then he got banged up yet again. From his cell in Dartmoor Prison, he sent a letter to Jack Spot, whom he'd heard of through other criminals. Spot was impressed by Hill's letter and told him to contact him when he got out. On his release, Hill – desperate for cash – teamed up with a character called John the Tilter and they pretended they were detectives in order to relieve a couple of crooks of their haul of stolen parachutes, which they then sold for £500.

Initially, Spot took Hill under his wing, but Billy Hill was a reluctant sidekick to anyone, let alone Jack Spot. Then in the late 1940s, completely out of the blue, Hill – who'd quickly amassed £10,000 of his own from a rapid turnaround of robberies following his release – surprised the London underworld by announcing he was off to South Africa. He informed Spot he wanted to set up a chain of speilers on his own, but he didn't want to step on Spot's toes. Within months of settling in South Africa, Hill was arrested for assaulting one of the country's most powerful criminals after a clash about paying protection money. Hill was thrown out of the country and headed back to England. When Spot heard the news, he shrugged his shoulders and told one associate, 'Well, he'll have to start all over again, won't he?'

At first Hill kept a low profile in the north of England. Then he and two of Spot's one-time associates, Sammy Josephs and Teddy Machin, stole a Manchester bookie's safe containing £9,000. The police were soon on his trail and Hill eventually gave himself up and got a three-year stretch in Wandsworth Prison. Jack Spot reckoned the jail term would teach Hill a lesson. In prison, Hill decided that once he'd served his sentence he'd form his own strong-arm gang and then stand shoulder-to-shoulder with Jack Spot. Hill reckoned characters such as Slippery Sam, Bullnose Bertie, Billy the Long-Reach and Iron Jemmy Spike would queue up to join him.

Soon after his release Hill opened several legitimate nightclubs while expanding his criminal activities and in 1952 he began organising robberies, eventually netting more than £500,000. He also ran a cigarette-smuggling operation from Morocco during this period.

One day in the mid-1950s, Ron and Reg Kray, their brother Charlie, and a pal called Willy Malone were at Fort Vallance, the Kray family home, when the phone rang. Ron picked up the receiver, and it was Jack Spot's great rival Billy Hill on the line. He said, 'Will you come over to my flat, quick as poss?'

'OK, Billy,' responded Ron. He then told the others, 'I think he's got some kind of trouble. Let's get over there.'

The twins picked up a shooter each and departed for Hill's flat in Bayswater, West London, with older brother Charlie driving. As he walked in, Ron said to Hill, 'What's the trouble? We've bought some shooters.' Hill laughed, left them in the lounge and went into his bedroom. When he returned he tossed £500 in brand new notes onto the table and told the Krays, 'Take that few quid for your trouble and cut it up between you. I was only testing. I wanted to find out if you would get here fast or if you would blank the emergency.'

Reg Kray later recalled, 'To me, Bill was the ultimate professional criminal. I like to think that in some ways I have come close to emulating him, but in many other ways he stands alone. There will never be another Billy Hill.'

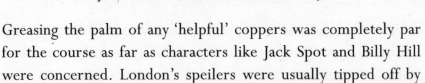

Greasing the palm of any 'helpful' coppers was completely par for the course as far as characters like Jack Spot and Billy Hill were concerned. London's speilers were usually tipped off by police for a 'fee' when a raid was on the cards, and Spot and Hill would then get 'a few mugs' in so that the regular customers escaped arrest.

Soho's brothel keepers were also helped by the police, who offered to 'adjust' certain evidence at a price. The payments covered what an officer might say in evidence relating to a police raid. Hundreds of Soho basement clubs were tolerated, thanks to their unofficial contribution to police funds. Uniformed policemen in Soho received up to £60 a week in bribes. (The average PC's wage was between £9 and £11 a week at that time.) Even in the courts, evidence was frequently 'cooked' by 'bobbies' to benefit the accused. Details of previous convictions were also suppressed on numerous occasions so that defendants were fined rather than imprisoned.

Jack Spot was later credited with introducing the policy of paying £20 a week to the wife of any member of his team who went to prison in his service. That way he could ensure the loyalty of many, although there would always be the bad eggs, prepared to 'grass me up for a score'.

Meanwhile, London's West End was booming. Spot and Hill were now running numerous protection rackets, taking their cuts on gambling and using their power bases for one main purpose – the survival of the status quo. They were really more like businessmen, drawing their profits from a discrete monopoly, and only became dangerous if they felt that their empires were being threatened.

The origins of Soho, London's so-called vice centre, can be traced back to the hunting grounds of the 16th century, when the cry of the huntsman gave the district its name. Grand town houses were then built in the 17th century, but the area has long since been associated with colourful outcasts, refugees and immigrants.

The first violent invasion of Soho was engineered by the Messina brothers who arrived from Malta in the 1930s and were nicknamed the 'Epsom Salts' (Malts) in cockney slang. The two eldest Messina brothers – Salvatore and Alfredo – were born in Valetta, Malta, and moved with their parents to Alexandria in Egypt where their father, Giuseppe, set up a chain of brothels. The remaining boys – Carmelo, Attilio and Eugenio – were all born in Alexandria, but when Giuseppe was expelled from Egypt he moved the entire family to London, having attained British nationality due to his Maltese citizenship (Malta was part of the British Empire).

Eugenio Messina founded the family's London vice empire by recruiting girls from the Continent, and as the operation grew he was joined by his other brothers. By 1946 the family's earnings from prostitution were at least £1,000 a week. When four other Maltese pounces (pimps) tried to muscle into the business by demanding protection money from the Messina girls, they were cut and maimed by Eugenio and his boys. When Eugenio was arrested for his part in the attack, he offered £25,000 to anyone who could smuggle him out of London before he was due to be sentenced. The Messina court case publicly exposed the family for the first time.

The Street Offences Act in the 1950s introduced new penalties against prostitution, but it drove the girls into the arms of a new gang of Maltese gangsters, run by 'Big' Frank Mifsud and Bernie Silver. These criminals provided flats to the girls at rents of £100 to £150 a week, situated above clubs in which the staff openly sent customers upstairs to visit the waiting 'models'. The Maltese hid behind nominees and expensive lawyers.

Soho grew to encompass dozens of brothels, 24 strip clubs, five 'blue-movie' cinemas and numerous sex shops. The Maltese oversaw a reign of terror in which enforcers ensured that the girls paid their rents, informants were kidnapped and beaten, while corrupt police officers kept the crime lords safe.

Bernie Silver and Frank Mifsud had earlier operated prostitutes, brothels and gaming clubs in the East End, particularly in the Brick Lane area of Stepney. Silver and Mifsud gained a real stranglehold on Soho through a strip club they ran in Brewer Street. Four prostitutes operated above the premises, and after the notorious Messinas departed in the early 1950s, Silver and Mifsud bought up Soho properties through nominees, so no one knew they were the actual owners.

Mifsud, who weighed 18 stone, was a former traffic policeman from Malta. He was suspected of arranging numerous beatings for rival pimps and prostitutes. 'When you heard Big Frank wanted to see you, it struck terror into the hearts of even the hardest men,' Scotland Yard's own dodgy detective Bert Wickstead later explained.

By this time, Soho's favoured tools of the trade were razors, knives, broken bottles, revolvers, hammers, hatchets, coshes and knuckle-dusters. Charing Cross Hospital employed a special staff of medical seamsters to deal with the gaping wounds made by these weapons. Victims seldom complained but harboured an urge to 'get even' with their attacker.

In the summer of 1954 Billy Hill, Jack Spot's biggest rival, bought himself a villa in Tangier, Morocco. He also acquired a luxury yacht with which he intended to run the occasional load of contraband – cigarettes, not drugs – over to Gibraltar and Spain. Spot presumed Hill was running away, but Hill had no intention of moving out of Soho and saw Tangier as nothing more than a sunshine retreat, combined with a lucrative sideline.

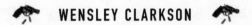

Within weeks of Hill's first trip to Morocco his luxury yacht, the *Flamingo*, together with its first load of illicit goods, sank in 'mysterious' circumstances as it crossed the Mediterranean from the North African coast to Spain. Hill wasn't on board at the time but was spitting blood because he suspected that Jack Spot had organised the sinking to teach him a lesson. Back in London, Hill told his boys that he wanted to increase the size of his gang so that he could start taking complete control of the West End. Spot was confused and infuriated by Hill's reappearance and failed to appreciate Hill's new manoeuvres. Hill put feelers out around various London gangs, and a number of meetings were arranged in West End pubs.

South Londoner Brian McDonald's gang the Elephant Boys had earlier formed a tentative alliance with Spot. They had established their reputation through a series of battles with other gangs in the 1920s, and by the 1950s had such a fearsome reputation that many gangs in other districts paid to hire their services. Most of them did not come from the Elephant and Castle area but from Walworth and the Old Kent Road, Kennington, Lambeth, Waterloo, Blackfriars, Peckham, Camberwell and Borough.

One of the few hard-men totally unimpressed by Billy Hill's grandiose plans to become King of the Underworld was Spot's old South London sidekick, Johnny Carter. He didn't believe the gangs could work together; they'd have to bury too many hatchets. Carter told other villains that he didn't want the 'ponces' (his word for safecrackers, pickpockets, pimps and con men) that Hill associated with calling the shots. Carter still thought Spot had the right idea: 'Chiv any bastard that didn't play ball.' A few days later, Billy Hill tried to join forces with the Italian mob, still based in Clerkenwell but not the force they'd been before the war. But when word got out, Johnny Carter cut Billy Blythe, Hill's emissary to the Italians, and the deal went up in smoke.

Then the increasingly short-tempered Jack Spot gave one of Hill's young tearaways a good kicking after he'd had the temerity to warn Spot not to show his face at one West End club. The man worked alongside fearsome freelance gangster 'Italian' Albert Dimes, whom Billy Hill had recruited as one of his top henchmen.

Within days, Spot and Johnny Carter started mouthing it off around Soho that Billy Hill was at the top of their brand new hit list. Hill heard the rumours and then publicly recruited 'Scotch' Jack Buggy — a nasty American-born chiv merchant based in Kentish Town — to go after Jack Spot. The cycle of violence and threats was picking up speed.

Brian McDonald, the leader of the Elephant Boys, stumbled on Buggy lurking outside the Galahad Club in Soho. He'd heard rumours about Spot being targeted by Hill. 'I walked right past him,' McDonald recalled. 'Buggy pulled a revolver from his overcoat pocket and pointed it at my face. I remember the metallic click as it failed to go off. He fled, but he couldn't outpace me. I brought him down by grabbing the belt at the back of his overcoat.'

MacDonald alerted Spot, and one of his henchmen ran a knife down Buggy's face and thighs, the only parts not covered by his heavy overcoat. McDonald continued, 'The road was busy, so we left him there. In time, he limped back to Kentish Town.' Buggy returned some years later, still making a nuisance of himself. Eventually, his body was found bobbing around in the Channel, off Seaford, Sussex — after he was shot, some say, on the orders of Albert Dimes.

Out on the racetracks, Jack Spot's power and influence took another body blow when a group of Italian bookies led by Dimes took over even more of Spot's pitches. Spot knew Dimes was connected to Hill, but he chose not to confront him with the facts.

One of the most legendary coppers of this period was Scotland Yard's Detective Chief Inspector Edward Greeno, a tall, square-shouldered man with a bucket head, bulldog features, a ready, all-knowing smile and small dark eyes that missed little. He was one of the hardest-nosed coppers in London, and knew it. An inveterate gambler, Greeno had been approached with more bribe offers than a good-looking dame got whistles.

But much to the consternation of London's gangsters in the 1940s and '50s, Greeno was as straight as he was tough. His trademark arrival on the scene of all crimes consisted of him stepping out of a black police Austin or Humber, allowing his driver to go park it, and striding forward in a snap-brim hat and raincoat. Greeno was a Flying Squad veteran who had earned countless commendations from judges and Scotland Yard commissioners. Fleet Street crime reporter Percy Hoskins even dubbed him 'the underworld's public enemy number one'.

Greeno took personal charge of all his investigations into robberies. He threw himself into the groundwork that he so adored and as often as not rounded up the usual suspects himself, once he'd worked out how they had committed their crimes. Jack Spot and Billy Hill were both top of his hit list. Often, after a big blagging, Spot was happy for the outside world to believe he was responsible. But underneath he was seething, because he knew that Billy Hill was usually the organiser of such jobs, and it was yet another feather in his rival's cap.

Greeno placed Jack Spot and Billy Hill under close surveillance throughout much of the late 1940s and early '50s. He'd been catching villains for 38 years and backing horses for 39. He once said, 'If I'd not backed so many winners, I couldn't have caught so many criminals, because at both sports you need information, which costs money. A man rarely turns informant just for the money, but he certainly does not remain one without it. And usually it was my own money.'

Greeno had a photographic memory that indexed 10,000 criminals in his mind, or so he claimed. And that index allegedly included every villain in the East End. He'd spent hours as a young bobby in an Aldgate teashop overlooking a nearby tram terminus, studying faces in the crowd. One of Greeno's earliest claims to fame was the arrest of two gangs of pickpockets run by Jack Spot's old schoolmate, Long Hymie, who'd worked the West End in eight- and ten-handed day shifts for months.

Greeno personally handled 12 murder investigations and solved them all, including the apprehension of cold-blooded child-killers Gordon Cummins and Arthur Heys. Greeno said, 'That 100 per cent record is even better than my record with Derby winners.' He was awarded the MBE in 1949. Greeno's philosophy was simple: 'When police officers say, "We know who did this, but we just cannot pin it on him," my answer is, "Nuts". Either they know or they don't, and if they do, then their job is to prove it. I was never rough for the sake of it, but when I saw trouble coming I forestalled it. I have given some villains awful hidings. I think if more policemen showed more villains that it is not only the lawbreaker who has strong arms, we would be nearer the end of this age of violent nonsense.'

Part of Greeno's campaign against Jack Spot involved pulling him in for relatively minor offences 'just to let him know' the police were closely monitoring him. On 23 September 1953 Spot was arrested in a west London telephone kiosk with a knuckle-duster in his pocket. He was fined £20 for possession of an offensive weapon. Spot admitted to the magistrates that he'd bought the knuckle-duster a fortnight earlier. The arresting officer later told reporters,

'To be pulled in, searched and then booked like some petty thief was an intolerable blow to Spot's high opinion of himself.'

So-called 'Kings of the London Underworld', Billy Hill and Jack Spot's early power had come from their skill in avoiding too much violence. Many of their biggest battles were never actually fought. More than anything else they were both extremely adept fixers, and they went out of their way not to offend the police. They also prided themselves on keeping their men in order. But the young, up-and-coming Kray twins made sure everyone knew that they didn't appreciate such subtleties. The Krays loudly said that they weren't going to promote a 'sensible understanding' with the police because their attitude was 'coppers are dirt'.

At that time, the twins were rumoured to have thrown down the gauntlet to some Islington rivals by heading up to North London in a van, armed to the teeth with guns and knives, intent on a showdown. But no one rose to the bait. The Krays even proudly told their great friend Billy Hill about the incident. The last thing Hill wanted was all-out bloodshed, but he knew that in the long term he could do nothing to stop the Krays and their mob from muscling-in on the West End. Hill started tipping off the twins about various businesses ripe for protection, and even told them about some potential robbery targets. Hill was blatantly feeding such information to the Krays to try to keep them off his back.

When the twins disappeared from Fort Vallance in the middle of 1954, rumours swept London that they'd been killed in a gangland execution sponsored by their numerous enemies. Then it was claimed that the twins had fled the country and were living it up in the Bahamas on a wedge of cash paid out by Billy Hill to get them off his turf. Hill laughed at that one because nothing could have been further from the truth.

The twins re-emerged unscathed a few days later when they set upon a rival gang in Clerkenwell. Ronnie Kray saw their smooth victory as a sign for the future and convinced himself that no one would now be able to prevent their eventual takeover of the West End.

Back on the racetracks in the 1950s, business was still booming. Small-time crooks earned a bundle working as bookmakers. Others spent entire weekends at point-to-point races, which were not so well policed. London criminals would go whenever there was a meeting and stand on a couple of boxes beside a post with a bookie's name on it and a board to write the odds on. This was known as a bookmaker's 'joint', but although it could be put up in seconds, villains still had to pay other spivs for it, plus the cost of the chalk and even the water to wipe the board clean between races.

The criminal scene in London during the 1950s remained a mixture of small-time gangs engaged in very localised protection rackets and illegal-gambling clubs (but mainstream gambling was legalised in 1960, which cut the ground from under the criminal element). Most were only one step up from petty crime and lacked any political connections with local government. But all this would eventually change.

A colourful and unusual character from the East End during the 1950s was Shirley Pitts, one of a rare breed of female professional criminals. She was into high-class shoplifting. Shirley and her 'girls' focused their attention on big West End stores like Harrods but made 'shopping' expeditions as far afield as Paris, Geneva and Berlin. When she died in 1992 Pitts was reportedly buried in an expensive dress, stolen for the occasion. There were wreaths from

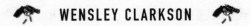

everyone in the London criminal underworld, and the flowers on the hearse were made up in the shape of a Harrods bag with the words 'gone shopping'.

Billy Hill's tough-guy hard-man Albert Dimes – already known as the 'King of the Points' – had built a fearsome reputation in London. In 1941 he'd been involved in the killing of Harry 'Little Hubby' Distleman following a brawl in the Old Cue Club in Frith Street, Soho, which had also left Distleman's friend Eddie Fletcher badly cut up. At that time, Dimes was sidekick to the psychotic Babe Mancini, who'd splattered the ceiling with blood as he slashed away at Distleman with his dagger. Dimes somehow escaped with a caution for unlawful wounding, although he was sent back to the RAF, from which he had deserted.

One of Dimes's favourite racecourse ruses was to find a gullible bookmaker and place bets with him just after the end of a race. His right-hand man at the time was a bizarre six-foot four-inch tall, broad-shouldered character called Prince Monolulu, who wore ostrich feathers in his hair. He was also reputed to be one of the racing world's greatest tipsters and sold his tips for a few bob at a time.

Albert Dimes also helped organise bare-knuckle boxing bouts at racecourses. Car-loads of gangsters would turn up at places such as Epsom with their own favourite fighter to take on an opponent. One Derby Day, Dimes oversaw a fight to the death between one of his boys and a 'pikey' (gypsy) on a field close to the track. Straight racegoers were barred from the ringside as the two fighters smashed each other to pieces for a £500 prize. More than ten times that amount changed hands in bets.

Dimes ran numerous other rackets on the streets of London. One involved a crooked doctor getting 18- and 19-year-olds exempted from National Service. The parents paid the 'fees' for this service, which depended on their wealth. The cash was split between a 'tame' doctor and the medic in charge of the examinations at a bent medical centre in Mill Hill, North London.

Dimes had also become expert at getting his hands on what were called dockers' tickets, or books (which enabled anyone to work as a docker at the quayside, loading boats and barges), which would then be sold-on for a fee. The 'charges' depended on the wealth of the 'client'. The dockers were paid vast wages compared with most jobs, even though the working hours were very short. Many dockers helped steal items like jewellery and watches, which were smuggled in from the dock areas without being cleared through customs.

Twelve men arrived separately at a flat in the West End at midnight on 21 May 1952. They knew they were to be part of a team of robbers but nothing more, until notorious London underworld boss Billy Hill entered the apartment and told them the assignment. Two hours later a man dressed as a postman walked through the gates of the main London Post Office in Eastcastle Street, just a stone's throw from the Old Bailey, on the edge of the City of London. He nodded at the men at the gate and headed towards a group of vans near the sorting office.

He picked out one of the vans, lifted the bonnet and broke a wire, which disconnected the alarm that could be set off by the driver if he was in trouble. Then he walked calmly out of the complex, got into a car and drove away. He went to a phone box and called the others at the flat to report that his part in the operation was complete. He had no idea what else was being planned. Soon after 3 a.m. two stolen saloons with false numberplates were handed over to the gang. The two cars were driven to Eastcastle Street with four

men in each vehicle. They pulled up in a mews on one side of the street and waited.

Then another member of the gang went to Paddington Station and watched the Post Office van with the disconnected alarm leave soon after 3.30 a.m. He phoned the flat. At a bomb-damaged garage in St Augustus Street, Camden Town, another gangster parked a van filled with empty apple boxes covered in tarpaulins. There was a large square gap in the centre of the boxes.

At 4.17 a.m. the driver of the mail van slammed on his brakes after a black Riley swerved in front of him. A green Vanguard then pulled up behind the van just as a man jumped out of the Riley and leapt towards the van driver's door, yanking it open. Two more men followed and hauled all three guards out of the van, attacking them with fists and coshes. The guards were then thrown to the ground. The three robbers climbed into the van and slammed it into gear while another villain climbed back in the Riley. The rest of the team jumped into the Vanguard and headed off with the other vehicles into Covent Garden, where they took a left into Floral Street. Another car was waiting around the corner in Rose Street. They got in and drove off behind the mail van at high speed.

At 4.32 a.m. the van pulled up outside the yard compound in Augustus Street. One man jumped over the gates and unlocked them. The other robbers followed the van into the yard while a lookout waited in the street. The mailbags were ripped open. Within half an hour they'd counted £287,000 in cash.

A brown van was then driven out of the compound into Camden Town Road, through the back of the City down to Spitalfields Market and south out of London. Just after midday the van turned into a country lane, and the £287,000 was shared between about 15 of the top criminals in the London underworld, including Billy Hill.

Clubs, dives, speilers, pubs, hotels and private homes were all kept under constant surveillance by detectives investigating the 'Big Job', as the Post Office van robbery quickly become known. A £10,000 reward was offered by insurers, who later increased it to £14,500, but this was chicken feed compared with what Billy Hill's team had scooped.

Hill knew he'd never be fingered for the Big Job. It just wasn't the way it was back in those days. Two villains were eventually charged with receiving in connection with the blagging, but they were both found not guilty. No one was ever successfully prosecuted for the Eastcastle mailbag robbery, and it remains one of London's legendary crimes.

Billy Hill's reputation as London's new top-dog gangster was further enhanced when he masterminded a robbery at the Holborn offices of the KLM airline on 21 September 1954. This time the robbers got away with two boxes containing £45,500 in gold bullion when a company lorry was hijacked during rush hour. Hill was the prime suspect, but at the time of the robbery he was in the office of *Sunday People* reporter Duncan Webb, telling his favourite journalist yet another version of his life story as 'Boss of the Underworld' for an article to be published the following Sunday.

A couple of weeks later, Hill even encouraged Webb to publish details of the KLM raid. He wanted the world to know all about this supposedly 'brilliant' criminal enterprise.

In early November 1954 Jack Spot met Webb in a Soho café and informed him that he wanted to write 'a story about the underworld' in retaliation to Hill's articles. Webb tactlessly told him that he wasn't interested and suggested that Spot go and see the

Sunday Chronicle. His dismissive attitude infuriated Spot, who then told Webb, 'If you do anything to interfere with this, I will break your jaw.' Spot then complained bitterly to Webb about another Fleet Street journalist, Hannen Swaffer, whom he claimed had made up a story about him in *World Press News*.

A few days later Webb was interviewing a contact in the Surrey town of Kingston upon Thames when he got a message to call a 'Mr Nadel' who said he was calling on behalf of 'Billy' and that Webb should 'Phone Holborn 9107'. When Webb did so, a voice said, 'Billy's in trouble.' A meeting was arranged outside a cinema in Tottenham Court Road. 'Billy' was, in fact, Jack Spot, who'd just used the public telephone in the bar of the King's Arms pub in Soho.

When he reached the cinema at 10.30 p.m. Spot walked straight up to Webb and said, 'Come on, it's bad.' As he walked down the street with Spot, one man moved alongside them and another behind. When Webb asked Spot what it was all about, Spot ignored him. Near Bainbridge Street, at the rear of the cinema, Spot turned, punched Webb between the eyes and said, 'Take that, you fucker. I'm runnin' this show.' Spot then grabbed Webb by the lapels of his coat and began shouting, 'I'll give you Billy Hill. I'll give you fuckin' Billy Hill.'

Warding off another blow to the lower part of his body by 'travelling it', in boxing parlance, Webb then saw what he thought was a knuckle-duster glinting in the neon light. As he tried to get away, Spot struck him in the stomach before missing with another blow. The following morning Webb went to Charing Cross Hospital where an X-ray revealed a fractured arm, which would be in plaster for months, and reported the incident to the police. When officers called at Spot's flat at Hyde Park Mansions later that day he told them, 'What's it about – that rat Duncan Webb? He's a dirty rat to the police and the public after what he has put in those articles.'

Spot was arrested and taken to West End Central Police Station. He was later fined for the attack. Duncan Webb was so shaken up by what had happened to him at the hands of Jack Spot that when he wrote a book about his journalistic adventures he avoided all mention of the incident or subsequent court case.

Shortly afterwards the *Sunday Chronicle* published a series of articles by Jack Spot. They were ghosted by Spot's new Fleet Street pal, reporter Vic Sims. Spot informed *Sunday Chronicle* readers that he was still the 'guvnor of guvnors' with a duty to make sure that trouble didn't flare up in Soho. Spot boasted in the newspaper that he'd even turned one of his clubs into an 'innocent little place' with a bar and a dance band and which was visited by celebrities such as Abbott and Costello and the boxer 'Jersey' Joe Walcott.

Billy Hill read the *Sunday Chronicle* with amusement. Duncan Webb had already told him that the articles were harmless, and they certainly didn't refer to anything Hill didn't already know about.

In January 1955 Jack Spot requested a 'friendly chat' with the Kray twins, because he knew they were on the rise. He had no idea that they'd already been in close touch with Billy Hill. Ronnie Kray's inflated ego was already crammed with dreams of 'ganglordship'. He wanted the war between Spot and Hill to worsen so that he and Reggie could surge through to 'rescue' the London underworld. They'd fuelled much of the tension themselves, thanks to a word in the right ears. After Spot left his meeting with the Krays he told his sidekick Moisha, 'Those two are real trouble. We'd better keep an eye on them.'

A month later Spot had further proof of the ever-widening gap between himself and Hill when a bank strongroom in London was torn open by a gang of highly professional villains. The basement walls were 22-inch-thick concrete, but the massive steel door of the safe was blown off. Easy-to-pass, one-pound, five-pound and ten-shilling notes were stolen, totalling £20,300. Everyone said that Hill's gang was responsible.

Then the Kray twins got themselves nicked for demanding money with menaces. As they were charged at City Road Police Station, Ronnie Kray made a reference to Jack Spot, which sent a shiver up the detectives' spines, because they weren't even aware of a connection between the Krays and Spot, let alone Billy Hill.

Ronnie Kray insisted to the police that he and his brother had been grassed-up by people they'd been 'blacking' (blackmailing or demanding money). Ronnie was also charged with possession of an offensive weapon – a sheath knife. Many years later the Krays concluded that Spot or Hill might have been behind their arrests. They believed that one of the two had grassed them up because they had wanted to teach the twins a lesson. And their money was on Jack Spot.

Meanwhile, Billy Hill was recruiting more toughies to add to the strength of his gang. They included Pasquali Papa and Tommy Falco, who'd already been working the main racecourses alongside Albert Dimes, Hill's number-one hard-man. Spot sneeringly told anyone who'd listen that Dimes 'couldn't bodyguard a flea'. But many figures at the races warned Spot that Dimes was making great inroads into his business. And Hill had yet another trick up his sleeve.

The Krays had been 'keeping an eye on things' whenever Hill was abroad, making sure no one got ahead of themselves. Meanwhile, Superintendent Herbert Sparks, the new police guvnor of the West

End, was trying to make a name for himself by cleaning up Soho. Sparks even used the new Prevention of Crime Act of 1953 to regularly pull in gangsters whom he thought were overstepping the mark. They were seldom charged with anything, but at least the police could fire a few warning shots across their bows.

The feud between Spot and Hill was now an open secret. Billy Hill recruited even more new troops from West, North and East London. And his henchman Albert Dimes brought on board two more notorious hard-men, Battles Rossi and Johnny Rice – the latter had once been in the Sabini Gang where he was known as 'Johnny Ricco'.

In the spring of 1955 Jack Spot invited the Kray twins to join him at the flat racing at Epsom, offering them race pitches and promising them introductions to bookmakers who'd work for them along with the clerks they'd hired. The Krays would keep a dollar (five shillings – 25 pence) in the pound profit. Spot told them that they wouldn't lose a penny. Traditionally the Epsom season was an annual outing for London gangsters, all of whom expected to make big bucks. Whichever gang controlled the leading bookies' pitches was guaranteed a percentage of the take from every other bookie on the course. Epsom represented the form sheet for just about every London villain worth his salt. A simple smile or brush-off showed the others who was on the up and up; a handshake made it clear that an old grudge had been long forgotten. Little went unnoticed.

Word had spread that Spot and Hill were at each other's throats, so everyone turned up. Spot had swallowed his pride by inviting the Krays, even though he had his suspicions about their motives. But he still didn't know for certain that they hated his guts. The twins were far from impressed. They'd only accepted Spot's offer for the hell of it. It might be interesting. 'Interesting' had become one of Ronnie's favourite words.

At Epsom, Spot found the twins a good bookmaker to 'mind'; all they had to do was turn up and stand by the pitch, keeping an eye on the percentage. The Krays parked their cars behind the pitches. Reg later admitted, 'Ron and I and a friend of ours, Shaun Venables, had two or three revolvers in a briefcase hidden away in the car, just in case of any gang warfare.' They also kept an eye on Billy Hill, who had the number-one pitch up by the winning post and was surrounded by minders. One of them was the notorious 'Mad' Frankie Fraser. Next to him was Billy Blythe, a wild man with a conviction for cutting a Flying Squad officer in the face.

As young as the Krays were, they were already up there challenging the big boys. They took a long, hard look at their so-called rivals and concluded they could take them all on at any time they felt like it. One Italian gang member sidled up to Ronnie Kray and told him, 'This lot mean business. You two must be stark staring mad to show up here with Spotty. If you want to kill yourselves, there are less painful ways of doing it.'

The twins laughed and offered the man a drink. When he'd gone, Ronnie turned to his brother and said, 'The way these old men worry, Reg. Fair makes you sick.' The Krays were constantly lurking right behind Spot, guns at the ready, so to speak. They predicted, absolutely accurately as it turned out, that more and more of Spot's henchmen would quit his mob and that he'd take to the bottle, which would be the beginning of the end of his 'reign'.

But Spot still dreamed of pulling off one huge job that would save his skin. He had a specific target, a West End bank, which had been carefully cased. Then he went looking for the right team to carry out the job. But everyone turned him down; even second-division villains didn't want to know. The word was out. Spotty was out of the loop.

A fence called Nukey told him, 'Everybody's been warned off you.' Nukey reckoned Spot's pals had stitched him up: 'They worked you out, Spotty. They've broken you. You're out, and the other bloke [Billy Hill] is in. He's sitting there on your throne and wearing your crown.' Nukey advised Spot to forget trying to put together a new gang.

Billy Hill's favourite hard-man Albert Dimes phoned Spot that same morning and told him to stay away from racetracks. Spot was furious and headed over to one of his favourite Soho clubs for a drink. He later recalled, 'But as soon as I walked in there was dead silence. Everyone looked at me and then looked away.' As he walked across the dance floor to talk to one familiar face, he heard others mentioning his name and then laughing behind his back. Spot was about to front up one of the offenders when he realised that there was nothing he could do about it.

Spot stumbled out of the club in a daze. He began walking across Soho, not even noticing the traffic whizzing by and the familiar faces on the street corners. A name was ticking over and over in his head: 'Dimes, Dimes, Dimes, Dimes.' Then he bumped straight into that slippery fence Nukey again, who told him that Dimes wanted to see him. Spot told Nukey to tell Dimes to 'fuck off' and then headed west. That night Spot didn't mention a word about what had happened to his wife Rita. But he slept so badly that the next morning – 11 August 1955 – she asked what was wrong. She thought he was sick and told him to stay at home. Spot ignored her.

At Spot's office later that morning, greaseball Nukey turned up yet again sowing the seeds of doubt and told Spot, 'You've got to go and see Dimes. If you don't go and see him, he's gonna do you up.' Spot was outraged. As he later recalled, 'I didn't know what I was doin'. The name Dimes kept ringin' again and again in my brain.' A few minutes later Jack Spot was striding through the West End with a worried look on his face.

Elephant Boys gang member Brian McDonald was on his way to a drinking club in Rathbone Place when Spot came out of Charlotte Street, just north of Oxford Street. Spot clapped a huge arm round McDonald's shoulders, squeezed him with his big fist, which was the size of a bunch of Fyffe bananas, and steered him back down Rathbone Place. Spot then offered to buy McDonald a salt-beef sandwich. McDonald agreed, none too enthusiastically. The two men walked out of Rathbone Place, across Oxford Street and into Soho Square. Spot nodded to familiar faces as they strolled.

As the two men turned into Frith Street, morning shoppers crowded the pavements, bustling in and out of stores. Barrow boys were selling their fruit, bookmakers kept an eye open for the police. Then he saw him . . .

Jack Spot blinked twice. He couldn't quite believe that the object of his complete and utter hatred was standing there just a few yards ahead of him: Albert Dimes, 36, sometimes known as Dimeo and a brother of Victor Dimes, notorious throughout Soho. Spot marched straight up to him. 'I want you, Dimes,' panted Spot. Dimes looked him straight in the eye. 'You been talkin' big,' snarled Spot. 'You been spreadin' the word around I'm to come and see you. You been talkin' like a strong-armed guy.'

'Take it easy, Spotty,' Dimes replied. 'Don't blow your top, mate.'

'You been talkin' too big,' repeated Spot.

'Let's go somewhere quiet and talk it over.'

'Don't treat me like a nobody. I've had my troubles. But I'm still a big man. I'm bigger than you'll ever be.'

Then Dimes quietly said, 'Face up to it, Spotty. You're fuckin' finished!'

'We'll soon see if I'm finished,' screamed Spot.

Dimes repeated his message: 'You're finished Spotty. What's

more, it's about time you were finished. You've had your day. And this is a final warning. Get the fuck out of here.'

As he spoke, Dimes gave Spot a big-enough shove to make the red mist descend.

Brian McDonald witnessed what happened next: 'He put one right on Dimes's chin. Italian Albert went down like a sack of spuds.' As Spot went to give Dimes a few more kicks, another man called Johnny Rocca grabbed Spot around the waist and tried to pull him off. McDonald then got involved. He explained, 'If I didn't, all my respect would have gone with everyone. I jumped on Rocca, and we pranced around like a couple of old-time dancers, not really wanting to mix it. He kept screaming at me, "Are you in this? Are you in this?"'

As Spot was hitting out at Dimes, his hand dropped automatically into his pocket – but he didn't have a blade on him that day. Precious seconds of indecision allowed Dimes time to recover. He came at Spot, punching him viciously, and soon a full-scale battle had erupted. A woman nearby screamed. Spot later alleged that was when he felt a sudden sharpness slice through his arm.

The two men fell over some vegetable boxes outside the Continental Fruit Store on the corner of Frith Street and Old Compton. Spot twisted his opponent's right hand away from him, but as he did so Dimes yanked back and sliced through the side of Spot's body. The two broke away from each other only to start grappling again, and, locked together, they tumbled into the greengrocer's shop. Customers shouted in alarm, but all Spot was aware of was Dimes's heavy breathing and the pain as something plunged in and out of him – over and over again. Across the street, Rocca and McDonald swapped a few more blows before Rocca tried to halt proceedings: 'Hold up, what's all this about?'

'I only came here for a salt-beef sandwich,' McDonald replied.

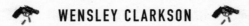

But inside the shop the battle was still in full swing. The proprietor's wife, Sophie Hyams, grabbed the heavy, cast-iron scales and hit Spot over the head, splitting his scalp open. Spot later claimed that he wrestled a knife from Dimes as he realised his opponent was trying to finish him off. Others claim Spot grabbed a potato knife and stabbed Dimes a couple of times. Whatever the truth, the two men fought with the desperation of two wild animals. But as they grappled, the strength was ebbing away from them both.

Dimes pulled away from his opponent and leaned, exhausted, against the doorjamb before tumbling out on to the pavement. Spot felt a searing pain in his leg and the warmth of blood filling his shoes as he also staggered out of the shop. Brian McDonald watched as Dimes made his way to a taxi, was helped in and driven away.

Meanwhile, Spot slithered slowly and painfully down a girder and then sat expressionless on the pavement. People looked the other way as they hurried past. Spot's neck, ears and head were bleeding, and there were chunks torn out of his 100-guinea suit. Spot eventually struggled to his feet and staggered a few yards before slumping into a nearby Italian barber's shop. 'Fix me up!' he told the attendant in front of startled customers, looking up at him from their swivel chairs. Spot grabbed a towel and dabbed roughly at his wounds. Then he collapsed unconscious on the floor.

Across the street, McDonald and Rocca took one last look at the scene and legged it. A few of McDonald's pals later put him in a taxi and directed it across the Thames to Borough. Spot was taken away by ambulance to Charing Cross Hospital. Within an hour, word had got round all the usual underworld haunts that Spot and Dimes had been involved in a fight. And as the names spread across the West End, people who'd earlier been talking openly about what had

happened suddenly lost their memories. It was about to be dubbed
'the fight that never was'.

At the two hospitals five miles apart, Jack Spot and Albert Dimes
lay grievously wounded. Both men were vulnerable to any
gangland attempt to knock them off. Spot was protected from view
by a yellow curtain, and two Yard officers remained close by at all
times. A lot of 'family', including nine 'brothers and cousins' and
three attractive women, turned up in the hours following the
attack, but were told they couldn't see Spot, who was by now
wearing blue-striped flannelette pyjamas. His head above his
hairline was covered in plaster and bandages, he had a black eye and
his throat between his Adam's apple and chin was also bandaged.
He was weak and on the danger list. The only words he could
muster for the police were, 'Can't remember what happened.'

At the Middlesex Hospital, Dimes was just as tight-lipped. His
left forehead cleft was cut open down to the bone, requiring 20
stitches. He also had minor lacerations of the chin and left thumb,
a wound on the left thigh and one in the stomach which just failed
to penetrate the abdominal cavity.

One of the few witnesses prepared to speak out said that one of
the two men had suddenly brought out a stiletto from his inside
pocket and had lunged at the other. Another witness claimed that
he had seen the attacked man seize the stiletto from the other. Then
there was the mystery of the so-called 'third and fourth men', who
detectives believed were present throughout the incident.
Detective Inspector Eric Shepherd of West End Central Police
Station took charge of inquiries. Flying Squad men and others with
long experience of the West End gang scene swooped on houses,
clubs and pubs across the capital in the hunt for witnesses.

In South London, another man was linked to the incident after
he was found lying beaten up on a pavement in Elephant and Castle

the night before the Frith Street fight. The man had been heard making threats against West End gang members, and police believed that the attack on him might have sparked some kind of turf war between gangsters. The victim refused to give his name and address and told police to call him 'Mister X'. He insisted the injuries were the result of 'an accident'.

Jack Spot suffered a total of nine stab wounds, including a punctured lung just a quarter of an inch from his heart. He'd lost pints of blood and his stomach had been turned into a sieve. So much air had seeped into his belly that he'd swollen up like a half-inflated balloon. Spot had also been stabbed over the left eye, in the left cheek, in the ear and neck, and four times in the left arm.

In hospital, Spot fell in and out of unconsciousness and was close to the point of death, while doctors worked furiously to stem the vast loss of blood. As Spot himself later recalled, 'I hovered in a grey, twilight world, punctuated by sharpness, the smell of anaesthetic and constant nausea.' As soon as he was pronounced well enough to talk, Spot told detectives that he didn't remember whom he'd fought with. It was more than his life was worth to reveal what had happened.

In the middle of all this, a swastika with a message from the Blackshirt movement – 'Remember 1936' – was delivered to the hospital with a bunch of black carnations as a reminder of the role Spot played before the war in leading a march against the Mosley Blackshirts on behalf of the Jews of the East End. It seemed as if Billy Hill wasn't the only one enjoying Jack Spot's pain.

At the Middlesex Hospital, Dimes was told that he and Spot would be charged with GBH [Grievous Bodily Harm]. He got so angry he told police, 'It was Jackie Spot. I'm not "prossing" [prosecuting]. Spotty does me up, and I get pinched. That can't be fair.' But later, in an official statement to the police, he would only refer to being attacked by 'a tall man . . . I don't know his name. I don't want to kid you, but in the struggle between us I must have cut him up with my knife. If I did use it, it was struggling for my life.' When Spot heard he would also face GBH charges, he told police, 'Why only me? Albert did me, and I get knocked off.'

In the *Sunday People*, Duncan Webb regaled readers with how over almost 20 years of covering crime he'd been slugged, kicked, lunged at with knives, shot at, knuckle-dusted and was once the target of a speeding automobile that raced onto the pavement of a narrow Soho street and tried to smash him against a building. He even reminded readers that Jack Spot had objected to one of his stories by attacking him in the street, and he'd ended up wearing a plaster cast on his broken right wrist.

Webb gleefully celebrated Spot's downfall in a *Sunday People* article headlined 'Jack Spot – the Tinpot Tyrant'. He wrote that at last 'the mob had discovered what I had known for years – that Spot is a poseur who had got away with it'. Webb was out for revenge following his earlier encounters with Spot. And Billy Hill enjoyed every word of it. Meanwhile, as Spot and Dimes lay in hospital, Billy Hill and his henchmen were taking over Jack Spot's pitch concessions at race meetings.

Fearing an outbreak of gang warfare, Scotland Yard flooded Soho with extra police. Traders were better protected than they had been for years. But nothing materialised. Spot and Dimes were both seen sitting up in hospital, receiving their friends and cronies and telling reporters to mind their own business, or words to that effect.

Across the Thames, other gang problems were flaring up. Pitched battles took place between gangs from Elephant and Castle and Deptford. Detectives believed much of the trouble had been caused by thriving street betting. Another South London gang invaded their

neighbour's territory and told the bookmaker 'runners' that in future all bets must be placed with bookies sponsored by them. A few nights later, the visitors, 30 to 40 strong, arrived ready to do battle. But a squad of 20 specially selected uniformed policemen were waiting for them, and any fighting was thwarted.

The evening after Spot's 'fight that never was', the Kray twins held a celebration drink at their favourite boozer, the Blind Beggar in Mile End Road. 'They were that happy to see Spot out of circulation,' one former Krays man explained years later. Around midnight, Ronnie Kray paid a visit to the Italian Club in Clerkenwell with his latest toy – a heavy Mauser automatic – and threatened one of Billy Hill's associates. It was all done for show to make Spot believe that they weren't involved in his beating and slashing. Back in the West End, police warned that it was highly likely the attack would spark fresh friction between London gangs.

Later that same day Spot posed for a photograph in the *Sunday Express* with wife Rita at his side. His arm was encased in plaster, his nose and mouth were twisted, and both eyes blackened. He told the paper, 'I'm the toughest man in the world. I am staying on in London. Nobody will ever drive me out.' Rita added, 'Let 'em all come. We're not scared.' Rita got £300 for the article, and neither of them meant one word of what they were quoted as saying.

There was a serious knock-on effect from the adverse publicity surrounding the string of violent underworld incidents featuring Jack Spot and his mob. MPs began asking questions in the House of Commons about whether 'effective steps were being taken by the police to prevent the operation of criminal gangs in the London area'. Mr Anthony Greenwood (Labour, Rossendale) asked Home Secretary Gwilym Lloyd George, 'How long have the public got to wait before the activities of these squalid, cowardly and small-time hoodlums like Comer, Dimes and Hill are going to be effectively curbed?'

On Monday, 22 August 1955, Spot and Dimes stood together in the dock at Marlborough Street Magistrates Court with three policemen sitting between them. At one stage Spot looked directly at Dimes, who didn't even glance back at him. During one later conversation Spot was heard discussing the possibility of paying a former Scotland Yard detective £1,000 to appear as a witness for him at his trial.

Shortly after the well-publicised magistrates court hearing, a Polish pilot, Christopher Glinski – whose exploits during the war had won him the Polish Military Cross and the French Croix de Guerre – presented himself at his local police station, West End Central. He claimed that he'd been in Frith Street and had seen Spot push the other man: 'Then the other man charged him. The other man took a knife out of his pocket. I saw the knife cut into his arm. Then I saw another blow cut his face. They got hold of one another and, together, staggered into the shop.' The police were somewhat bemused by Glinski's account but took a statement and warned him that he could well be asked to appear as a witness in the forthcoming trial.

What they didn't realise was that Glinski had just visited Spot's flat at Hyde Park Mansions for 'a chat' with some of Spot's associates, including his gang members Moisha Blueball and Sonny the Yank. He'd then agreed to go to the police.

Another visitor to Spot's flat, in the company of Moisha and Sonny, was an elderly parson, The Reverend Basil Andrews, who, despite his outwardly respectable persona, had heavy gambling debts. At a previous meeting with Sonny, engineered by a fellow gambler, 'Tall Pat' MacDonough, Andrews had insisted that he had witnessed the Spot-Dimes fight. Sonny the Yank told Andrews that he could earn himself 'a decent wedge' by saying a few words: 'I saw Dimes with the knife.'

In Spot's flat, Moisha Blueball was equally persuasive. The Reverend Andrews later recalled, 'He said, "You say this," and "You say that," and "Splendid!" They seemed very delighted about it all. In fact, they told me they had a bottle of champagne to celebrate with after it was all over.'

Over the following days Moisha Blueball gave the Reverend Basil Andrews a total of £63 (it should have been £65, but Moisha couldn't resist cheating the churchman out of a couple of quid). Moisha also promised the elderly cleric that he 'would never want' and 'would always be provided for' if Jack Spot got off.

Shortly before the Spot and Dimes trial started at the Old Bailey, Spot's wife Rita visited him in Brixton prison where he pleaded with her to leave London. But Rita was in no mood to compromise their future and told Spot she'd done everything in her power to make sure he'd be acquitted. After an emotional, tear-filled visit, Rita left the prison with her head still held up high.

That same day Billy Hill visited a Brighton bookie called Sammy Bellson, the 'guvnor' of Brighton racetrack and a supposedly close friend of Jack Spot. Hill and Mad Frankie Fraser were collecting money for Albert Dimes's defence. They wanted Spot to realise how popular Dimes was. Bellson – said to be worth at least £80,000 – made a generous contribution of £500 because, as he later explained, 'I knew what would happen if I told 'em to fuck off.' Ironically, Fraser was arrested by Scotland Yard detectives later that same day after police heard rumours that he was about to shoot another of Spot's supporters who was also at the Brighton races that afternoon.

Hill had no trouble persuading many of Spot's henchmen to contribute to Albert Dimes's defence. Names like Teddy Machin and Jackie Reynolds were happy to drop Spot like a brick. Hill even encouraged them to see Spot in prison and tell him to his face why they were joining Hill's mob.

On 19 September 1955 Spot and Dimes were found not guilty of GBH at their Old Bailey trial.

Spot had been defended by (Dame) Rose Heilbron, who died in December 2005 aged 91, one of the most celebrated defence barristers of the post-war years; no woman before her enjoyed anything like her success rate at the criminal Bar, and she later became the second woman only to be appointed a High Court judge.

She won her first murder acquittal in 1946, aged 29. Three years later, having just taken silk, she became the first woman to lead in an English murder trial, defending the Merseyside gangster George Kelly in the Cameo cinema case. Kelly had begun by sneering, 'I want no Judy defending me.' But although he was eventually convicted and sentenced to hang, he praised Heilbron for her painstaking defence, which also led to her being named the *Daily Mirror*'s 'Woman of the Year'.

In 1951 Rose Heilbron successfully defended Anna Neary, accused of murdering a woman in her bath. The following year her client Mary Standish walked free from court after standing trial for the murder of her husband. Another client, the Knowsley Hall footman, escaped the gallows on the grounds of insanity after shooting two men dead and seriously wounding the Countess of Derby in the smoking room of her stately home. Rose Heilbron's bold decision to call a psychiatrist as the only defence witness was considered a masterstroke.

When Jack Spot was eventually found not guilty of stabbing

Albert Dimes in Soho in the so-called 'fight that never was' in 1955, he told reporters gathered outside the Old Bailey, 'If you want something to write about, write about Rose Heilbron. She's the greatest lawyer in history.'

At 10.40 on the night of 2 May 1956, Jack Spot and Rita, and a friend called Paddy Carney, were walking back from the pub to their apartment at Hyde Park Mansions. As they approached the block, three cars screeched to a halt 30 yards further up the street. Rita heard the sound of people running behind them. Moments later at least half a dozen men — some with handkerchiefs tied loosely around their faces — emerged from the dark and steamed right into Spot. One was Billy Hill's psychotic sidekick Mad Frankie Fraser. Spot hit the deck in seconds as a cosh ripped open a gaping wound in his skull. Then he felt sharp pain tearing at him as blades sliced through his flesh.

Rita let out an ear-piercing scream before flinging herself at the attackers. She kicked and scratched them to try to get them to pull away from her husband. Spot scrambled back onto his feet and started hitting back, as a few local residents emerged from nearby homes.

That was when Rita spotted the shillelagh being used on them. It was the one she'd brought back from Ireland and which her husband had insisted on giving to Billy Hill as a gift. She also recognised a tearaway called Billy Blythe amongst their assailants. The men hastily scrambled back towards their cars before driving off.

Rita grabbed her husband's arm and dragged him up the steps. With blood streaming from his face and body, and one ear flapping in the wind, Spot tried to focus on the front door of the mansion block. Then he collapsed as everything went black.

Mad Frankie Fraser later insisted that there was no intention to murder Spot: 'The thing was to teach Spotty a lesson. He wasn't important enough to kill. The death penalty was about, but you couldn't care less about that because you could easy have killed him by mistake anyway. That's the chance you take. But the purpose was to let him see what a loudmouthed chump he was.' Usually, Fraser was paid cash up front for such an attack, but on this occasion he'd waived his fee because he knew that once word of the incident spread through the London underworld his reputation would be second to none.

Within hours of the attack Frankie Fraser had hotfooted it to Brighton. From there, Billy Hill had arranged for him to fly to Ireland and had rented a doctor's house on the outskirts of Dublin. Meanwhile, Jack Spot was once again rushed by ambulance to hospital, this time St Mary's in Paddington. Semiconscious and with Rita at his bedside, he was immediately given blood transfusions and emergency surgery.

The manipulation of court cases and juries continued unabated. Take the trial of Mad Frankie Fraser for that later attack on Jack Spot, which was heard before Mr Justice Donovan at the Old Bailey on 9 June 1956. Billy Hill rounded up a bunch of his boys who'd been cut by his great rival Jack Spot and arranged for them to sit in the public gallery. As Fraser later explained, 'They were there to let Spotty know. He went white when he saw them.'

Court officials had a special buzzer warning system installed to call police reinforcements to any part of the building in case there was trouble. As with the previous trials, this one got Fleet Street banner-headline coverage. And the stench of corruption reached inside the Old Bailey itself. Early on in the proceedings prosecutor Reggie Seaton, QC, asked Fraser an awkward question, which Fraser hadn't 'squared' with one of his tame witnesses. Fraser then got a message to his 'dodgy' counsel, Patrick Marrinan, to make sure that what had been said was conveyed to the witness waiting outside the court. Marrinan stood up, bowed to the judge and indicated that he wished to go to the lavatory. Outside, Marrinan saw the tame witness and told him what Fraser had said. That witness later gave exactly the same evidence as Fraser.

Billy Hill – sporting his customary shades and snap-brim hat – and his mob made their temporary headquarters at the Rex Café opposite the Old Bailey, where they drank tea, smoked cigarettes and monitored proceedings. Many looked as if they'd walked off a Hollywood movie set: broad-shouldered, broken-nosed and razor-slashed characters, who swaggered in front of press photographers and muttered threats for the benefit of anyone who cared to listen. They also watched the police who were watching them.

At the end of each day Billy Hill reported back to the Kray twins at their billiard hall in the East End. The Krays assured Hill that there was no way Jack Spot would ever be allowed to make a comeback.

The jury eventually decided on a verdict; Fraser and his sidekick were brought back into the dock looking tense and pale. Then the verdicts were announced: 'Guilty . . . Guilty . . .' As Mr Justice Donovan gave each man seven years, he told them, 'I have been affected by what I have just been told. Otherwise sentence would have been much longer.'

Billy Hill's legal pal Patrick Marrinan QC, who'd climbed the ladder to become a barrister after studying law at Queens University, Belfast, was the son of a Royal Irish Constabulary officer. He'd been a well-known face at Belfast clubs and greyhound racetracks for years. Marrinan was also a keen boxer who was heavyweight champion of the Irish universities. In 1942 he'd been convicted of harbouring uncustomed black-market goods in

Liverpool. This had held back his ascendency to the Bar until 1951. Marrinan was a greedy, unscrupulous character, but he appealed to the likes of Billy Hill.

Mad Frankie Fraser and others regularly socialised with the QC at Billy Hill's luxury flat overlooking the Thames in Barnes, southwest London. Fraser later recalled, 'He was a good drinker: he'd start with Guinness and go on to Irish whiskey. I think Marrinan was a rebel. It was the unfairness and corruptness of the legal profession he fought against. Also, he got better money from fighting hard for a case. Billy Hill was intelligent enough to recognise this.' And, on the face of it, the evidence against his boys on this particular occasion was not impressive.

Marrinan managed to rub the police up the wrong way at every opportunity. In the summer of 1957, Scotland Yard's Tommy Butler – later head of the Flying Squad – had Marrinan's phone tapped because of concerns about the lawyer's close ties to Hill and other mobsters. Marrinan was disbarred on evidence provided by those phone taps and moved back to Ireland to try to start a new life.

Mad Frankie Fraser got his monicker after viciously attacking Jack Spot during the fight on Praed Street in Paddington on 2 May 1956. That was the incident which really brought Fraser to the attention of London's underworld. He was born in London in 1923 to a Canadian dad and Irish mum. Fraser was called up during the Second World War, only to desert his barracks and disappear on numerous occasions. And it was blackouts and rationing which most encouraged his development into a criminal. It also helped that London's streets were virtually police-free, because most men had left to fight the enemy. In 1941 Fraser 'knocked off' a hosiery store near Waterloo Station and ended up in borstal. Soon after his release he was nicked again for shop-breaking and got a 15-month

prison sentence. Later, Fraser regularly joked in interviews that he'd never forgive the Germans for surrendering.

His eventual 'associations' ranged from the Krays to the Great Train Robbers to the Brinks-Mat robbers, as well as road-rage killer and crime boss Kenny Noye. He was also one of the Richardsons' notorious gang of 'torturers'. From his mid-teens onwards, he spent 32 of his next 40 years in prison.

After the war Fraser was involved in a smash-and-grab raid on a West End jewellers and got a two-year prison sentence, served largely at Pentonville. It was during this sentence that he was first certified insane and sent to the Cane Hill Hospital, London, before being released in 1949. During the 1950s he took part in more bank robberies and spent more time in prison. He was again certified insane while at Durham Prison and this time sent to Broadmoor. Fraser uncharacteristically stayed out of trouble and was released in 1955. But then he got a seven stretch for 'chivving' Jack Spot.

The antics of Billy Hill and Jack Spot, and the emergence of gangs like the Krays, brought with them a resurgence of Scotland Yard's Flying Squad, originally set up by Detective Inspector David Goodwillie in 1918 to deal with an influx of American and Continental crooks. Criminals soon dubbed it 'the heavy mob', and it handled some of the Met's most high-profile cases, concentrating on armed robberies.

In the squad's early days London was experiencing a crime wave following the release of large numbers of men from the armed forces, many of them hardened to violence after the carnage of the Western Front. Shortly after the end of the First World War, in 1919, Inspector Walter Hambrook led a team of 12 detectives given special dispensation to arrest criminals anywhere in the

Metropolitan Police District. This unique squad maintained surveillance on the streets from a horse-drawn carriage van, which was actually a canvas-covered Great Western Railway van with spyholes cut in the side. The squad struck fear into the underworld by nabbing known criminals, including housebreakers and pickpockets, off the streets. The 'heavy mob' also went undercover in pubs and clubs, where informants provided information on other criminals. It was the first time the police had officially used criminals in such a way. As a small unit of Branch C1, Central CID, they were known as the 'Mobile Patrol Experiment' until being re-named the Flying Squad in 1921, on account of their abilities to 'swoop' on criminals.

Those early units enjoyed rapid crime-busting success and in 1920 were provided with two motor tenders capable of a top speed of 35 mph. (The speed limit at the time was just 20 mph.) A *Daily Mail* journalist then referred to them as 'a flying squad of picked detectives', and the name stuck. The Flying Squad has now been in existence so long that the Squad's nickname in rhyming slang the Sweeney (from Flying Squad/Sweeney Todd, the notorious Fleet Street barber who turned his customers into meat pies) is now generally regarded as a cliché.

The Flying Squad's main function to this day is to detect and prevent armed robbery and other so-called professional crimes. They even use specially trained drivers, recruited from the uniformed divisions of the Met and given the honorary title of Detective Constable while serving in the Squad. By 1929, The Sweeney had evolved into a superbly organised London police unit of 40 officers led by a C1 Branch Detective Superintendent. Their exploits went on to figure in a number of British films, and in the mid-1970s the squad was eulogised in a popular TV series *The Sweeney*, starring John Thaw and Dennis Waterman.

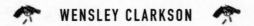
The Flying Squad chief at the end of the 1950s was Tommy Butler, an unmarried, 24-hours-a-day policeman, who had little or no interest in anything other than police business. He often worked into the early hours in his office at Scotland Yard, and lived on sandwiches and food from the police canteen. He looked like a concentration-camp survivor, and in his twisted mind everyone was a potential criminal – it was only a matter of time before they were all behind bars.

His respect for justice and fair play was nonexistent. Other policemen feared him, not because he was an upstanding officer, which he was most definitely not – he had taken his share of 'bungs' – but because of his single-mindedness. It was this fear that stopped him rising to a higher rank in the force. To head the notorious Flying Squad he had to be made a chief superintendent, but he was not allowed to go any higher by his superiors, who blocked his promotion.

These days, Butler's unusual methods would be easily exposed by standard forensic science. But rewritten statements and the planting of 'bent' evidence regularly helped convict many so-called criminals in the 1950s and 1960s.

PART 2
1960–80: BLAGGERS, BENT COPPERS AND TORTURE

The infamous Charlie Wilson

'He was a drunkard and a bully. I done the earth a favour.'
RONNIE KRAY, EXPLAINING WHY HE NEVER REGRETTED
MURDERING GEORGE CORNELL

PETER RACHMAN'S NAME IS SO SYNONYMOUS with bad housing that it even features in some English dictionaries:

Rachmanism: Landlords buying up slums to fill with immigrants at extortionate rents; named after Rachman, a notorious racketeering landlord in Notting Hill in the 1950s and 1960s.

Rachman and his gang of henchmen acquired many slum properties in West London, particularly around the Notting Hill area, which in the 1950s and '60s did not have the hip-and-trendy image of today. His policy was to acquire tenanted buildings, and his gang then used violence to evict sitting tenants so Rachman could fill the squalid properties with immigrant families from the West Indies who were crammed into tiny flats at extortionate rents because the 'colour bar' effectively prevented them finding other accommodation.

Rachman's infamy came about largely by accident. At the time of his death in 1962 he was not widely known outside of Notting Hill. It was only during the controversial Profumo Affair, a year later, that his name started to make the headlines. His mistresses included Mandy Rice-Davies, who owned the infamous mews house in Marylebone where she and Christine Keeler entertained their clients, including the then Secretary of State for War, John Profumo, and also a Russian embassy attaché who was, allegedly, a Soviet spy.

The call girls made the front pages, but it was his treatment of his other tenants that made Rachman notorious. When one group of Rachman's tenants in Bayswater refused to leave, the roof of their flat was stripped off. As details of his seedy property empire emerged, the call for legislation to outlaw unscrupulous practices became unstoppable. Rachman was himself an immigrant, born in Poland in 1920, the son of a Jewish dentist. He escaped the Nazis but spent a horrific time in a Russian labour camp before fleeing to England.

Around 1960 Ronnie Kray learned about Rachman and decided to milk him. One night, Ronnie and a bunch of his pals crashed a party Rachman was giving in Soho. After a bit of minor terrorism Rachman agreed to pay protection money to Ronnie to prevent 'trouble' arising among his rent collectors and enforcers. Rachman paid his first instalment to Ronnie via a cheque, which bounced, and then disappeared when Ronnie came searching for him. Sure enough, this sparked off some trouble in Notting Hill. Rachman's rent collectors were beaten up, and his enforcers were attacked by Kray enforcers. As Reggie once commented, 'His rent collectors were big, but our boys were bigger.' His empire was in danger of disintegrating, but Rachman was a clever man who understood perfectly the mentality of someone like Ronnie Kray. He realised that once he started paying protection, it would never stop. He needed to offer a bigger carrot, one that would get him off the hook for good.

Rachman was connected to a man called Stefan de Faye, who owned a gaming club called Esmeralda's Barn in Wilton Place, a fashionable street off Knightsbridge. Rachman 'sold' Esmeralda's Barn to the Kray brothers over the head of de Faye, who had no choice but to accept the deal when the Krays came knocking.

Rachman's own home in Hampstead, North London, was furnished in lavish, Louis XV style, and the house became the venue for decadent parties and a byword for conspicuous consumption. He owned six cars; his wife was given a red Jaguar, his mistress a white one. After he'd pocketed the rent takings, he'd drive around the capital in a white sharkskin suit and hand-stitched crocodile shoes, usually with a fat cigar in his mouth.

A mythology grew up after his death in 1962 as details of his

property empire became public. One story suggested that he had not died and that his death certificate had been forged, leading to questions in Parliament. Hard evidence to prove that he was alive, or to back up tales of his violent rent-collecting methods, proved difficult to come by.

In 1960 a young gangster was murdered in a highly publicised incident at the Pen Club in East London at which well-known South London villain Joey Pyle was present. That shooting was a wake-up call for Scotland Yard, who realised that they needed to know much more about 'the enemy'. As a result, CIB (Criminal Intelligence Branch) was formed to coordinate information about organised crime. Until then the police had little or no idea who they were up against. Up-and-coming young gangsters were already giving them a run for their money.

Also in 1960 the Jockey Club decided to introduce legal betting shops to every High Street, effectively wiping out the illegal gambling dens and street-corner bookies that had been so much a part of Jack Spot and Billy Hill's reign. As the big-credit bookmakers prepared for the legalisation of off-course betting, the smaller bookmakers and their protectors were being squeezed out of the picture. But with these changes, new 'industries' sprang up for gangsters like the Krays. A favourite racket was the protection of the newly opened betting shops. Then there were the one-armed bandits – fruit machines – which were installed in shops and clubs across the capital. A new criminal era was dawning, and gangsters such as Billy Hill and Jack Spot were already yesterday's men.

The new Betting and Gaming Act provided a legal basis for casinos and bookmakers. Overnight, illegal bookmakers, who were raided by police once a year, became legitimate. Opening at a rate of 100 a week, there were 10,000 betting shops established within just six months. One thousand casinos were opened in the first five years.

However, the Act was poorly worded and allowed almost anyone to open a casino in the UK, with disastrous consequences. As a result, many of the casinos became a cover for criminal activity. The film star George Raft, a childhood friend of notorious Vegas mobster Bugsy Siegel, fronted the Colony Club in the West End for the mob, while casino 'advisers' moved to the UK from Chicago and Miami.

In the 1960s London's gangsters naturally became heavily involved in the gambling industry. The Krays visited underworld bosses in New York to 'research new business opportunities'. They returned to London obsessed with demanding protection money from London clubs. According to the FBI there was even a summit between known mafiosi and London's gangs in the British capital to discuss the running of London clubs. Gambling junkets were organised by the mob, selling package casino breaks in London.

By the early 1960s the Krays – lacking the 'formal' training of Jack Spot and Billy Hill – were steaming through the underworld like runaway Chieftain tanks. They wanted control of every important criminal enterprise in the capital. The twins liked everyone to know that they wouldn't tolerate disloyalty. A lot of people got cut, and the word went out: don't fuck with the Krays. They ignored the fact that Jack Spot and Billy Hill's power had come from their ability to avoid violence. The Krays weren't politicians who negotiated their way out of aggravation. They thrived on confrontation.

Violence and fear were like a drug to the Krays, and they needed very regular fixes. If they had to knock someone off to prove a point, then so be it. As Ronnie later explained, 'We weren't playing kids' games any more.'

It was said in the West End that 'the dogs' were after Jack Spot with a vengeance. Spot had edged closer and closer to bankruptcy. Much of his legendary bravado had been replaced by basic fear. He slept badly and often lay awake at night replaying the fights and razor attacks that had dominated his life over the previous 30 years. And his drinking was getting heavier.

Now calling himself John Colmore, his birth name, Jack Spot eventually got himself a job running a small furniture business off the Gloucester Road in Kensington, West London, and moved into a shabby two-room flat above the shop. He kept photos of his family on his mantelpiece as a reminder of the good old days when he was King of the Underworld. And with more time on his hands than he'd ever had before, he started working out how the Krays had been so instrumental in his downfall.

Spot died a broken man in the early 1990s.

The 1960s saw a substantial growth in armed bank robberies. Back then, blaggers usually consisted of a group of 'loners' who came together for a particular job and then shared the takings and went into hiding for a while. Normally, the rule was that the fewer people who were involved, the fewer mouths to blab. And while the 1960s saw some spectacular heists, none could match one incredible 'job' in 1963 for sheer audacity and cunning.

The Great Train Robbery still dominates worldwide criminal history, even though many robberies have overtaken it in purely financial terms. Put simply, nothing can match the sheer drama of this legendary crime. Just the mere notion of robbing the Glasgow-to-London mail train in Buckinghamshire, just north of the capital, was outrageous.

A gang of South London blaggers believed they could hold up a train on a busy line in the English countryside like a bunch of cowboys in the Wild West. No wonder the Great Train Robbery went on to captivate the public's imagination and the world's media, not to mention elevating one gang member, Ronald Arthur 'Ronnie' Biggs, to the status of a modern-day folk hero.

Yet the robbery itself was devised by an unnamed Frenchman, renowned as a master criminal technician when it came to planning audacious crimes. In 1962 he 'sold on' the 'crime of the century' to an old-school villain serving time in prison with Bruce Richard Reynolds, a London antique dealer and prominent thief. Reynolds spent the final few months of his sentence hammering out the final details on a master plan to pull off what would become known as the Great Train Robbery.

Within days of his release, Reynolds had put the plan to his best mate, Douglas Gordon Goody, a smooth-talking, dandy London hairdresser and part-time thief, known in the capital's underworld as 'a brilliant operator'. Reynolds then formed a team of villains called 'The South West' gang. But they quickly realised they would need to expand if they were to pull off this once-in-a-lifetime opportunity, so they embroiled happy-go-lucky ex-boxer and club owner Ronald 'Buster' Edwards and one-time bookmaker and hard-man Charles Frederick Wilson.

The now legendary Ronnie Biggs didn't actually join the team until long after the so-called big boys. Small-timer Biggs was trying to 'go straight' at the time by using the carpentry skills he'd picked up in prison. But Biggs couldn't resist Bruce Reynolds's exciting description of the robbery, especially the £40,000 share, which would have bought four or five houses back then. Reynolds needed to recruit a diesel locomotive driver, and Biggs came up with one from his local railway yard in South London, where he'd been working as a builder. The driver, known as 'Peter,' also couldn't resist the prospect of tens of thousands of pounds. Bruce

Reynolds believed he was now in a perfect position to launch his audacious raid.

The robbery itself went very smoothly, apart from the fact that one gang member hit mail train driver Jack Mills over the head with a cosh, and some years later Mills was said to have died as a result of that injury. However their loot, estimated at £1 million, was soon burning a hole in the pride of the British establishment, and the entire gang were eventually rounded up by police. The only one to plead guilty was Roger Cordrey, who got 20 years, even though he paid back every penny of his £80,000 share of the proceeds.

The Judge, Mr Justice Edmund Davies, refusing to ignore the injury inflicted on driver Jack Mills during the robbery, told Cordrey, 'Let us clear out of the way any romantic notions of daredevilry. This is nothing less than a sordid crime of violence inspired by vast greed . . . anybody who has seen the nerve-shattered engine driver can have no doubt of the terrifying effect on the law-abiding citizen, of a concerted assault by masked and armed robbers in lonely darkness.'

An incredible worldwide media circus followed the trial of the other gang members at the offices of Aylesbury Rural Council. During the case, all the defendants pleaded their innocence and one robber even claimed he'd only ever heard of the raid 'in the papers'. But the jury saw through their lies and the gang were sentenced to a total of 307 years, most members getting between 20 and 30 years each.

Great Train Robber Buster Edwards hanged himself at the age of 63 on 29 November 1994 in a lock-up garage near the flower stall he had run for many years at Waterloo Station. He had a serious drinking problem and was suffering from depression.

Fellow Great Train Robber Roy 'The Weasel' James died of a heart attack on 21 August 1997 after a catalogue of problems in the

1990s, culminating in January 1994 when a court heard he'd shot his former father-in-law three times and pistol-whipped his ex-wife in a row over their divorce settlement. James was jailed for six years for the attacks.

Bruce 'The Colonel' Reynolds wrote his autobiography, which was published in 1995, and now lives in a modest flat in Croydon, South London. He keeps a low profile but occasionally appears on TV to talk about his memories of the Great Train Robbery.

In the same year as the Great Train Robbery, a West End Central police officer called Detective Sergeant Harry Challenor was exposed as one of the decade's most notorious 'bent coppers'. He'd planted knives, hatchets and iron bars on dozens of innocent citizens. He even claimed to have 'found' explosive detonators at the home of one so-called bank robber. The evil deeds of Detective Challenor – a Freemason – only came to light after he arrested a group of youths demonstrating against a visit to London by Queen Frederika of Greece. Challenor claimed he had found pieces of brick in their pockets, with the clear implication that they'd intended to throw the bricks at the Queen or policemen guarding her hotel. But all the youths were cleared when expert analysis showed that there was no brick dust in their pockets. Challenor ended up in the dock charged with conspiring to pervert the course of justice, alongside three junior constables who'd worked with him. Challenor was eventually found unfit to plead and sentenced to be detained in a mental hospital 'at Her Majesty's pleasure'. The other constables got three years each.

Mad Frankie Fraser was released from prison in the early 1960s when he met Charlie and Eddie Richardson, members of the notorious Richardson Gang from South London and rivals to the Kray Twins.

Fraser later claimed they helped him avoid arrest for the Great Train Robbery (in which he played no part) by bribing a policeman.

By this time the Richardson brothers were well-established crime kings south of the Thames and fast expanding. Charlie and Eddie, from Camberwell, were running Peckford Scrap Metal Limited, while also making a small fortune fencing other people's stolen goods, including many of the watches and jewellery from smash 'n' grab raids in the West End.

All this helped swell the Richardsons' coffers. Soon they were spreading into the West End drinking clubs and even goldmines in South Africa. Boss Charlie Richardson impressed all he met because he had the ability to be socially acceptable everywhere he went – either at upmarket West End clubs or on the back streets of South London.

The Richardsons' tough-guy father served in the merchant navy, and mum Eileen ran a sweetshop, bringing up her children in a 56-shilling-a-week council flat on an East Dulwich estate. Both Richardson brothers had been excellent boxers in their youth. At the age of 14, Charlie Richardson found himself the head of the family when his father walked out on his mother, two younger brothers and a sister. When the school leaving age was raised from 14 to 15, Charlie went AWOL, because he'd been planning his adulthood for years.

The Richardsons eventually moved into Soho with a very profitable fruit-machine business called the Atlantic Company. The brothers shrewdly made the tinderbox Mad Frankie Fraser a partner in Atlantic after he'd earned a fearsome reputation in the 1950s as London's premier hard-man, having notched up a list of victims headed by Jack Spot, as detailed earlier.

Mad Frankie Fraser was 39 in 1962 when he emerged from his seven-year sentence for cutting Spot at Albert Dimes's behest. On his release, Dimes and Billy Hill gave Fraser a party at the Pigalle Club in Piccadilly, with singer Shirley Bassey and Winifred Attwell, the ragtime pianist, as guests of honour. Then the Richardsons persuaded him to join forces with them.

By the early 1960s Charlie Richardson had a string of companies and an office in London's swish Park Lane, with nearly 100 employees. On paper, he was a millionaire, and he'd gathered round him some of the toughest faces in the country and formed them into a fearsome gang.

Just like the Krays, the Richardson brothers adored mixing with celebrities and wheeler-dealers. One night their henchman Jimmy Moody gave a Krays aide a hiding for daring to attack one of the Richardsons' best pals inside their beloved Astor Club. Moody pinned the man to a wall with an axe and told him not to be a naughty boy ever again. The axe didn't even merit a raised eyebrow in the club.

Charlie Richardson was raking in so much money he could afford one of the biggest houses in Denmark Hill in southeast London, which had once been owned by Canon William Fenton Morley, the Rural Dean of Leeds. No wonder many people in his manor referred to Charlie in virtually royal terms. He even got himself a Dobermann pinscher to guard his impressive house, and he kept a well-stocked bar in the lounge for whenever his team popped round for a chat. The wallpaper was blood-red and the furniture surprisingly tasteful and traditional.

Charlie, chubby faced and always neatly dressed in a pressed 50-guinea suit, dreamt of being another Al Capone. He led an empire built on fear. Richardson and his gang meted out their own brutal rough justice and created their own set of laws. 'Trials' were held in shabby warehouses they called 'courtrooms'. Sadistic punishments included tooth pulling, beatings, stabbings, burnings,

being nailed to the floor, having toes ripped off with bolt cutters and being electrocuted into unconsciousness. If victims were too badly injured, they would be sent to a doctor who'd been struck off the medical register and they would not dare ever talk to the 'Old Filth'.

Members of the Richardson team often stood around laughing and jeering as punishments were handed out. The process became known as 'taking a shirt from Charlie', because of Richardson's practice of giving a bruised and bleeding victim a clean shirt so that he could go back home without arousing too much attention.

Charlie Richardson was happy to tell anyone who'd listen that he and his gang, 'Kept crime in our area down and controlled what people got up to. We performed a social service.' Brothers Charlie and Eddie believed in the so-called good old days when, 'You could leave your door open when you went out. We had no muggings and no local burglary. If there was any, I would find out who did it and give them a smack in the mouth before the Old Bill ever heard about it.'

The escape from Winson Green Prison of Great Train Robber and notorious South London gangster Charlie Wilson guaranteed he would go down in the annals of crime history. In the spring of 1964, when Wilson arrived at the prison, about two miles from Birmingham, it was home to nearly 800 inmates, and almost half those slept three to a cell. From a distance, the prison was like a little toy fort perched on a hilltop overlooking England's second-biggest city. The drab-grey walls were separated only by a pair of massive iron-studded wooden gates. This medieval, high-walled encampment was, like its star prisoner, infamous for its silence. Winson Green had, until a couple of years earlier, been the scene of regular hangings when the death penalty was still the law of the land.

Lurking in the back of Wilson's mind was an escape plan. Soon after arriving at Winson Green he'd begun stealing sugar from the prison canteen and scattering it outside his cell, so that when the prison was silent at night he could hear a faint scrunch as the screws came to look at him through the spyhole in the door. In this way he could time their comings and goings. Wilson noted that at weekends the older officers were replaced by younger, more vigorous screws who might prove a problem during a breakout. Charlie also smuggled into his cell some of the black grease used in the workshop to water-proof mailbag straps, which he used to blacken the bulb in his cell because the round-the-clock-light rule was making it difficult for him to sleep properly.

At 5.30 p.m. on 12 August 1964, Charlie Wilson was given a supper of bread, cheese and soup. At 7.30 p.m. he drained his nightcap cup of cocoa and whispered to himself, 'Here's to the outside world.' Then he settled down to read a book on ancient history – his latest favourite subject – which he'd borrowed from the prison library. At 9.30 p.m. it was lights out and Charlie climbed into his bed. He immediately closed his eyes, but as he later explained, 'For the next few hours, my ears became my eyes.' He didn't know exactly what time they'd come for him, just that it was going to be that night.

In fact the escape team was already in the vicinity in a Ford Zodiac and a converted petrol-tanker lorry, which was to become Wilson's temporary home. Elsewhere in C Block, prisoners lay awake, including one with a tiny transistor radio, modified so that it would transmit rather than receive. Its range was only about 400 yards, but it was enough. Just then a third vehicle – a fake taxi fitted with a radio receiver – arrived in the street outside the prison. The driver and its one passenger received a faint message from the radio: 'Screw's been to Wilson's cell'. That information would be reported back each time the guard visited Charlie's cell throughout the night.

Outside, the blue Zodiac carrying three men and a woman stopped by the corner of the prison overlooking the canal. Then the petrol tanker pulled up one block from the prison. Three of the team – armed with a set of duplicated keys – met outside the prison wall.

Back inside his cell Charlie Wilson couldn't do anything to prepare for the escape team in case it was noticed by the warden carrying out checks every 12 to 15 minutes. At approximately 2.35 a.m. one of the two officers on duty in Charlie's C Block went to the kitchen to prepare the breakfast porridge, leaving the prison open to a serious breach of security because the five night staff patrolling the wings were locked in and carried no keys.

At 3 a.m. the three-man escape team dumped their equipment on the ground. Then all three pulled black-stocking face masks over their heads, with holes cut out for their eyes. A grappling hook was flung upwards against the outer wall, which the men scaled and then dropped into the exercise yard outside B Block and headed towards where Wilson was incarcerated.

Less than a minute later the men knocked night security officer William Nicholls unconscious with a cosh and tied him up with nylon rope. Then they used a duplicate key to open the outside door to B Block. This was followed by another key to open the steel grille door behind it. At 3.08 a.m. the raiders used a key specially cut for the job to open Wilson's cell so quietly that the next-door inmate heard nothing. As the door swung open, the three men burst in.

Wilson pulled on a roll-necked black sweater, a pair of dark trousers, plimsolls and a balaclava. Then he followed them out of the cell, past the trussed-up warder towards the centre of the prison before cutting back through A Wing and past the prison bathhouse and down some stairs. The locksmith stayed an extra two minutes to re-lock all the doors.

Wilson and his jailbreak team got out of the prison in under three minutes. Half a minute later he was in the fake petrol tanker, where he found three mattresses, pillows and blankets. Within an hour, he was in a private plane heading for France.

One of the first people to be told about Charlie's escape was Tommy Butler, still head of the Yard's Flying Squad. Under him, 300 men continued investigating the Great Train Robbery and were still looking for Buster Edwards, who was then 34, and his wife June, plus the other suspected robber on the run, Bruce Reynolds. Butler was not in the least bit surprised: ever since the end of their trial he'd been predicting one of the train robbers would escape. Wilson's breakout undoubtedly elevated his status in underworld folklore. And as the hours turned into days following his escape, it was the mighty Establishment who were being increasingly blamed for it.

Halfway across the globe, in Mexico City, one of the two train robbers who hadn't yet been arrested – Bruce Reynolds – was leaning back on a park bench with his feet in the sun when he opened his three-day-old English newspaper to see the headline 'JAIL BUSTERS FREE TRAIN ROBBER – THEY KNOCK OUT GUARD, OPEN CELL, GIVE PRISONER NEW SUIT'. As Reynolds recalled many years later, 'I just thought to myself, "Nice one, Charlie!" His success filled me with pride. We'd finessed the Establishment yet again.'

A couple of weeks after his escape, Wilson moved from the French countryside to an apartment in Paris. He decided that he needed a disguise, because Interpol had now joined the hunt for him. He didn't leave the Paris flat for a fortnight while he grew out

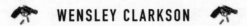

his prison-cropped hair before dying it jet black. On the run in Europe, Charlie Wilson read about the Establishment's problems with relish. Sure, he was a professional criminal, but he also loved poking two fingers at the 'beaks' who ran his country.

In July 1965, 11 months after Charlie Wilson walked out of Winson Green prison, Great Train Robber Ronnie Biggs pulled off an equally outrageous escape from Wandsworth Prison in South London. This was to be as dramatic as Charlie's had been smooth. As prisoners exercised in the prison yard, a furniture van drew up alongside the wall of the prison and an armed man leapt on to the roof of the vehicle. Then he dropped a tubular ladder into the prison yard below. Four prisoners ran towards the ladder, scrambled up it and jumped down on to the van. Biggs and the three other inmates then exited through a hole in the roof into the back of the lorry, and half a mile later split up and fled in three waiting cars.

Ronnie Biggs's escape was without doubt another nail in the Establishment's coffin. A headline and story in the **Daily Express** summed it up perfectly: 'FREED AT GUNPOINT: The Train Robbers snatched another of their £2,500,000 gang from prison yesterday – at gunpoint, in daylight, in public, in the heart of London.'

Biggs's successful breakout, despite the supposed 24-hour lockdown imposed on all the train robbers following Wilson's escape, simply added to the robbers' legendary status. How could they keep humiliating the Establishment and expect to get away with it? Biggs's escape was also good news for Wilson, because the police switched much of their attention away from him. The headlines that followed Biggs for many years turned out to be even bigger and bolder than those for Wilson. Some of the robbers were deeply unhappy with Biggs because they said his escape made it even harder for them to plan similar breakouts, with the police and Home Office cracking down on security in prisons across the land after the fiasco. Ronnie Biggs used plastic surgery to change his appearance and moved to Spain, then Australia, before settling in Brazil.

In November 1965 Charlie Wilson flew into Mexico City to meet his old Great Train Robber pals, Bruce Reynolds and Buster Edwards. Reynolds barely recognised Charlie when he went to meet him at the airport. Reynolds later recalled in his autobiography *Crossing the Line*, 'He had always been big, over six foot and powerfully built, but he turned up with a fantastic tan, ginger hair and a dyed ginger beard. He also wore small wire-rimmed glasses, which looked incongruous, and I thought, "My God – what have you done to yourself?"'

Wilson told Reynolds and Edwards he'd chosen Canada because he knew his wife, Pat, 'wasn't too keen on foreigners', and the city of Montreal seemed the best place for them. Wilson said Mexico would never have been suitable because he hated not being able to speak the local language and wasn't too keen on the food, either. Pat and the girls were still back in England at this time, but Wilson told his old friends he was certain he could 'smuggle 'em out' to start a new life in Canada.

In early January 1966 Wilson flew into Montreal via Brussels as a new immigrant using a fake passport in the name of Ronald Alloway. His wife and their three daughters eventually joined him there, and they lived in peace and harmony in a small town just outside Montreal. As Bruce Reynolds later recalled, 'The Wilsons were a very happy family. Chas idolised his wife Pat and their three daughters. His family life was, and always had been, sacrosanct. Sure, he played around, but never to the detriment of his wife and family. In all respects, he was a great father and a good husband.'

But in January 1968 the tenacious Tommy Butler got a tip that Wilson was in Canada, and he and a team of Royal Canadian Mounties swooped. Wilson's life on the run was over.

In early February 1966, South Londoners Eddie Richardson and Mad Frankie Fraser approached the management of a club called Mr Smith's in Catford, southeast London, with a proposition that they could 'assist' in keeping order there. A few days later, Richardson brought some suitable 'employees' to the club for a meeting to rubber stamp the arrangement. Eddie's older and more powerful brother Charlie was away on business in South Africa, otherwise, many have since insisted, the spiral of violence that was to follow might never have occurred.

It had all begun on a quiet Sunday a few weeks earlier when 39-year-old James Andrews, a known associate of the Krays, was shot and injured from a passing white car outside his home in Rotherfield Street, Islington, North London. Fingers were immediately pointed at the Richardsons. The impetuous tinderbox Eddie Richardson later insisted that he wasn't interested in starting a war with the Krays. Certainly, a couple of days after the Andrews shooting he seemed more concerned with his unwritten contract to 'look after' Mr Smith's. The Richardsons' and Mad Frankie Fraser's company Atlantic Machines had agreed to put slot machines on the premises. Mr Smith's, one of the largest nightclubs in London, was so named because its low prices catered for the 'Mr Smiths' of this world. The furniture was classy and the lighting as mean and moody as the regulars.

Opened in October 1965, with Diana Dors – Britain's answer to Marilyn Monroe – providing the cabaret, Mr Smith's was soon a runaway success and packed out most days and nights of the week. It housed a restaurant, bar, dance floor, two bands, a vocalist and cabaret. There were also tables for gaming – boule, blackjack and dice. But by February 1966 there was a definite feeling of tension on the premises. Many of the staff and customers had already been removed by the management, who felt trouble was brewing. One night, staff spotted a man with a gun in a shoulder holster under his jacket as he used the phone in the reception.

At around 10 p.m. that same evening Mad Frankie Fraser and Eddie Richardson walked into the club with their associates, including a henchman called Ronnie Jeffreys. The atmosphere immediately changed. All of them noticed well-known local face Billy Hayward drinking in another corner with a man called Henry Botton and one of the notorious Hennessey brothers, Peter. Billy Hayward's boys from Abbey Wood were known as 'a right bunch of nutters' around the Deptford and Lewisham areas. Their henchman Hennessey was dubbed a loudmouthed braggart. The Krays considered the Haywards to be on their team, even though they came from the wrong side of the river.

Just then, Richardson henchman Jimmy Moody – another Atlantic [the Richardsons' company] employee – strolled into the club with associate Harry Rawlings and approached Fraser and Richardson's table. He told them he was planning to rob the club's casino and had come in to case the joint. Fraser thought Moody was kidding and told him, 'We're gonna be employin' the doormen, and we'll be helpin' them, not hinderin' them – forget it.'

Moody immediately backed down, and Fraser later admitted he couldn't tell if Moody had been serious about the robbery plan. Meanwhile, Billy Hayward closely watched Moody's movements inside the club and looked paranoid that something was about to happen. By 3.30 a.m. Moody, Fraser, Eddie Richardson and their pals were the only ones left in the club besides Billy Hayward and his associates. Then one of Richardson's team spotted a .410

shotgun strapped inside Billy Hayward's jacket. Within seconds insults were being traded and trigger fingers started twitching.

The club's owners then asked Eddie Richardson to politely inform Hayward it was closing time and he should leave. Staff rang a local taxi firm to send several cars to take customers away. Richardson then tried to assert his authority on the proceedings. Eyeing up Hennessey as he spoke, Eddie Richardson spat, 'No one gets another fuckin' drink without my say-so.' Then he smashed a bottle on the table... 'Unless you want some of this.'

Seconds later the two men ripped off their jackets and steamed into each other for a brutal stand-up fight on the dance floor. Thirty feet away Hayward's friend Dickie Hart was stroking the trigger of his .45 revolver. Eddie Richardson was still hammering Peter Hennessey into the floor when Billy Hayward tried to pull out his sawn-off, but it got caught up in his coat. Jimmy Moody then grabbed a heavy glass ashtray and smashed it over Hayward's head, knocking him out. That's when someone shouted, 'Shoot the bastards.' Hart panicked and started firing in all directions. Within seconds the club was echoing to a hail of gunfire, with men hiding behind tables and others lying injured. Chicago had come to London in 1966.

One blast of the shotgun peppered Eddie Richardson in the buttocks. Another bullet hit a chair leg and another the roof. A fourth shot tore into the shoulder of Moody's mate Harry Rawlings, bursting an artery. Staff scrambled for the exits, knocking over tables and chairs, as more screams and shouts rang out. As people moved out through the doors and into the street, the fight still raged, with men firing from behind walls and hedges. To the crack of revolvers was added the blast of another sawn-off shotgun. At least eight guns were in action. Detectives responding to a flood of 999 calls later found trails of blood splashed on pavements and walls outside the club exits.

Back inside the club, Mad Frankie Fraser yelled at Hart that Rawlings was badly injured and demanded that an ambulance be called. Hart agreed but then saw Jimmy Moody approaching and let off another shot. Moody ignored it and leaned down to try to help Rawlings by tying a handkerchief around his arm in a tourniquet to stop the blood draining out of his body.

Moody and Ronnie Jeffreys then carried Rawlings out of the club. Fraser walked in front of them as cover. Dickie Hart followed behind with his gun panning nervously in all directions. Suddenly, Fraser punched Hart hard in the mouth, grabbed his wrist and tried to take the gun, which went off, shooting Fraser in the thigh. As bulldog Fraser knocked the gun away from Hart's grasp and collapsed in a heap with a shattered thigh bone, another shot rang out.

One of Billy Hayward's men yelled, 'You're fuckin' mad, Frank.'

Fraser was pulled to his feet by another associate and hopped on one leg 300 yards down the street before collapsing into a thick privet hedge. Dickie Hart had caught a bullet from his own gun during the struggle with Fraser and staggered off in the opposite direction. In the middle of all this mayhem, the Richardsons' henchman, Jimmy Moody, rolled up in his silver Mark 2 Jag as more shots rang out. But Moody was oblivious to the danger and headed for his injured pals. By this time more than 20 people were embroiled in a deadly free-for-all. Gunshot victim Dickie Hart even managed to kick a few more people before collapsing on the pavement. Billy Hayward staggered from the scene with his gashed head pumping blood in all directions. Hennessey and another man crawled off into the night.

Jimmy Moody and Ronnie Jeffreys bundled Eddie Richardson and the badly bleeding Rawlings into his Jag and pulled away from the mayhem. A few minutes later, Moody dropped an unnamed man off near the Rotherhithe Tunnel, apparently trying to lay a false trail for the police. Then he took the wounded Eddie Richardson and Harry Rawlings to the casualty department at East Dulwich Hospital.

The body of Dickie Hart lay crumpled under a lilac tree outside 48 Farley Road. He'd been shot in the face and some of the 'opposition' had played football with his head. It wasn't a pretty sight. At first, police mistook his corpse for a sack of old potatoes. A preliminary postmortem later showed that he'd died as a result of a .45 bullet wound in his chest close to his heart.

Meanwhile, Mad Frankie Fraser – the most badly injured apart from the dead man – lay under a privet hedge, where he'd buried himself for camouflage, in his bloodstained, 70-guinea Savile-row suit, with an open razor in his top pocket. A police constable called David Emberson found Fraser lying face down behind the hedge. When he tried to turn him over, Fraser yelled out in pain: he had been lying on the gun that had killed Dickie Hart.

Flying Squad chief Tommy Butler was outraged by the shooting and swore to track down the culprits. Butler – known as a '24-hour copper with the brain of a don and the memory of an elephant' – was going to need all his skill and experience to sort out the Mr Smith's shootings before anyone else got hurt. Meanwhile, Eddie Richardson, Mad Frankie Fraser and Harry Rawlings remained at East Dulwich Hospital, suffering from gunshot wounds, along with Moody's ashtray-victim Billy Hayward. The four men were all put under a 24-hour police guard 'for their own protection'.

The day after the Mr Smith's affray, armed detectives swooped on Jimmy Moody at his aunt Edie's house in Auckland Hill, West Norwood, in South London, after an anonymous tipster spotted his gleaming silver Jag parked in the driveway. Moody was so shocked to have been tracked down that he put up little resistance as detectives cuffed him before bundling him into the back of a Black Maria.

However, the battle of Mr Smith's paled into insignificance compared with the war that was just about to erupt. Rumours began sweeping across the Thames of a revenge attack by the remaining Richardson soldiers, said to be preparing to hit the Krays outside The Lion pub in Tapp Street, Bethnal Green, the following Saturday.

But the guns of gangland were to come out again even sooner. This time the venue was the Blind Beggar pub in Whitechapel. It was already well known as the favourite haunt of Ginger Marks, whose disappearance after being shot near the pub in January 1965 had first increased tensions between the Krays and the Richardsons.

Drinking gin-and-tonic in the Beggar a couple of nights after the Mr Smith's shoot-out was 38-year-old George Cornell, described as a car dealer from Camberwell. He'd crossed the Krays after working for them and then going back south across the river to join forces with rivals, Charlie and Eddie Richardson and their psychotic associate Mad Frankie Fraser.

Earlier, the twins had tried to muscle in on the Richardsons' manor, until Cornell was dispatched to the East End to tell them they weren't welcome. The Krays played ball, but Ronnie later said he took umbrage at the way Cornell had handled the 'problem' for the Richardsons. In fact, Ronnie was nursing a king-sized grudge, and following that shoot-up at Mr Smith's Club, convinced himself that a heavyweight response was in order.

On the evening of Wednesday 9 March 1966, Cornell and a sidekick called Albie Woods went to see their pal Jimmy Andrews in hospital, after he'd lost a leg in the Mr Smith's shoot-out. Rumours were flying around that Cornell was the man who'd shot

down Dickie Hart at Mr Smith's. Driving back from the hospital, Cornell and Woods popped into the Blind Beggar for some refreshment. It just happened to be on Whitechapel Road, right in the heart of Krays' territory.

Around the corner, one of the Krays' 'spies' walked into The Lion – nicknamed 'The Widow's – and told Ronnie Kray that Cornell was on the manor. Ronnie was so incensed he barked out orders to brother Reg's driver, John 'Scotch Jack' Dickson, and his right-hand man Ian Barrie, and they marched out of The Lion. Moments later they were charging towards the Blind Beggar in a black Ford Consul, stopping off en route to pick up some guns.

A few minutes later Scotch Jack pulled up outside the Blind Beggar in the Consul. Ronnie Kray and Ian Barrie walked straight into the pub to find Cornell sitting at the end of the bar with three associates. A Walker Brothers record was playing, aptly enough entitled 'The Sun Ain't Gonna Shine Any More'. Cornell, with drink in hand, saw Kray approaching from the door of the saloon bar and just had time to say, 'Look who's here, the fat poof,' before Ronnie drew a pistol out of his right-hand overcoat pocket, levelled it at Cornell's head and fired a 9 mm bullet squarely into the centre of his rival's forehead. He was dead before he even hit the ground.

Cornell's two associates dived to the floor just as Ian Barrie pulled out an automatic and fired two bullets into the wall above their heads. Then Kray and his associate calmly strolled back outside to their waiting car.

Rumours that Cornell's killer was Ronnie Kray ensured that the Krays and the Richardsons brought down the shutters on their so-called glamorous, high-profile lifestyles and returned to what they knew best – cold-blooded intimidation and revenge. Crime reporters started getting threatening phone calls warning them to lay off the two families. Gangster clubs closed down overnight, and the celebrities – who'd made it their business to knock around with the villains – suddenly fled all the usual haunts.

On 11 March 1966 the police officially confirmed a link between Dickie Hart's death at Mr Smith's and the shooting of George Cornell at the Blind Beggar. Detectives also believed that a third man had been 'marked for murder' by the same gangs. Police were anxiously trying to trace the unnamed man before he was killed.

With Flying Squad chief Tommy Butler at the helm, it was clear Scotland Yard would come down hard on the gangsters threatening the peace on London's streets. But the police were handicapped by the wall of silence maintained by all involved. Many officers were openly blaming the warfare on changes in the UK laws, which had allowed roulette and other games to be set up in clubs.

And Ronnie Kray never regretted the death of George Cornell. 'He was a drunkard and a bully. I done the Earth a favour,' he explained many years later. Kray believed he had the 'right' to shoot Cornell dead because it was a battle between soldiers of crime who knew the risks they were taking. The police quickly rounded up the twins and held a series of ID parades. But fear of the Krays crossed all boundaries and a series of so-called witnesses failed to identify the brothers and police had no option but to release them. So, for the moment, their reign of terror would continue.

Following arrests in connection with the Mr Smith's gunfight, Jimmy Moody, Eddie Richardson and Billy Hayward appeared before magistrates in Woolwich on 17 March 1966. They were charged with making an affray and possession of offensive weapons. The badly injured Mad Frankie Fraser was charged with murdering Dickie Hart.

Tommy Butler said all four should be kept in custody because of the gravity of their offences and fears about their own safety. Others, including Henry Rawlings, 35, of Logs Hill, Chislehurst, Kent, who was recovering from his injuries, faced similar charges. Ron Jeffreys, 29, described in court as a Covent Garden porter, of Ferndene Road, Herne Hill, southeast London, was also charged with causing an affray in the same incident.

Shortly after the start of the Mr Smith's trial at the Old Bailey in early July 1966, Charlie Richardson – now back from South Africa – gave his strong-arm boys a list of all the jurors' names. Richardson instructed them to find out where they lived and 'pay them a little visit'. Charlie boasted that one woman witness had already accepted a bribe. The first witness to take the oath even had to be ordered to attend the court after he refused to give evidence.

It was later revealed that a juryman was twice approached by different people to give a false verdict. Before the hearing was resumed on 6 July 1966, the judge and other court officials examined police reports about attempts to nobble the case. The judge refused to abandon the trial but told the court, 'I wish to stress as strongly as I can that you are here to try the defendants on evidence that you hear in this court and this court alone.' Police guards were immediately put on all the jurors' homes.

In the public furore following the Mr Smith's shooting, Flying Squad chief Tommy Butler and his hand-picked team of detectives heard from a terrified informant that the Richardsons were holding torture sessions to punish other criminals. They were determined to track down more witnesses before the Richardsons and their team of gangsters started exerting 'pressure' on anyone brave enough to give evidence against them.

Police investigating the torture allegations swooped on Charlie

Richardson's Georgian mansion in southeast London at dawn on 30 July 1966. In all, a total of eight men plus Richardson's common-law wife Jean were arrested, although she was later released on bail. There was stunned disbelief in southeast London that 'untouchable' Charlie Richardson had been arrested on these new, much more serious charges. Many in the area believed the entire police force was in the Richardsons' pocket and there'd be no witnesses prepared to speak out against him and his gang. Many also presumed Richardson would buy off the judge in the case.

Shortly after Charlie's arrest, an Old Bailey jury found Eddie Richardson – described as a 30-year-old chemist of Mead Road, Chislehurst, Kent – guilty of causing an affray at Mr Smith's. He was sentenced to five years in prison. Mad Frankie Fraser was acquitted of murder charges, although he was found guilty of fighting and making an affray and also got a five-year sentence.

The police were disappointed about the acquittal of three other defendants in the Mr Smith's trial but felt certain that they would nail down the entire gang at the main torture trial scheduled for early the following year. The Krays were buoyant and even more confident that they were now the Number One crime family in London.

Mixed in with all this death and destruction on the streets of London were some even more evil characters, such as Eastender Frank 'Mad Axeman' Mitchell, said to be as strong as a fork-lift truck. Mitchell's criminal career kicked off at just 17 and was peppered with spells in prisons as well as Rampton and Broadmoor mental institutions. 'He wasn't really crazy, he just had the mind of a child, and just like a child he liked to throw a few tantrums,' the Krays' website (www.thekrays.co.uk) helpfully explains.

On the run from Broadmoor, Mitchell once held an elderly couple captive in their own home using an axe stolen from their garden shed. Bizarrely, Mitchell insisted the elderly pair watch TV while he supped a cup of tea with the axe neatly balanced across his knees. Hence the nickname 'The Mad Axeman'.

Mitchell eventually surrendered and was incarcerated in Dartmoor Prison, in Devon, after being given an extra life term for the kidnap of the couple. He was soon deemed 'uncontrollable' by guards who gave him a wide berth, enabling him to serve his sentence with little or no interference from authorities. Mitchell even got out of Dartmoor on daily work details and was known to pop into a local pub for a pint alongside a friendly warden.

Nine years into his life sentence, Mitchell – now aged 37 – requested a release date but was turned down by the then Home Secretary. According to many of his associates, including the Krays, that was when the Mad Axeman felt it was time to take some drastic measures. Mitchell had originally first encountered the twins many years earlier in Wandsworth Prison. The hard-man began sending letters to Ronnie Kray, venting his anger about not being given a review date for his case. Then Reg turned up at Dartmoor in disguise, with a boxer called Ted 'Kid' Lewis, to screen boxing films to the inmates, including Mitchell. The governor was so delighted he asked both men to come back 'any time', unaware that one of them was the notorious Kray, hatching an audacious plan to 'spring' their most famous inmate.

Just a few days later – on 12 December 1966 – Mitchell strolled out of Dartmoor to be picked up by a limo and driven back to The Smoke by Krays associates, Albert Donoghue, 'Mad' Tommy Smith and Billy Exley. Mitchell – kitted out in a new suit – was taken to a London hideout but then changed his mind and ended up at his pal Lennie Dunn's flat in Canning Town in the East End. The gang then mounted a campaign to help Mitchell cut his sentence by flooding newspapers with protest letters so that they'd publicise his case.

The Kray twins later insisted Mitchell's breakout was purely to highlight his lack of a release date. Initially they were convinced if they could keep him out long enough without him getting into trouble, then the government would have to consider his case. Meanwhile, members of the Krays' entourage were obliged to keep Mitchell under lock and key in Dunn's flat. They even provided a pretty young hostess from the Krays' Winston Club, to satisfy Mitchell's sexual needs. She didn't bat an eyelid at the nationwide hunt for the so-called 'evil criminal' and it was later claimed the couple even genuinely fell in love.

But years of roaming the moors while serving his prison sentence meant Mitchell couldn't handle being holed-up in a tiny flat. In many ways it was worse than being inside, and the Krays' gang started to seem more like prison screws than fellow criminals. Mitchell's regular guards, Scotch Jack Dickson and Billy Exley, soon reported his unhappiness back to the Kray twins.

Ronnie later claimed that Exley and a gang of London-based Greeks offered to get Mitchell out of the country for a fee. But Mitchell proved such a handful they had to get rid of him, according to Ronnie. It was Exley who was said to have eventually fired the fatal shot.

Many years later it was revealed that it was Krays' gang member Albert Donoghue who convinced Frank Mitchell that he was invited for Christmas at Ronnie's pile in Kent and they picked him up in a waiting van. Sitting opposite him was Krays' associate Freddie Foreman and his pal Alfie Gerrard. As the van drove off, Mitchell was torn apart by 12 bullets. Donoghue later claimed he delivered £1,000 cash to Foreman on the twins' behalf. However, Foreman says to this day that no money changed hands, as he'd done it 'as a favour for one of the chaps'.

Reggie's Kray's personal life was also proving to be quite a handful at this time. His troubled marriage to wife Frances was less than a year old, but already his bride, exhausted by the strain of Reggie's lifestyle, had attempted suicide on two occasions. On 6 June 1967 the pair booked a holiday to Spain in an attempt to make a fresh start. But the following day her brother found Frances dead after she'd swallowed a massive overdose of barbiturates.

Reggie Kray immediately took solace in drink, and his behaviour deteriorated, to the alarm of the Firm. He shot a man he thought had insulted Frances (fortunately, he was so drunk he merely wounded him) and shot another man in a Highbury club in a drunken argument. Worried gang members began to drift away from the Firm, and the increasingly paranoid Ronnie became convinced others were out to challenge his authority.

As the 1960s progressed, the number of armed robberies in London increased dramatically. Part of the reason was the fact that banks sought to become more welcoming for customers. Out went the old grilles and the high walls; in came open-plan branches. The new designs were a honey-pot for thieves. And widespread corruption in the police, especially at Scotland Yard, did not help. So many bribes were being dished out to informers and the underworld that the Met began to collude with crime rather than solve it. As Bobby King, an armed robber in the 1960s and early '70s, once put it, 'If you learnt the Flying Squad was involved with the police investigation, you started to feel a bit better. You knew you could always do business with them for cash.'

Harry Roberts, now 69, is still serving a life sentence for the murder of three policemen in Shepherd's Bush, West London, in 1966, even though his 30-year tariff expired many years ago. In

April 2005 the Law Lords ruled against his sentence appeal by a majority of three to two. Roberts was jailed for murdering Police Constable Geoffrey Fox, 41, Sergeant Christopher Head, 30, and Detective Constable David Wombwell, 25. The officers were gunned down in front of children playing in a street after the policemen had pulled over a van containing Roberts and two other men, following an armed robbery. The murder of the three plain-clothes officers was one of the most high-profile crimes of the 1960s.

Roberts was transferred to an open prison in 2001, in what was thought to be a prelude to his release. But he was frequently alleged to have been involved in drug dealing, bringing contraband into prison and other illegal activities, which jeopardised his release. He was sent back to a closed prison after another review from then Home Secretary David Blunkett, who viewed material withheld from Roberts. At the time of writing, yet another appeal has just been turned down.

East Ender Jack 'The Hat' McVitie specialised in ripping anyone apart who dared upset the Krays. At the Regency Club, owned by close pals of the Krays, McVitie was renowned for once stabbing another villain just to send a message that the Krays were top dogs. He was also known to wave sawn-off shotguns at criminal rivals. McVitie's nickname came from his habit of always wearing a trilby hat over his bald patch. However, by 1967 he was hitting the booze, and swallowing back handfuls of the amphetamines, 'speed', which he also regularly sold to other criminals. He'd also taken £100 from Ronnie to murder another rival with a promise of another £400 once the job was complete. McVitie was so wrecked by drink and drugs by this stage that he never carried out the killing or repaid Ronnie his cash. Big mistake.

So when, on 28 October 1967 'The Hat' showed up at party in a Stoke Newington basement, he was signing his own death warrant. Already in attendance were the twins plus their sidekicks, the deadly brothers Chris and Tony Lambrianou. Many believe this fearsome mob already knew McVitie was on his way and that the twins had specially lined up the Lambrianou brothers to teach 'The Hat' a lesson he would never forget.

Within minutes of McVitie's arrival at the party, Ronnie verbally laid into him. Then Reg followed up with a pistol to his head. No one was surprised when, seconds later, Reg squeezed the trigger. But the gun jammed. Reggie held it there for a moment or two before grabbing a knife from a nearby table and plunging it deep into 'The Hat's' stomach, impaling him to the floor in the process. He expired seconds later. McVitie's corpse was eventually wrapped in a quilt and driven south of the river by Tony Lambrianou, with brother Chris in convoy. 'The Hat's' body eventually showed up outside St Mary's Church, near the Rotherhithe Tunnel. The twins blew a gasket because it was just a stone's throw from the home of their old pal, South London gang boss Freddie Foreman, which could have proved quite an embarrassment.

In 1969, two years after Jack 'The Hat' took his final breath, the Krays found themselves facing an Old Bailey jury who deliberated for six hours and 55 minutes before returning a unanimous guilty verdict after the longest (39 days) and most expensive murder trial held in a London court. Others found guilty of the killing included the Lambrianou brothers plus associate Ronnie Bender and the Krays' elder brother, Charlie. Freddie Foreman and Cornelius Whitehead were found guilty of being accessories to the killing. Another man, Tony Barry, was found not guilty and set free. Krays' henchman Albert Donoghue had earlier pleaded guilty to being an accessory to murder.

GANG WARS OF LONDON

The judge recommended that the twins should be detained for a minimum of 30 years – the longest sentences ever passed at the Old Bailey for murder. Brother Charlie got ten years while the Lambrianou brothers and Ronald Bender were sentenced to life. Fred Foreman got ten years and Cornelius Whitehead seven years. Albert Donoghue got two years.

In April that same year the Krays returned to court to plead not guilty to the murder of Frank 'Mad Axeman' Mitchell. This time they were acquitted, although Reggie was convicted of plotting Mitchell's escape from Dartmoor, 11 days before he died.

A lot of the Krays' problems were initially caused by allowing those demons in Ronnie Kray to spark excessive violence and insane acts of revenge. Many put it down to Ronnie's sexuality, which was the centre of gossip following a 1964 newspaper report about how Scotland Yard was tipped off that Ronnie was having an affair with top Tory, Lord Boothby. Ironically, the newspaper couldn't substantiate the claim and paid the peer £40,000 in an out-of-court settlement. But the rumours bugged Ronnie Kray to such an extent that when George Cornell branded him a 'fat poof' in the Blind Beggar in 1966 he couldn't resist the urge to shoot him dead. A few hours later Ronnie boasted to one criminal, 'Always shoot to kill. Dead men cannot grass.' He then added chillingly, 'Cornell was the only one to call me a poof, and he is dead.' It's now emerged that Ronnie had dozens of sexual partners while in and out of prison. He even fell in love with a young Arab boy on a trip to Tangier to see his Fifties gangland hero Billy Hill.

The twins remained incarcerated for the rest of their lives; Ronnie died in 1995 and Reg in October 2000 after more than 30 years in jail. Older brother Charlie passed away in his prison cell in

April 2000 after being sentenced to 15 years for masterminding a £69-million cocaine-smuggling plot.

One-time king of the London underworld, Billy Hill, maintained a reasonable lifestyle throughout the 1960s, even making occasional guest appearances at some of the Krays' clubs. Hill also grabbed a few more headlines, thanks to his friendships with upmarket socialite Lady Docker, evil property landlord Peter Rachman, and Profumo girl Mandy Rice-Davies. But most of the time he kept a low profile at his home in Spain, steering clear of the ruthless 1960s gangsters who'd taken over his turf.

Hill returned to England in the early 1970s and ran an upmarket nightclub in the respectable commuter belt town of Sunningdale, Berkshire. Then, in 1976, he split up with long-time love Gypsy Riley and took up with a black nightclub singer. When she committed suicide a couple of years later, Hill shut himself away in his flat in Moscow Road, just a stone's throw from where Spot had once lived at Hyde Park Mansions. He was racked with remorse and blamed himself, because he left her after a row and returned home the following day to find her body.

Hill died on New Year's Day 1984 at the age of 74. Jack Spot described him as 'the richest man in the graveyard', and former love Gypsy Riley arranged the funeral. None of his old underworld cronies were informed until after the cremation service. Hill had arranged for the 12-year-old son of his last lover to inherit his entire fortune. Hill also made a settlement with Gypsy, with whom he'd lived during his heyday. Part of the deal was that she should look after the boy. The Krays sent their condolences from their cells. Without Billy Hill, their reign of terror would never have got off the ground.

Aggie Hill, Billy Hill's ex-wife, prospered well following Hill's decision to quit London for Spain. Her only setback came when Selwyn Cooney, the manager of her New Cabinet Club in Gerrard Street, was murdered in February 1960 by Jimmy Nash, whose brother Johnny reckoned he was on his way to becoming the new boss of the underworld (although the Krays would no doubt have disagreed). In the 1970s, Aggie moved to Jersey where she opened a nightclub and became a wealthy and respected member of the community.

Albert Dimes abandoned the racetrack for the even more lucrative business of supplying fruit machines to nightclubs in the early 1960s. He became friendly with Hollywood star Stanley Baker and through him was introduced to movie director Joseph Losey. Dimes worked as an adviser on Losey's 1960 movie *The Criminal*, in which Baker played the leading character – a combination of Dimes, Hill and Jack Spot. Dimes always reckoned that he never fully recovered his health following the 'fight that never was' in Soho. He died of cancer in his home in River Street, Islington, in 1972 at the age of 57.

After Mad Frankie Fraser was sent down at the infamous Richardsons' torture gang trial, he became involved in so many violent incidents in prison that he ended up having to serve his full 19-year sentence. During a total of 42 years served in more than 20 prisons in the UK, Fraser was involved in riots, fights with prison officers, other inmates and even a number of attacks on prison governors. During the Parkhurst prison riot in 1969, Fraser was earmarked as a ringleader and, following extensive injuries, ended up in the prison hospital for six weeks and was given extra time in prison for his violent behaviour.

Fraser finally got out in 1985 to be greeted by his son James in a Rolls Royce. But it wasn't long before he was skating on thin ice again. In August 1991 Fraser was gunned down outside Turnmills nightclub, in Farringdon, North London, but miraculously survived.

These days, Fraser – now in his eighties – is more of a criminal celebrity than a violent psychopath. He's regularly seen on TV and even wrote a bestselling autobiography. He also hosts his own gangland tours of his favourite killing grounds, including the Richardsons' scrapyard, Turnmills, the Hackney streets where the Krays grew up, and notorious spots such as the Blind Beggar pub where Ronnie Kray ended the life of George Cornell. How the mighty have fallen.

Notorious chiv-man Teddy Machin – one of many gangsters whom Jack Spot accused of turning Hill against him – was severely wounded when two shotgun blasts were fired through the window of his home in Canning Town in 1970. Later, it emerged that Machin – by then 60 years old – had upset the son of one of his numerous female lovers.

By 1970, the then Labour Government felt obliged to act against gambling's overt criminal connections. A classic example was when Hollywood actor George Raft was deported because of his mob connections. That same year the new Gaming Act became law, which closed all the loopholes of the earlier 1960 Act. Now all gambling, including bingo and 'one-armed bandit' slot machines, needed a licence and were placed under the stewardship of the Gaming Board, backed by the Home Office.

It was now a legal obligation to take out membership of a casino 48 hours before playing, and all promotion of gambling was curtailed. The number of licensed casinos in Britain crashed from well over 1,000 to 120 within just 12 months of the new legislation, which many branded the most restrictive gaming regime in the western world. However, London remained a vital gambling capital, and the changes in the law caused nothing more than a slight lull in the popularity of gambling, as it evolved into a vastly profitable leisure industry.

By the mid-Seventies, high rolling, big-spending, oil-rich Arabs playing for high stakes had turned London casinos back into a boom industry. Some were so desperate for mega-rich customers that they sometimes resorted to dirty tricks. Clubs including Ladbrokes and the Playboy had their licences revoked and had to shut down.

Then corporate gamblers moved in and, thanks to the latest mass-merchandising techniques, managed to give betting a less sleazy image, selling it as the latest form of family entertainment at a time when Las Vegas was being redeveloped as 'Disneyland for Adults'.

In 1974 Scotland Yard's Jack Slipper sparked a diplomatic incident after flying to Rio de Janeiro to arrest Great Train Robber Ronnie Biggs following a tip-off from the *Daily Express*. Slipper hadn't told anyone of his plans, including the Brazilian authorities, who were so furious they went out of their way to prevent Biggs's extradition, helped by Biggs himself, having fathered a child in Brazil. Eventually Slipper returned to London empty-handed.

Biggs eventually returned to Britain voluntarily in 2001 after suffering a stroke. He was immediately taken back to prison. After eight years in custody he was finally released in August 2009 and remains, at the time of writing, still seriously ill. Speaking after informing his father of Slipper's own death two years ago, Biggs's son Michael said his father respected Mr Slipper as a gentleman and an 'old-fashioned copper'.

In the late-1960s the Met seemed content to largely ignore Soho's sleazy pornographers, while seeking prosecutions against hippie magazines *Oz* and the *Little Red Schoolbook*. Detective Chief Inspector George Fenwick, of the Yard's notorious 'dirty squad' even told Home Secretary Reginald Maudling that the Soho porn barons were part of the fabric of West End society and therefore not worth pursuing.

Outrageously, Fenwick went on to claim that *Oz* and the *Little Red Schoolbook* were deliberately targeted at children and young people because they promoted 'the alternative society'. But the Home Secretary eventually described the Yard's performance in Soho at that time 'as leaving a good deal to be desired'.

As the Yard launched its biggest-ever anti-corruption drive, Fenwick went on the offensive and accused the national press of unfairly hounding the Met. Then in 1969 an investigator for Lord Longford's unofficial inquiry into pornography named seven so-called porn barons as bribing police officers, and the Home Office's relationship with the Met never truly recovered.

Some years later, further inquiries into bribery and corruption severely damaged the Met's reputation. The Flying Squad, the Regional Crime Squad and the Criminal Intelligence Branch (C11) were all accused of high level corruption. Armed robbery gangs and high-ranking detectives in specialised units were said to be working together. Hard-hitting new Met Police Commissioner, Sir Robert Mark, appointed the Assistant Chief Constable of Dorset Constabulary, Leonard Burt, to investigate the allegations.

Labelled Operation Countryman, 200 officers were seconded to the special corruption taskforce. The inquiry eventually grew so big that extra officers joined the Countryman operation from all over the UK. However, many among the Met's rank-and-file police officers refused to cooperate. After six years and a cost of £4 million, Operation Countryman led to more than 400 police officers losing their jobs during or after the investigation, although not one officer ever actually appeared in a court of law as a result of these proceedings.

Operation Countryman revealed an extensive and tangled web of corruption. Bribery was endemic, especially between officers and those notorious Soho pornographers. The Flying Squad was later integrated into the Organised Crime Group, an elite unit which tackles major criminals, and underwent a huge cultural change, even recruiting more women. But the damage inflicted on the squad almost 30 years ago was immense.

Probably the most notorious husband-and-wife team to take a chunk out of the Soho sex trade in the 1970s was Jimmy and Rusty Humphreys. James William Humphreys, born in Southwark in January 1930, eventually helped bring about the downfall of those bent coppers whom he'd been bribing for years in the West End. His wife Rusty, one-time stripper and chorus girl, was a good businesswoman who encouraged her husband to expand his empire of strip clubs in Soho. By 1969 the Humphreys were so well in with the Met that they were guests with senior CID officers, including the Yard's Commander Wally Virgo, at a bash at the Criterion restaurant in Piccadilly.

Two or three tabloid newspaper exposés later, and Jimmy and Rusty Humphreys had told the world how one Commander Ken Drury had accepted an invite to their villa in Cyprus. This eventually brought about the resignation of Drury from the Yard and helped bring down the whole crooked house of bent West-End coppers taking bribes. In 1976, Drury, Virgo and ten other officers were arrested and eventually convicted to between four and twelve years in prison.

Freemasonry is a subject rarely discussed by the Met Police, London's judiciary, or even the many criminals who also claim membership – ironic that, as the Masons like to be known for their stance in favour of 'morality, fraternity and charity'. But they are certainly a force to be reckoned with, having between 3 and 4 million members in Britain plus more than ten times that number worldwide. The Freemasons make sizeable donations to charity as well as looking after the interests of their own brethren, and their relatives, whenever bereavement or sickness strikes. The Masons are an all-male domain as well as being predominantly middle class, due mainly to the high cost of membership. Hence, Freemasons tend to be businessmen and 'professional' people, such as policemen, bank managers, lawyers and senior civil servants.

The Masons openly claim direct links to the Middle Ages, encouraging the impression they are a society filled with mysticism. However, Freemasonry's real beginnings came with the emergence of a growing middle class in the 17th century. In those days it was seen as the perfect gentlemen's club, providing many influential people with a distinct identity which came from their inner fears and hatred for the ever increasing influence of the working classes.

Today, Masons overtly push their clan forward in business to achieve promotion and increase their wealth and influence. And there is no doubt the police corruption which led to Operation Countryman was heavily influenced by pressure from a Masonic City-of-London police commissioner in the 1970s, who conveniently ignored the activities of numerous corrupt Freemasons under his command.

They call it a firm within a firm. As their favourite verse goes:

Is a Brother off the track?
Try the Square;
Try it well on every side.
Nothing draws a craftsman back
Like the Square when well applied.
Try the Square.
Is he crooked, is he frail?
Try the Square;
Try it early, try it late;
When all other efforts fail,
Try the Square to make him straight —
Try the Square.

At one stage it was so bad that any detective after a share of the cash regularly extorted from Soho's sleazy, profiteering pornographers, used membership of the Masons as the perfect cover. C1 – aka the 'Porn Squad' - was a unit within the CID's central office and detectives were literally queuing up to join it. The C1 commander responsible for selection from 1964 until 1972 was Detective Chief Superintendent Bill Moody – a keen Freemason, naturally. Incredibly, Moody had been fronting one of the biggest-ever investigations into police corruption while at the same time accepting huge bribes from many of Soho's notorious porn barons. He was the ultimate turncoat.

And there were numerous other classic example of 'bent coppers', including Detective Inspector Leslie Alton, also a Freemason. He bullied other officers to pull in weekly cash payments from the West End pornographers, then made them share it out amongst his colleagues. From 1970 to 1972 the C1

'Porn Squad' overlord was another Mason, Commander Wally Virgo. As previously mentioned, he was jailed for 12 years for corruption, although later freed after the appeal court announced that the judge's summing-up had been 'unduly hostile'.

Virgo encouraged all his officers to become Masons. Freemason colleagues of one member – Detective Inspector Anthony Kilkerr – even came up with a convincing explanation for the £20 of pornographers' pay-off money planted in Kilkerr's desk drawer each week. They claimed, during one police corruption trial, that the crisp fivers were simply whip-rounds to help Kilkerr afford to pay his Masonic initiation fees. That lie said it all about the brethren. Kilkerr never touched the money, which had made others suspect he was a 'spy in the camp' in the first place. His untarnished reputation so infuriated fellow detective Peter Fisher that he told Kilkerr he would make sure he was dragged down with his crooked colleagues.

The classic phrase 'firm in a firm' has long since gone down in the annals of Met police corruption. But the words were first immortalised by Detective Sergeant John Symonds on a secret tape-recording made by two *Times* reporters in 1969. On the tape, Symonds allegedly said: 'Don't forget always to let me know straight away if you need anything because I know people everywhere. Because I'm in a little firm in a firm. Don't matter where, anywhere in London, I can get on the phone to someone I know I can trust, that talks the same as me. And if he's not the right person that can do it, he'll know the person that can. All right? . . . That's the thing, and it can work – well, it's worked for years, hasn't it?'

The tape was used to back up the claims of a small-time thief who told journalists Symonds was extorting cash out of him. Symonds was immediately suspended and charged, but in 1972 he got a tip-off from a fellow Mason that his trial was to be brought forward, and he fled abroad. Seven years later Symonds returned and was tried, convicted and given a two-year jail sentence, but would continue to allege he was a classic sacrificial lamb, thanks to corrupt coppers running the CID at that time.

Among those who led Scotland Yard's high profile anti-corruption drive in the 1970s were Deputy Assistant Commissioners Gilbert Kelland and Ron Steventon, later head of A 10 – both Freemasons. However, they refused point-blank to favour their brethren, although Kelland spent the first 25 years of his police career in uniform, which meant he was much less likely to allow his Freemasonry to influence his police work. It was inside the plain clothes CID that Mason bribery and corruption seemed to flourish. None of this would have been uncovered if it not been for an officer who was neither a detective nor a Freemason – Commissioner of Police, Sir Robert Mark. He was obsessed with fully stamping out corruption for the first time in a century – whoever the officers were.

But the long arm of the Masons stretched far and wide. When one squad of police raided a notorious West End hostess club frequented by prostitutes, one of club's owners appealed to the detectives in classic Masonic terms, 'on the square'. They'd clearly expected to be let off. One officer later said he ignored the approach and went ahead and charged the club owners, only to watch them be acquitted at their eventual Old Bailey trial. He was, understandably, appalled.

By 1977 the so-called Soho porn wars had led to highly publicised Old Bailey trials revealing corruption spread across London's CID, involving many officers who were Freemasons. The 12 detectives who were eventually jailed included two commanders, one chief superintendent and five inspectors.

The 1970s also marked the emergence of a new criminal elite – the blagger. In 1972, armed robberies in London totalled 380. By 1978 it had risen to 734, but by 1982 it had more than doubled to 1,772 – a 366 per cent increase in just a decade. Some of the names behind this veritable crime boom included George Davis, Bertie Smalls, Billy Tobin, Ronnie Knight, Freddie Foreman, Mehmet Arif and Mickey McAvoy. They were barely known to the wider public, but to the police they all qualified for the title of 'Top Blaggers'.

Their ascendancy within the capital's criminal hinterlands came amid constant and ominous questions being asked about their enemies, the Flying Squad, and indeed the whole Metropolitan Police. Tough-guy Commissioner Sir Robert Mark had ruthlessly stamped down on his detectives in such a way that they were now unable to take any risks. 'A good police force,' he told them in one speech, 'is one that catches more criminals than it employs.' Mark had pulled apart what he considered the infected areas of his force until he was left with little but the bare bones.

London was supposed to be filled with sharp-eyed detectives determined to win back the streets after all those gangster-filled years of the 1960s. Scotland Yard's very own crime buster in the Seventies, Detective Chief Superintendent Albert Wickstead, aka the 'Grey Fox', head of the Yard's Serious Crimes Squad, mounted raid after raid in 1973, which resulted in 235 officers taking 93 men and one woman into custody.

But the Flying Squad's glamorous, hard-nosed image had been seriously knocked back, leaving all detectives wide open to accusations of corruption in the form of a detective either turning a blind eye to what was going on in return for a cut of the action or – if the information led to the recovery of stolen property – pocketing some of the reward money claimed on the informant's behalf. A strategically placed officer could also, for a fee, ensure bail was granted, hold back evidence and details about past convictions from a court, or pass on to a person under investigation details of a case being made against him or warnings about police operations in which he could become compromised. Corrupt officers also held onto a proportion of whatever valuables they recovered during an inquiry.

The Flying Squad was also rumoured to regularly haul in villains whom they knew had committed a particular crime, even when there was no way of proving it. They approached some gangsters to help them frame other high-ranking police officers, just before they were due to give evidence in major trials. The aim was to smear their names to such an extent that their evidence would be seriously questioned in court.

In the mid-1970s, newly appointed Deputy Assistant Commissioner David Powis ordered a crackdown to stop corrupt policemen from creaming off reward money meant for informants. In future, all payments amounting to more than £500 would be handed over by the Deputy Assistant Commissioner himself. Also during the 1970s, jury nobbling and interference with star witnesses became an almost weekly occurrence at London's big courts, including the Old Bailey. The Director of Public Prosecutions regularly objected to bail applications by villains on the basis that there was a 'strong fear' of interference with witnesses.

Another disturbing new element had crept into the London underworld – the supergrass. Perhaps the most notorious of all was the controversial 'chit-to-freedom' that bank robber Bertie Smalls negotiated from London's law-keepers. Characters like Smalls played their cards close to their chest. His chips were times, places,

hauls and Christian names. Smalls and other grasses believed that what they had to offer would be enough to win the most important gamble of their lives – freedom. Smalls was one of the most hated men in the criminal underworld. Richardson gang henchman Jimmy Moody told one criminal associate that he'd, 'Gladly kill that bastard for nothing. He's vermin and should be wiped off the face of this Earth.'

In May 1974 Smalls helped convict seven men at the Old Bailey of robbing the Barclays Bank at Ilford of £237,736 and Barclays' Wembley branch of £138,111. After that, he was guarded by 12 armed detectives at a secret hideout 24 hours a day, knowing full well that a £60,000 contract had been put on his head.

One of the most shocking professional hits of the mid-1970s was the assassination of East London haulage contractor George Brett and his ten-year-old son Terence. One day in 1975 father and son had left their Upminster farmhouse in Essex accompanied by a man in a bowler hat and business suit who drove a Mark 2 Jag. They were never seen again.

More than a year later an underworld informant told detectives they'd find the father and son's remains under concrete at Mount Pleasant Farm, in Hornchurch, Essex. The source also claimed that proceeds of armed robberies amounting to half a million pounds could be found in the same site. But a massive search operation proved entirely fruitless.

Another gangster victim of a professional killer at this time was East End crook William Moseley, whose dismembered body was washed ashore in the Thames Estuary in the summer of 1975, and in August that year the body of 37-year-old armed robber Michael Cornwall was found in a grave in a wood in Hatfield, Hertfordshire. He'd been shot in the head.

Back in the 1970s robbery had a certain class to it, even though the actual crime remained almost as brutal as it is today and involved armed villains, who've always openly admitted that they considered shooting a policeman as fair game 'in the theatre of war'.

In the long, hot summer of 1976, a well-respected East London armed robber called Charlie 'Chopper' Knight went on a recruitment drive. Knight asked his pal, former Richardson gang henchman Jimmy Moody, if he was interested in being the strong-arm man for his team of robbers looking to hit the lucrative security-van 'market'. Initially, this band of highway robbers would always strike on a Thursday, which was wages day, so they became known as the 'Thursday Gang'. Their total haul would eventually exceed £2 million, making them the most successful team of robbers in criminal history at that time.

The team assembled by Chopper Knight had first worked as a unit two years earlier under two Scotsmen – Alex Sears and Sammy Benefield. They were the only survivors from the original gang. The idea was to run a group of London-based robbers capable of operating nationwide – from the capital to as far north as Dundee in Scotland and from Essex across to the Midlands.

Chopper Knight, then 38, wasn't the overall 'Mr Big' as such. A hard-core committee of criminal faces financed and selected the jobs to be done, checked details of layout and security, and then suggested the right men for the job. But Knight was the self-acclaimed general – the man who'd pull each job together. Charles Roland Knight – aka 'The General', aka 'Top Cat' – had been robbing since the 1960s. Short, well built and with a round deadpan face that gave little away, he got his main nickname when his mother sent him into the garden every day when he was a child to chop wood. Police later said he could have become a millionaire businessman if he'd used his talents more honestly.

Other robbers recruited by Chopper Knight included John William Woodruff, 41 at the time, aka 'Big Bad John', who had a classic East End background. This lofty, softly spoken, mousy-haired former builder had been on the robbery scene for years but had a weakness for booze. Woodruff was given an eight-year sentence for what was one of the first-ever security van hold-ups in London's Shepherd's Bush in April 1968. Then there was Tony Knightly, then 36, a highly respected, experienced and utterly dependable villain. Knightly was a very sociable fellow – even the police admitted that he was 'a good bloke to go and have a beer with'.

And there was also Bernie Khan, 34, a robber with a difference: he was half Indian. Small and wiry, he was a cheeky chappie with an appetite for life. He and Knightly were the self-appointed 'technicians', the men who'd actually grab the loot, while heavier characters like Jimmy Moody waved their weapons in the air. Another gang member 'Big' John Woodall, who was 50 at the time, had not long been out of jail when he was recruited by Chopper. Woodall had once been a big name, so it was quite a comedown for him to be back on the streets. There was also Alex Sears, a wheelman with a penchant for rally driving. Other robbers came in and out of the South London-based gang as it sparked terror and stole fortunes up and down the country, but these characters were the self-appointed first team.

All jobs were meticulously planned during meetings in pubs and clubs; vehicles were the most vital preliminary tool for any big robbery; and the gang stole hundreds during their reign. A well-stocked arsenal of weapons was also essential. And there was a jester-like range of disguises, including ginger wigs, coloured spectacles, false beards and large moustaches. Some robbers said they'd even be prepared to dress up as women to confuse potential witnesses.

Moody and the gang's other strong-arm men were expected to fire their weapons if necessary – usually revolvers and shotguns – to at least scare security van personnel into cooperating. They also used sledges, hammers and iron bars to shatter windscreens. Gang member Sammy Benefield provided an arsenal of weapons by breaking into a gun shop in Ingrave, Essex, and stealing one Browning 12-bore semiautomatic shotgun, one Mossberg 12-bore shotgun, one Winchester 101 shotgun, one Manufrance perfex semiautomatic 12-bore shotgun, one Manufrance 12-bore pump-action shotgun, one Remington pump-action shotgun and one Savage 12-bore shotgun.

The gang also had a number of 'bent' security guards on side, including Brian McIntosh, employed by Security Express as a driver/custodian. After Chopper paid McIntosh's family a visit, the frightened driver started giving the gang valuable tips. McIntosh provided Moody and Knight with details of security van movements, which alone helped the gang eventually net more than half a million pounds. Another 'friendly' security guard was Brian Upton, employed by Group 4. He was introduced to Chopper by an associate called Kenny Clark through his love of fishing.

It was a daring robbery in the Blackwall Tunnel, under the Thames, on 29 September 1977 that made Scotland Yard really sit up and take notice of the gang. In the raid, Moody dressed up as a policeman to create a gap in the traffic and force a security van to stop just past the bend, about two-thirds of the way into the tunnel. At the same time two of the robbers staged a crash behind them to block the tunnel just before the bend. The gang used three stolen cars and a stolen van to surround the security wagon. The team had done their homework, because once inside the tunnel the security van's radio was useless. 'PC' Moody then leapt out of his car and 'confiscated' the keys of several backed-up motorists at gunpoint so they couldn't drive off and raise the alarm.

Three of the gang – including Moody – were armed with sawn-offs, one with a pistol and another with an axe, which was used to smash the security van window to force the crew to cooperate. But what few villains mentioned was that Jimmy Moody attacked the custodian of the money, felling him with a shotgun butt during the job. He was so badly injured that he ended up drawing a disability pension.

The Blackwall Tunnel job provided robbers throughout London with a new phrase that summed it all up – 'the buzz'. That's what they experienced thanks to the thrill of pulling off the robbery, and it was an expression that many criminals (and police) would use subsequently. As one of the gang later explained, 'The buzz on that job was better than any drugs. All that adrenalin pumping through you was fuckin' incredible, and the feelin' of elation once you'd snatched that cash was out of this world.'

The transfer of the money into the getaway vehicle was always done with precision timing, because the longer it took, the more likely it was that the police would arrive, and nobody wanted a shoot-out. The gang escaped from the Blackwall Tunnel that day with almost £100,000 in wage packets destined for Greenwich hospitals. Only a small fraction of the cash was ever recovered. Once the money was divided up at a flophouse, within hours of the crime being committed, the team made a point of going their separate ways.

But not every job the gang touched turned to instant gold. Their next robbery was at a mill on the Lea Bridge Road in East London, where they planned to hold up a security van, again delivering at least £100,000 in wages. Chopper, Moody and the rest of the team, armed with shotguns, sat tight in two vehicles and waited for the van to show up one grey afternoon in the early winter of 1977. When the vehicle finally appeared it stopped nearly 300 yards away from the delivery point they'd been told about. The gang looked at each other for a moment before driving their cars in for a hijack, but by the time they got to the van the guards had driven off without even realising how close they'd come to being robbed.

Knight now believed that the gang needed to devise a new method of robbing, one in which the custodian's keys wouldn't even have to be used. Knight, Moody and the rest of the team compared security vans to sardine cans – difficult to open without a key. So they came up with the ideal solution: a chainsaw. Thus was born the 'Chainsaw Gang'. The first job was a disaster – the chainsaw failed to fire up because no one had remembered to electrically charge it properly before the job.

On 15 August 1978, Jimmy Moody, Chopper Knight, Bernie Khan and the rest of the nine-man team met at Moody's flat in Hackney, the gang's 'out' (safe house), to discuss their biggest job to date. Chopper gave his men a final briefing before they all left the flat separately – at one minute intervals – to head for the stolen vehicles, parked in pre-designated spots within a few hundred yards of the flat.

Bernie Khan drove a Ford Escort in a six-vehicle convoy as it headed across the river and into the South London suburbs en route to Banstead, Surrey. Then Khan was caught at a red traffic light. 'Suddenly there's a siren, and I see the police in my rear-view mirror,' he later recalled. 'I thought, "Fuck it, my time's up. I'm gonna get a pull".' Khan pulled his car over, got out and waited for the police.

Khan's team-mates had seen what had happened and watched from a safe distance. 'I had enough equipment on me to get convicted for goin' to rob,' explained Khan. 'I was a gonner.' The police car floated right past Bernie Khan without giving him a second glance. 'I couldn't fuckin' believe it. They didn't even look

at me.' It was a false alarm. Khan got back in the Escort and the robbers' convoy continued. Eventually, the gang stopped next to a small forest on the outskirts of Banstead on the Sutton Road, right in the heart of the Surrey countryside. Khan recalled, 'We was early, so we set the motors up in their right positions.'

Over in Banstead, two of the robbers' vehicles were shadowing the Security Express van from the moment it left the bank in the High Street. Khan explained, 'We picked it up at the bank at around 11. We had a car in front and a car behind the van.' Less than a mile out of Banstead, on the Sutton Road, the car in front of the security vehicle put on its right blinker so that the van had to slow down. Khan explained, 'Now the van's caught in the middle and having to slow down. Then another of our cars being driven by Jimmy Moody pulls out of a side turning to stop all the traffic behind the security van.'

Just then the robbers' own Sherpa van – covered in dents to made it look as if it had been in an accident – pulled out of another nearby lane and screeched to a halt alongside the Security Express vehicle. Three robbers with sawn-offs emerged, surrounded the van and blew its tyres out with their weapons. 'Then I jumped out with all our tools,' Khan recalled. 'We'd already warmed the chainsaw up earlier that morning, because sometimes they didn't start easily.' All the men were wearing flesh-coloured latex gloves and a variety of masks and helmets.

Chopper Knight got out of a Ford Granada and stood to attention with a stopwatch in his hand. Pressing the button, he said, 'Three minutes, gentlemen.' Chopper knew only too well they had to get the cash and move very quickly. Perhaps surprisingly, at least three of the robbers – Khan, Knight and Knightly – were not even armed. Khan later explained, 'That wasn't our job. Jim and the others were the hired guns, not us.'

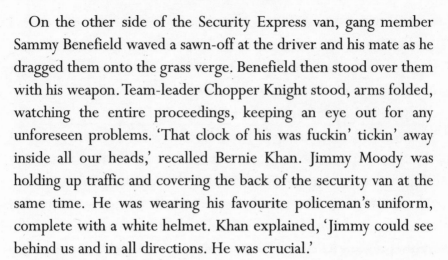

On the other side of the Security Express van, gang member Sammy Benefield waved a sawn-off at the driver and his mate as he dragged them onto the grass verge. Benefield then stood over them with his weapon. Team-leader Chopper Knight stood, arms folded, watching the entire proceedings, keeping an eye out for any unforeseen problems. 'That clock of his was fuckin' tickin' away inside all our heads,' recalled Bernie Khan. Jimmy Moody was holding up traffic and covering the back of the security van at the same time. He was wearing his favourite policeman's uniform, complete with a white helmet. Khan explained, 'Jimmy could see behind us and in all directions. He was crucial.'

By this time Khan had pulled his cutting goggles over his balaclava and he and Tony Knightly got down to work. 'We've got all the gear on,' recalled Khan. 'We look well professional, and that fuckin' grinder is makin' a hell of a racket.' The security van staff looked terrified when Khan fired up his chainsaw. 'As we're cuttin' away, there's lots of smoke 'n' noise.'

'Two minutes, thirty seconds,' bellowed Chopper to his men.

Khan was still cutting away at the outer skin of the van. 'The hole had to be big enough to get those money bags out,' he explained. 'It was a precision cut.' Gang member John Segars remained on lookout in the driver's seat of another backup car parked alongside the security van. Just then, one of the security-van guards tried to get up from the grass verge where he'd been ordered to lie down. Segars jumped from his vehicle and panned his sawn-off into the air, saying, 'Don't fuckin' move!' The van driver ignored the order. Segars let off a warning shot, and the driver dived back onto the ground.

'Two minutes!' screamed Chopper Knight, consulting his stopwatch, completely ignoring the incident.

Khan explained, 'That's when I got through the outer skin and was trying to bend it open so we could get into the cash. I remember turning to see if everything else was all right. I saw Jim waving at the traffic jam behind us. What a fuckin' impressive sight he was.'

'One and a half!' shouted Chopper.

Khan and Knightly then started pulling the money bags out of the van and transferring them straight to the robber's van. They later discovered there was £25,000 in each bag. Behind them, Jimmy Moody continued waving his sawn-off in the direction of an increasingly irate group of motorists. 'GO! GO! GO!' screamed Chopper, before blowing his football ref's whistle, just in case anyone hadn't heard him. The nine robbers piled into three vehicles, leaving three other cars behind. They were careful not to exceed the 30 mph speed limit as they drove away from the scene of the robbery.

At 6 p.m. on the evening of the Banstead robbery, 40 bags of cash containing a total of almost £800,000 were carried up to Jimmy Moody's flat at 38 Lexfield Court, Pownall Road, Hackney, in a plastic body bag with a zipper down the front. Bernie Khan recalled, 'We arrived in the three motors and lugged the cash up the stairs over our shoulders. We were all fuckin' knackered. The old buzz had long since gone.'

When Khan walked into Moody's flat he was astonished to see that Moody's 13-year-old son Jason was at home. Khan said, 'Jason just sat there watchin' us, which was really out of order because there shouldn't have been anyone else in that out. But no one dared have a go at Jim because we was all shit-scared of him.'

The entire transaction at Jimmy Moody's flat – including handing the money to each gang member – took just 20 minutes.

In 1976 the £8 million Bank of America raid in Mayfair, in the heart of London's West End, became the world's biggest robbery. It later emerged this was the gang's second attempt and nothing, it seemed, could deter them from their mission. The gang's 'inside man' was an electrician employed by the bank.

At the Bank of America trial, Judge Alan King-Hamilton pledged that none of the gang would ever get to spend their massive haul. Yet only £500,000 of the loot was ever tracked down. Two of the team – safe-cracker Leonard Wilde and Peter Colson, 32, a used car dealer – were eventually sentenced to 23 years and 21 years respectively. They also faced criminal bankruptcy orders of £500,000 each. Others criminals connected to the raid were sentenced from 18 years for robbery to three years for receiving stolen goods. But alleged mastermind Frank Maple left Britain shortly after the raid and travelled to Morocco, which had no extradition order with the UK. He has never returned to London to face his accusers.

By the mid-1970s, various families in South London were wielding great influence following the downfall of the Richardsons: the Tobins, the Hennesseys, the Smiths in Deptford, the Frenches in Lewisham, and the Porritts and their so-called cousins, the Reddens. 'Flash' Harry Hayward had the Harp of Erin pub, the Frenches had the Deptford Arms, and Peter and Bernie Hennessey ran the Dog and Bell. In 1966, Peter Hennessey had served ten years for warehouse breaking, and his brother Bernard had a conviction for conspiracy to rob. Third brother Mickey, friend of notorious gangster Alfie Gerard, was later involved in a massive drugs smuggling case.

But it was the emergence of families like the Arifs that really proved the benchmark. They'd come over from their native northern Cyprus already steeped in crime and were determined to make their own chilling mark on London.

The Securicor van had been shadowed all over southeast London as it picked up takings from more than a dozen shops in March 1976. Then, as the vehicle drove up the busy A2 dual carriageway towards its depot in Powdermill Lane, Dartford, Kent, a gang of southeast London robbers in two stolen cars forced it off the road.

Brandishing sawn-offs, the team ordered the Securicor guards out of the van and helped themselves to more than £100,000 – which was decent money in those days. Then the windscreen was smashed with a sledgehammer. However, when the robbers started spraying bullets around, one of the guards was hit and later died. The gang escaped by scrambling up an embankment. A number of motorists even photographed them. The police soon rounded up all the usual suspects. This was the terrifying, deadly robbery that put the Arif family on the map.

Ozer Arif – then 28 and a minicab proprietor of Layard Square, Southwark – was later charged with murder along with two other men. Murder charges against Bekir Arif – then 22 and described as a butcher of Hawkestone Road, Rotherhithe – were withdrawn, but he was arrested for robbery, stealing cars, and possessing guns without certificates and disposing of them.

In May 1977 Ozer Arif pleaded not guilty to the murder charges at the Old Bailey. At the end of a four-week trial, the jury also found him not guilty of wounding two other guards with intent to cause them grievous bodily harm and possessing shotguns with intent to commit robbery. Bekir got a five-stretch after admitting to robbery. Later, the police proudly announced that they'd broken the back of the Arifs. 'This is the best news we have had for a long time,' they boasted to reporters. 'We reckon we've nipped them in the bud.'

They couldn't have been more wrong.

After Ozer Arif's acquittal, the boys in blue tape-recorded an

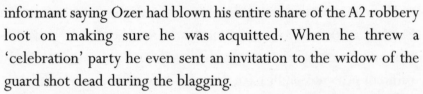

informant saying Ozer had blown his entire share of the A2 robbery loot on making sure he was acquitted. When he threw a 'celebration' party he even sent an invitation to the widow of the guard shot dead during the blagging.

The Arif family and their army of associates have gone on to make millions, thanks to a series of blaggings, highly lucrative drug-trafficking operations, and a whole bunch of legitimate businesses set up with stolen cash. One retired thief taker who's spent half a lifetime digging into the Arif family background told me a few years back that the brothers' father was given a new identity by the British Army in Cyprus when he became an informant for the British back in the 1950s. 'That's how the Arif family came to live in southeast London. Bloody ironic, isn't it? We helped set up the Arifs as one of the most awesome gang of villains ever seen in London.'

The emergence of the Arifs as a force to be reckoned with in the 1970s came when the family ran a café off Deptford Broadway, right in the heart of their adopted homeland of southeast London. Eldest brother Dogan soon earned himself a reputation as a hardman with a chirpy sense of humour and a fondness for sticking sawn-offs in people's mouths when he wanted to make an important point.

One of the first times Dogan did this was in a pub in Rotherhithe in 1979. Witnesses swear to this day that he pointed his sawn-off right in his victim's face before panning the weapon at the fellow's shoulder and squeezing the trigger. Not one customer in that pub remembered seeing anything when the police later arrived on the scene. Frightened witnesses always get confused, and the Arifs had just created a pub full of frightened witnesses. If the police had tried to get a Photofit from the descriptions provided by those punters, they'd have ended up searching for the Elephant Man.

Then, Dogan's kid brother Dennis walked into another tavern in South London and confronted a man who owed him money. Dennis pushed his Uzi into the man's face before playing a sick and twisted game of pizzicato on his victim's belly with a flick knife.

Like many other gangsters, the Arifs used fear as their number one weapon. They could be seen strutting around their manor like medieval warlords, building a reputation as bandits who specialised in violent crimes with maximum profits. During those early days the Arifs also built up vast reserves of cash from legitimate businesses, such as jewellery and menswear stores, kebab houses, a restaurant and a nightclub. Their club – the Connoisseur – was a legendary nightspot on the Old Kent Road, decorated in black and shiny chrome.

One day, Dogan and Dennis Arif ran into a heavy bunch of coke dealers at the Connoisseur and took it upon themselves to 'confiscate' the merchandise. It turned out that these fellows had been transporting the drugs for the mafia, who were not happy when they heard what had happened. Dogan and Dennis barricaded themselves inside the club with submachine guns and spent two tense weeks in a stand-off, refusing to budge until all parties had reached a satisfactory agreement.

Older brother Dogan even used Arif money to support and manage his own football team, Fisher Athletic. Under his guidance the Docklands club achieved remarkable success a few years back. They were promoted out of the local league into the GM Vauxhall Conference, and, with sponsorship money pouring in, they got within a whisper of the old Fourth Division. It is believed that they club were unaware of the source of this money. Today they have long since severed any ties they once unknowingly had to any criminal organisation.

In 1988 the police once again tried to come down on the Arifs like the proverbial ton of truncheons. They even set up a special squad reinforced by men from the Customs investigation branch with the express purpose of getting the Arifs off the streets. Then Dogan was arrested after riding shotgun on a lorry which was alleged to contain £8 million-worth of cannabis, although customs officers had already removed the drug and replaced it with chipboard. To this day, Dogan swears blind that he was not on for that job. He was eventually convicted to a nine-year sentence and his associates still say that he was never on the lorry tracked by the cops and customs officers. He later appealed against his sentence, and it was reduced to three years.

In many of the pubs and bodybuilding gyms of southeast London it's said that the Arifs have always been clever at stashing away their millions before the long arm of the law can lay its hands on the money. And the Arifs might have kept a cleaner sheet if Dogan and his brothers hadn't made the fatal error of getting directly involved in their own action. Behind the scenes, Dogan and his brothers wanted complete and utter respect, so they were obliged to get involved in a few tasty gangland battles as a matter of honour. 'They felt they had no choice but to come out fighting,' said one former Arif associate. 'They wanted other faces on the manor to know they don't take no shit off no one.'

In November 1990 the Arifs hit the headlines once again when Dennis, Mehmet and brother-in-law Anthony Downer tried to rob a Securicor van in Woodhatch, near Reigate in Surrey. The Flying Squad had been given a tip-off in advance and lay in wait when the Arif family members, and another sidekick, struck. They were all arrested on the spot, except for robber Kenny Baker, who was shot dead by the police after he and Mehmet Arif decided not to throw down their weapons. The gang was carrying a Brazilian-made revolver, a 12-bore Browning shotgun, a US Army self-loading

Colt, an Enfield Mark II revolver and a Browning 1922 pistol. Later that same day the police raided a house in Streatham, South London, where they seized a further small arsenal of weapons, including three sawn-offs and a submachine gun. Mehmet eventually put his hands up to the attempted blagging, but Dennis refused to cough, although he was later found guilty in court.

What really shocked other southeast London faces at the time was that Dennis and Mehmet had bothered to dirty their hands by going 'across the pavement' when they already enjoyed millionaires' lifestyles in their own area.

'New Krays Smashed' read the massive front-page headline in **The Sun** back in December 1991 when Dennis and Mehmet were finally sent down after trying to rob the security van carrying £1 million. The police proudly screened video footage of the arrest and tried to suggest that the Arifs were now a spent force. But others knew that they were far from dead and buried. Shortly after the brothers were sent down, a heavyweight contest was declared between a brace of southeast London gangsters. Many of them suspected that it might have been one of their rivals who had grassed up the Arifs and their gang of robbers.

Round one kicked off in March 1991 when the Arifs' cousin, Abby Abdullah, walked into a William Hill bookies in Bagshott Street, Walworth, with his bull terrier on the end of a lead. Minutes later a hitman squeezed off two rounds from his 9 mm Browning, after Abby was pointed out by a helpful punter. Abby even tried to use another customer in the betting shop as a shield, but was shot again in the back as he ran from the premises. He managed to stagger 400 yards to a friend's house on the Kingslake Estate, where he collapsed at the front door. That's when Abby whispered the names of his alleged killers. Soon, half the manor had heard the rumour that he'd named two local brothers, from nearby Bermondsey.

Abby was rushed by air ambulance to the Royal Hospital, Whitechapel, where he was pronounced dead shortly after arrival. When the news was broken by the Arif brothers to their father, Yusef, who treated Abby as a son, he went ballistic, and the word 'revenge' was on everyone's lips. In June 1991 police from a special crime unit nicked one of the brothers for the Abby shooting. They later claimed he told them, 'I didn't mean him to die. I didn't mean it.' Then, one night in the Connoisseur a well-known face was shot. This victim survived but, naturally, refused to say who shot him. Three days later, in King's College Hospital, he spewed up the bullet that had grounded him, only to then promptly swallow it again. 'He wanted to stop us doing forensic tests on it,' one plain-clothes cozzer explained helpfully.

Dennis and Mehmet Arif were now serving 18- and 22-year sentences at Parkhurst Prison on the Isle of Wight for the armed blagging. They'd turned the facility's maximum security D-wing into a drugs den and virtual no-go area for staff.

Dennis and Mehmet were even rumoured to have mobiles and a couple of guns in their cells. Some Parkhurst staff got so spooked that they asked for outside protection from the brothers. The screws feared attacks on their families after clashing with the Arifs on D-wing. Another time, a warden was injured after skidding on two packets of cocaine lying in a corridor. And those staff who still patrolled the Arifs' wing found they could no longer use the specially installed security viewers to take a look inside cells. 'All the spy holes are blocked by curtains, paint or paper,' groaned one fed-up officer.

In October 1997 Bekir Arif was pulled in by detectives investigating a plot to flood the streets with more than £10-million worth of heroin. The cozzers claimed that they had found 95 kg of the drug piled up in the front room of a south London house they'd raided. Detectives reckoned Bekir was running a major drug-trafficking and distribution network. Car dealer Bekir was charged with conspiracy to supply heroin

In May 1999, Bekir, now 46 and living in a £250,000 house in Petts Wood, Kent, was jailed for 23 years after being convicted of conspiracy to supply heroin. The court was told that Bekir had used his second-hand car business as a front to supply £12 million-worth of heroin. The court also heard that the police had spent a year watching his car business in Rotherhithe and a nearby flat.

In court, Bekir – known by now as 'The Duke' – insisted that he was nothing more than a 'Del Boy' businessman. It didn't help when prosecutors pointed out that Bekir was splashing out 30 grand a year for an executive box to watch his favourite football team, Arsenal. Judge Geoffrey Grigson told Bekir, 'Your role was plainly that of principal, and your conduct was as cynical and dishonest as has been your defence. In my view, there is no mitigation.'

A few years back I met up with Dogan Arif at his business address, a fruit-and-cigarette-machine service centre in a dead-end street just off the Old Kent Road. 'I'll see you on the cameras and come and get you,' he told me on the phone an hour before our meet. As I slowly drove my old jalopy towards a brick wall that marked the end of the road, I wondered what he really meant. The idea of Dogan Arif 'coming to get me' sent a shiver up my spine.

In the not-too-distant past, Dogan's favourite way of attracting anyone's attention had been to stick a gun in their face and ask questions later. As one-time unofficial godfather of the Arif family, his reputation precedes him with everyone from the major faces in London to the police at Scotland Yard. The CCTV cameras that pan the end of the lane where he has his one-armed bandit warehouse command a view of run-down buildings and lots of broken glass scattered across the pavement. It's just a stone's throw from his family's old club, the Connoisseur. As I slung my old Merc up on the curb, a Dobermann the size of a small donkey came bounding out of a side door. Just then, a tall, dark-haired, bull-necked bouncer-type yanked the pooch back into the front office of the warehouse. Inside, a pretty girl in her early twenties offered me a cuppa and told me that Dogan would be out 'any minute'. It was all very civilised.

Then the man himself emerged, grinning and full of charm. He walked me through the small warehouse, filled with flashing machines, into his office. Compact and muscular, he moved with an athlete's roll, instantly reminding me that he was once a talented footballer. Many people reckon Dogan could have made it as a pro, but he had bigger fish to fry. It turned out that Dogan was still annoyed he'd been arrested for the £8 million puff deal back in 1988. His brief reckoned that if he'd been anyone else the conviction would have been completely thrown out.

Dogan told me that he'd turned over a new leaf – gone straight. One old thief taker I know still calls him 'the thinking man's gangster'. While Dogan was banged up in Parkhurst, the governor even encouraged him to talk to prison visitors because he had such a sharp take on life inside.

'Sometimes it'd be nice to wipe out the past,' Dogan told me. 'But you can't do that, can you? People never let you forget. That's just the way it is. You have to take life on the chin.'

Dogan Arif believed the big London families of the 1980s and '90s were on the way out: 'They had principles and respect. The police could keep things under control 'cause people were predictable. Now there are hundreds of operators all over the place climbin' on the bandwagon. It's too easy, by half. Let's say Billy Bloggs has a transport company. He'll move a consignment of drugs. Suddenly, he's got more money than he's ever dreamed of. Now he's in the underworld. He's got to have soldiers. But he doesn't know what he's doing. He knows nothin' about it, but he's in it. It's chaos. There's no respect and no control. You can't blame the public if they want the police to throw the rules out of the window. And they do. They infiltrate, they pay big money to grasses. There's electronic surveillance, MI5. If you have things you care about – a family – don't even think about it any more.'

Dogan blames a lot of his problems on the over-the-top 1980s: 'Everyone had money in the '80s. Everyone was spending like crazy. There'd be kids with five grand in their pocket. They'd say, "Give us a gram of Charlie. What the hell, make it five grams." They'd ask me for it. I'd sling them out, the idiots.'

The Arifs were not to be crossed . . .

The Old Bailey has seen countless high-profile gangster trials down the years, but one of the most outrageous was the murder trial of actor-gangster John Bindon. The west London hard-man was accused of stabbing to death south London villain John Darke during a fight in a drinking den called the Ranelagh Yacht Club, just a stone's throw from the Thames in Putney. Bindon was eventually caught after going on the run to Dublin, where he finally gave himself up to police.

On 10 December 1978, Bindon, 41, was charged with murdering mobster Darke following his return to London. The next day, Bindon – slumped and still in pain from injuries caused during his battle with Darke – made his first court appearance in the dock at Horseferry Road Magistrates.

The following year, on 23 October 1979, Bindon was tried at the Old Bailey, when he was also charged with causing an affray at the Ranelagh Yacht Club, along with Darke's associates Raymond

Bohm, a 39-year-old builders' merchant from Kezia Street, Deptford, and George Galbraith, a 30-year-old scaffolder from Welford Court, Westbury Estate, South Lambeth. They all denied the charges.

The jury heard that Bindon had lain spread-eagled on the floor of the Yacht Club pleading for his life in the middle of his fight with Johnny Darke. The court was also told that despite severe wounds Bindon had fought back, stabbing his attacker to death with a hunting knife belonging to his then girlfriend. It was alleged that Bindon was hired on a £20,000 contract to kill Darke, a police informant. But two key witnesses – Bindon's friend Lennie Osbourne and Darke associate Ernie Begbe – had disappeared.

Then up stepped another of Bindon's close friends, a Fulham bank robber called Alan Stanton. But no one at the Old Bailey that day realised Stanton was close to Bindon. Donning serious-looking spectacles, Stanton had originally been called as an eye witness to describe Bindon's attack on Darke, but Stanton cleverly turned around the prosecution's questions and ended up telling the court that Bindon was the victim of an unprovoked attack.

On 13 November 1979 the jury announced that John Bindon was not guilty of Johnny Darke's murder. There were cheers from the public gallery. The jury also found Bindon not guilty of manslaughter and an affray charge. Both his co-defendants, Bohm and Galbraith, were found guilty of affray charges. They got three- and four-year sentences respectively. But the courtroom drama wasn't over quite yet. As everyone filed out, Galbraith's mother strode across the lobby and delivered a smart left hook to the jaw of Vicki Hodge, Bindon's lover, then tugged her tousled-blonde hair and screamed, 'You vicious cow. You're a mockery to this trial.'

After his acquittal, the *Daily Mirror* laid on limousines for Bindon, Vicki and their entourage to whisk them away from the

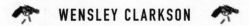
court. A party was then held at the *Mirror*'s palatial high-rise headquarters in nearby Holborn Circus. Ever the professional, Vicki had ensured that they would be financially rewarded for all the heartache of the previous year by signing a deal with the *Daily Mirror* for a 'kiss 'n' tell' story following Bindon's acquittal.

Meanwhile, south London crime boss Charlie Richardson was still languishing in jail, although, rather like 'Mad Axeman' Frank Mitchell, he believed he'd been unjustly refused a release date by the Home Office because of the controversial nature of his crimes. So, no one in the London underworld was surprised when, in 1980, Richardson walked out of an open prison. While on the lam he even dressed up as Santa Claus and gave out presents to children to try and publicise his bid for parole from prison. Richardson remained on his toes for nearly a year before giving himself up. Less than three years later he was granted day release to help the handicapped and permitted to spend a weekend with his family. Richardson's eventual full release from prison came in July 1984.

PART 3
1980–95: DRUGS, SEX AND GOLD BULLION

Kenny Noye, the
Brinks-Mat Robbery
mastermind

John Bindon,
photographed with
Princess Margaret

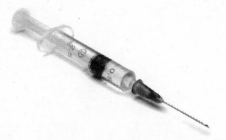

'Drugs were where the money was. It was like hittin'
the jackpot once they came on the scene...'

VETERAN LONDON GANGSTER

THE £7 MILLION SECURITY EXPRESS RAID in April, 1983, was the largest cash haul in British criminal history — until the Brinks-Mat raid a few months later. A £500,000 reward was immediately offered for the capture of the six-man team, who literally carried away tons of cash from the company's east London headquarters. Hooded gang members toting sawn-off shotguns overpowered a lone guard at breakfast time on the Easter Monday bank holiday. Over many hours, coins and bank notes in the company vaults were carefully loaded onto three vans. Employees turning up for work in the middle of the raid were taken prisoner by two gang members.

One of the brains behind the robbery was Freddie Foreman, probably the most legendary face to emerge from the Kray twins' era and then graduate into major robberies during the 1970s and '80s. Foreman was born in 1932 and raised in war-torn South London. He left school at the age of 14 and started working in a factory. He later explained to this author, 'I was humping fuckin' hundredweight sacks up ladders and things for the princely wage of £4 a week. So I had to go out and do a bit of thieving.'

At 16, Foreman ended up in the No 1 court at the Old Bailey where he received a lengthy sentence for theft. It was the first of five appearances he would make at the most famous criminal court in the world. By his mid-twenties Freddie was a professional armed robber whose 'firm' was responsible for some of London's most lucrative crimes of the late 1950s and early '60s.

In 1961 Freddie Foreman and his team held up an armoured truck in Bow Common Lane only to find two guards armed with handguns, and a policeman with an Alsatian, all inside the vehicle. The blaggers hit back with pickaxe handles as the cops started firing. As Foreman later explained, 'It was the turning point in the crime scene, because from then on you never pulled out on the street without a shotgun.'

In the early 1960s Foreman became a close friend and associate to Ronnie and Reggie Kray. When the twins were imprisoned for life in 1969 Foreman was convicted of being an accessory to the murder of 'Jack the Hat' McVitie and sentenced to ten years in prison. On his release, with remission, in 1975, detectives quickly rearrested Foreman for the murder of Ginger Marks. But the following October he and three others were cleared of the killing and Foreman moved abroad, first to Tenerife and then to the United States, where he remained until January 1982 when he moved to Spain.

Then, in 1983, Foreman took part in the £7 million Security Express raid, which has since been acclaimed as one of the most brilliant robberies ever committed. Within days Foreman hotfooted it abroad. Eventually he turned up back on the good old Costa del Sol, where he cut a smart figure in his silk suits and dark glasses, smoking cigars. Some people even reckoned that the renowned British gangster flick *The Long Good Friday*, with Bob Hoskins playing the lead, was based on Foreman's own life story.

Foreman was eventually extradited from Spain to face charges for the Security Express job back in the UK. He was jailed for nine years. He's lived a happy and peaceful retirement at his home in London since his release in the mid-1990s.

Then, just few months after the Security Express job came the most legendary robbery of the decade.....

Only CCTV cameras and spotlights mounted on the walls of Unit 7, a steel-and-brick box on a scruffy trading estate near Heathrow Airport, caught the attention of curious onlookers. But when the huge orange-and-white armoured shutter doors rolled open, the building's real purpose was revealed. Chunky, dark-blue Brinks-

Mat vans, with barred and tinted windows, came and went from the well-protected loading bay day and night. Unit 7 held one of Britain's biggest safes, used to store currency, precious metals and other high-risk consignments when they were en route for Heathrow Airport.

At 6.25 a.m. on Saturday 26 November 1983 it was pitch black and icy cold as a new early morning shift of workers kicked their heels and blew clouds of mist, waiting for 6.30 a.m. to arrive. Then an automatic timer neutralised the high-tech alarm system, allowing the keys to be inserted without triggering flashing lights, bells and alarms linked to the local police station and other security companies.

Four guards arrived and greeted each other. A fifth was late and still hadn't arrived when the man who would supervise the day's work drove up. This so-called 'keyman' entered the unit alone, locking the door behind him, leaving the crew outside while he collected another key, which shut down the alarm system covering the perimeter walls and windows. The four guards went to the rest room to take off their coats. One of them paused briefly to switch on the radio room aerials and the CCTV cameras before re-joining his mates.

Just then the doorbell rang. It was the missing guard. He was ten minutes late. The guards heard the keyman go downstairs to let him in. He said he'd overslept, then, mumbling something about having to use the toilet, he disappeared downstairs again. It was by now 6.40 a.m.

'Get on the floor or you're fuckin' dead.' A masked man filled the doorway of the rest area and virtually spat out the words in a heavy south London accent. He aimed his 9 mm Browning automatic straight at the guards. Three of them dived for cover. The armed robber was white, about five-feet eight-inches tall and clean shaven, wearing a trilby and a dark car coat, or anorak, over a black blazer, black trousers and a black tie. He had on a yellow balaclava hitched over his head to cover everything but his eyes.

For a second or two nothing happened, then the gunman jerked his gun arm upwards and, with a silver blazer button glinting in the light, smashed the gun down on the back of one guard's head who hadn't gone to the floor quickly enough. Then he beckoned through the open door to someone waiting outside, and at least three more robbers stormed into the room.

'Lie still and be quiet,' ordered the original blagger, as his henchmen started yanking the guards' arms behind their backs and handcuffing them, then locking their legs together at the shins with heavy-duty masking tape. Cloth bags with strings were then pulled down over the guards' heads and fastened around their necks. One guard saw enough of the main robber to spot the herringbone pattern of his tweed hat and the crispness of his starched white shirt. He even noticed a lock of fair hair sticking out from under the balaclava as one of the bags was dropped over his head. Keys and watches were also snatched from the guards.

Then another voice spat out, 'Get that radio tuned in. If you hear anythin', tell us.' He must have been the boss. A radio crackled through frequencies until it tuned into a Met Police wavelength. No alarm calls had been made. Just then the keyman felt his shirt pulled up to his chin and a hand tugging violently at his waistband. 'Breathe in deeply or I'll cut you,' said a voice. Just then a knife sliced through his belted jeans from the buckle to the crotch. A rag was waved under his nose.

'Do you recognise that smell?' It was unmistakable. The next instant he felt petrol stinging his groin area. 'Do as I fuckin' say, or I'll put a match to the petrol and a bullet through your fuckin' head. You live in a flat in Ruislip High Street above a TV rental shop.

We've been watching you for nine months and settin' this up for twelve. Now, let's get on with it. You've got two numbers.'

It was all over in moments, and the alarms were rapidly neutralised. The team was in. Inside Unit 7's vault the robbers found a carpet of drab grey containers, no bigger than shoeboxes, bound with metal straps and labelled with handwritten identification codes. There were 60 boxes containing 2,670 kg of gold worth £26,369,778. There were also hundreds of thousands of pounds in used bank notes locked in three safes. One pouch contained traveller's cheques worth $250,000. In the other was a stash of polished and rough diamonds worth at least a hundred grand.

The atmosphere was buzzing as the team moved the gold out to the side of the loading bay and into their waiting vans. Sure, they'd expected riches, but nothing like this. The Brinks-Mat robbery, ruthless in its conception and brilliant in its execution, had just landed them the biggest haul in British criminal history, a caper the tabloids soon labelled the 'Crime of the Century'.

Within 48 hours Lloyd's of London announced they'd pay two million quid for information leading to the return of the Brinks-Mat gold, which had already leapt in value by more than £20 an ounce in the hours since the robbery. The police soon narrowed down their list of suspects to some of the most notorious gangsters in and around southeast London. They had two folders, each containing 12 photographs of the main men. Many of them are featured elsewhere in this book, which is why they're not named here. But most were never even caught, and those tens of millions of pounds were reinvested in everything from cocaine and ecstasy shipments to brothels and a handful of major blaggings and building developments on the up-and-coming Docklands development property scheme.

'Brinks-Mat made the names and fortunes of many of today's

most ruthless gangsters,' said somebody who should know. 'It's the stuff of legends . . .'

In December 1984 Brian Robinson and Mickey McAvoy were each sentenced to 25 years in prison for committing the Brinks-Mat robbery. Anthony Black, who turned informant on the gang, got six years and a new identity. Others who handled the gold, including Garth Chappell, got ten years, while another lesser-known character who allowed his company to be used in a false tax claim received a suspended sentence of 12 months for conspiracy to evade VAT on the gold.

The after-effects of the Brinks-Mat robbery continued to ripple through the underworld, encapsulating both police and criminals alike. One tragic victim of that fallout was Detective Constable Alan 'Taffy' Holmes, a stocky, 15-stone, gregarious, broken-nosed, rugby-playing Welshman who drank to excess. He had a wife and children plus a mistress, although colleagues insisted he'd been a loyal copper throughout his 26 years of service. One workmate later said Taffy believed 'a problem shared is a problem solved'. But others admitted he did sometimes have 'misguided loyalties'. His father-in-law noted Taffy always liked to be liked by everybody. When Holmes shot himself dead in his back garden early one morning in July, 1987, a tangle of personal and work problems came to the surface. Not to mention Holmes's membership of the Masonics, although that was never disclosed during the inquest into his death, which concluded that he'd taken his own life.

However, it was revealed that Holmes had been investigated by the anti-corruption squad, CIB 2, which was probing links between a detective commander and the notorious south London criminal Kenneth Noye, who'd been convicted of avoiding the VAT on some

of the 'Brinks-Mat' gold bullion stolen in 1983. Noye had also been acquitted of murdering an undercover policeman in the garden of his Kent home. It's alleged that CIB 2 arranged for another officer to secretly tape-record Holmes talking about police corruption. Holmes plunged into depression after being told about the tape. Five days before he died, the inquest into Holmes's death later heard, the detective returned from an all-day grilling by CIB 2 in a very distressed state. He referred to a colleague he considered a friend but who, he said, had 'let him down and told lies about him'. The inquest heard that Holmes said he was going to kill that man and then kill himself. Holmes, it was disclosed, had recently encouraged the same officer to join his own Masonic lodge where he – Holmes – was Lodge Master.

Deputy Commissioner John Dellow led dozens of Scotland Yard mourners at Holmes's funeral, where he received full police honours. One colleague spoke at the service about how Holmes 'had a face as hard as granite but a heart as soft and vulnerable as a butterfly'. Dozens of wreaths at the service included several openly signed by Freemason police officers, as well as numerous police stations and squads. One Mason inscription read: 'To our brave, wonderful and worshipful master who chose death rather than dishonour his friends and workmates.'

There were a lot of shrewd, artful crooks around in London when a seismic shift in criminal opportunity presented itself in the mid-1980s: the whole of Europe discovered cocaine. Coke was about to become the fashionable drug of choice for people from all backgrounds. The cocaine business had already turned dozens of Colombians into multi-millionaires; now some of London's best-known 'faces' believed it was their turn to grab a piece of the action. With the US cracking down heavily on the cocaine flooding across their borders, Spain was the new gateway for much of Europe's supplies. In London, many criminals had bold plans to become the big boys in Europe, controlling the drug flowing into Britain via Spain and South America.

So, a small group of greying, middle-aged London villains chased a piece of the European-wide, multi-million-pound drug industry based in their backyard. The profits were phenomenal. Cannabis, for example, cost £250 per kg in North Africa and could be sold in the UK for upwards of £4,000. An investment of £20,000 in a shipment of cocaine would bring a return of £160,000. Usually, four investors worked together to buy 100 kg at a time.

The peak year for cocaine use in the United States was 1985. The decline that came after that prompted the Colombian cartels' decision to turn their attention to Europe as the next main territory to conquer. The money generated by street sales of cocaine – all cash and carry, no cheques, credit cards or charge accounts – had made the coke trade one of the industrial colossuses of the world. And London was soon making a bid to be the new global centre for the drug.

Cocaine sold at £60 a gram – that's just a twenty-eighth of an ounce, 15 to 20 modest lines' worth, sufficient to induce a heightened sense of wellbeing for an evening in a party of four. The 50 tons of the drug sold in London in 1985 would be 'cut' up to four times by successive dealers to eventually generate retail revenue of something in the region of £10 billion a year. The cocaine business was the sixth largest private enterprise in the US Top 500. Companies such as Boeing, Proctor and Gamble, and Chrysler Motors were rated after cocaine on the 'rich list' of industries. By the mid-1980s there was so much profit and so many shipments going into London that villains calculated they could afford to lose one-third of their product and still make tens of millions of pounds in profit each year.

Initially, many London crooks were happy to 'buy into loads'. That meant making a living from partly financing other people's deals and having virtually no direct contact with the actual drugs. They also frequently took a 20 per cent stake in large consignments of cannabis from Morocco. But in order to get the really big money, these London faces knew they'd have to get their fingers dirty. A classic example of this type of villain was former Great Train Robber Charlie Wilson, who moved to southern Spain in the mid-1980s. On one occasion the south Londoner got a call about 15 tons of Lebanese cannabis resin hidden in a cave on the Costa Brava by a bunch of young London wannabes. He organised a search party to drive up the coast and locate the drugs, steal them and then sell them through to the UK. Robberies were a thing of the past for Charlie. He knew drugs would line his pockets with gold from now on.

Wilson contacted associates, including his old mate Jimmy Rose, whose 'Rose Organisation' was by now renowned for being able to transport virtually anything across continents without any problem. Rose's and Charlie's relationship went back to the 1950s when they were banged up together in prison. Charlie Wilson also met with the notorious Haynes family of drug smugglers. Michael Haynes, from Egham in Surrey on the outskirts of London, was part of an international family-run drugs ring. Haynes, then 41, was later arrested on the French border with a woman associate after being tailed from the Costa del Sol. Police found 36 kg of cannabis hidden in secret compartments beneath his car.

Other gangs of London smugglers were extremely adept at persuading innocent 'one-off' couriers to smuggle drugs into Britain by plane, knowing full well that there were other smugglers on board with much more valuable consignments of drugs. These so-called 'mules' would sometimes be sacrificed to customs inspectors so that the big-time smugglers had more chance of getting through. Another smuggler's trick was to get a lorry to pick up a perfectly innocent-sounding cargo and then tip off the local police, who'd arrest the driver who had no idea that the concrete blocks he was carrying contained cannabis.

'That kept the cozzers happy for a while because they think they're winning the battle against drugs, while all the very big consignments are still getting through,' explained one veteran smuggler. On Spain's Costa del Sol, London faces regularly rented villas near the sea and turned them into temporary 'drugs warehouses', while at least half-a-dozen cars were being prepared to carry narcotics – which had been delivered by boat the previous night – back to the UK.

London's gangland was well and truly hooked.

Tony White – one of South London's most powerful villains – was a classic bank robber turned drug baron. White, now in his sixties and nicknamed the 'King of Catford', was cleared of involvement in the Brinks-Mat robbery in the mid-1980s, although the Old Bailey jury dubbed him a 'dishonest man with an appalling criminal record' who had come into substantial wealth after the raid. Following Brinks-Mat, White was sued by Lloyd's of London in the High Court after they named him as one of the Brinks-Mat gang, and he was ordered to pay them millions of pounds in compensation, although no one knows to this day if he ever came up with any of the cash. White moved to Spain after Brinks-Mat. His house on the 'Costa del Crime', appropriately called the 'Little White House', was a massive spread, and he even sent his children to the expensive fee-paying school. White was later arrested by Costa del Sol police on money laundering charges. When detectives raided White's mansion, they found a secret Scotland

Yard surveillance report allegedly implying he had a number of senior British police officers in his pocket. He was eventually released after a long legal wrangle.

White was later seized at gunpoint by Spanish police at Madrid airport in June 2003 over an alleged plot to smuggle £4 million worth of cocaine into Spain. White was eventually released and all charges were dropped.

Another legendary face whose criminal career seems to perfectly sum up the ganglands of London from the 1960s onwards is Mickey Greene, born and bred in northwest London. He's recently been described by the Republic of Ireland's Criminal Assets Bureau as 'one of the world's biggest cocaine traffickers'. Greene has become so adept at escaping justice since his days as a notorious armed robber in London 30 years ago that he's been nicknamed 'the Pimpernel' by authorities. Greene is the classic Mr Big with alleged links to the mafia and Colombian drug cartels.

His grand-looking hacienda just east of Marbella is worth more than £2 million, and he's even got a friend to live in one of the nearby houses to keep an eye on the property whenever he's on his travels. Michael John Paul Greene was born in 1942 in Wembley to a family originally from Ireland. His criminal reputation began in 1972 when the notorious London supergrass Bertie Smalls named him as leader of a gang of robbers known as the Wembley Mob – then the UK's most successful team of armed robbers. Greene was eventually jailed for 18 years for his part in the 1970 robbery of a bank in Ilford that yielded £237,000, although he was suspected of involvement in numerous other crimes.

Greene was released on parole after serving seven years of his sentence and was soon back in the thick of things. He teamed up with old Wembley Mob partner Ronnie Dark and they developed a lucrative VAT scam on gold Krugerrands, which made Greene and his pals £6 million in under a year. Greene then turned up on the Costa del Crime, where kidnaps, robberies and killings were being ordered by some of Britain's most notorious villains. Back then, Greene was living in a luxury penthouse in the La Nogalera building in Torremolinos and driving a white Rolls-Royce and a red Porsche. He also had his own yacht and had become a regular at many of Marbella's most exclusive restaurants and clubs.

By the mid-1980s Greene was already worth tens of millions, and owned 11 yachts and half-a-dozen luxury motors besides his Rolls-Royce and Porsche. Greene still described himself as a car dealer but now lived lavishly at a huge villa near Marbella. Known as the original 'medallion man', he also part-owned a nightclub overlooking the marina at nearby Puerto Banus and spent much of his time cruising the port looking for blonde dollybirds. There was even a rumour he kept £1 million in French francs hidden in a box in the flowerbed of his Marbella villa. British customs agents have been pursuing Greene for years.

During the 1980s Greene started building up a vast drug empire by running narcotics into Europe from North Africa, using Spain as his centre of operations. He was arrested by Spanish police in 1987 after two tons of hash was seized. But Greene was given bail and fled to Morocco, leaving behind the powerboats and yachts allegedly used to run drugs from North Africa to Spain.

A few months later Greene turned up in Paris, and Interpol were alerted. French police swooped on his swish Left Bank apartment where they found gold bullion and cocaine –but no Mickey Greene. He was later sentenced in his absence to 17 years in jail for drug possession and smuggling. Greene's next stop was California where he rented Rod Stewart's mansion under an alias; Stewart clearly had no knowledge that his tenant was a villain. A few months later FBI agents knocked down his front door as he was lounging by the pool and arrested him. Greene was put on a flight bound for France to fulfil that jail sentence, but he disembarked when the plane made a stopover at Ireland's Shannon Airport, and, using his Irish passport, slipped unnoticed past customs men and headed for Dublin, where he had many contacts. Greene then took full advantage of the weak extradition laws between the Republic of Ireland and France at the time and settled in Dublin.

He even splashed out on a massive £500,000 farmhouse just outside the city. Then, in 1995, Greene ran a red light at a busy junction in his Bentley and killed a taxi driver called Joe White. Greene was fined and banned from driving, but there was uproar in the local press because he was not given a custodial sentence, despite the death of an innocent man. Under mounting pressure, Irish police made it clear that they were planning to grab Greene's assets, including his farmhouse property, so the Londoner disappeared once again. It was later claimed during another criminal's trial in London that Greene bribed two witnesses in the death-crash court case to keep himself out of jail.

Shortly after leaving Ireland, Greene turned up once again in southern Spain. It was also widely reported that he'd managed to slip in and out of the UK using forged passports on numerous occasions between 1997 and 2000. There were also persistent rumours that a senior Scotland Yard detective was supplying information to Greene in exchange for thousands of pounds in bribes.

Then, in February 2000, Greene's Irish lawyer was shadowed to the Spanish city of Barcelona by UK Customs agents who'd been investigating Greene's links to the mafia, Colombian drug cartels, and a massive worldwide drug network importing narcotics into Britain. When Greene turned up at the Ritz Hotel he was immediately arrested by UK Customs and Spanish police and transported to the nation's most secure jail in Madrid. At first, both Spanish and UK police hailed the arrest as Greene's swansong. An extradition hearing was set, and it seemed just a formality that he would be heading home to London and a long stretch inside. Newspapers at the time estimated Greene's personal fortune to be at least £50 million. It was also said that he had evaded arrest on the Costa del Crime for a couple of years by wearing a disguise and using a false identity.

Besides being wanted in the UK, Greene also still faced the long prison sentence back in France for earlier drugs offences. It then emerged that Greene had invested many millions of pounds into legitimate businesses in Spain, all financed by his frenzied multi-million-pound drug deals on the Costa del Crime. Despite this, Greene told many associates he couldn't resist the 'buzz' of committing crimes.

And Mickey Greene isn't known as the Pimpernel for nothing; a few months after his dramatic arrest in Barcelona, a Spanish court refused to extradite him after insisting that UK Customs did not have enough concrete evidence to mount a prosecution. Mickey Greene was once again a free man. Rumours of bribes swept the Costa del Crime.

At the trial of supergrass Michael Michael at the Old Bailey in 2001, prosecutor Nicholas Loraine-Smith named Mickey Greene as a major drugs baron. Following his court case, Michael had good reason to fear the wrath of Mickey Greene. It was said in court that Greene had organised the murders of two other criminals. First to die was hard-man Gilbert Wynter, who disappeared from his north London home in 1998. His body was rumoured to have been disposed of in a car crusher or in the foundations of the Millennium Dome. Then a notorious finance chief for a London criminal family was shot dead outside his home. Michael told customs investigators that they were both killed after double-crossing Greene in a half-million pound cannabis deal.

In the same Old Bailey court case one of Michael's cash couriers, a woman called Janice Marlborough, also said that Greene was 'head of the tree'. Even today, Greene is described in Interpol intelligence reports as 'a highly dangerous criminal mastermind'. Greene denies these charges.

These days, Mickey Greene still spends some of his time on the Costa del Crime, although sources in Spain say that he is planning to spend more time in Costa Rica, where he owns yet another luxury home. He's also rumoured to be planning a property purchase in Thailand. As one of those involved in his Barcelona arrest has said, 'Mickey's a survivor, but you can be sure he's watching his back very carefully.'

One of Greene's closest mates in the Costa sunshine was chirpy south Londoner Frank Maple – tall, grey haired and extremely stylish in a 1980s sort of way. Maple fled the 'Big Smoke' to Spain after being named as the brains behind the Bank of America robbery in 1976. He also spent three years in an Austrian jail for a £100,000 hotel robbery. He's now believed to be living a happy but quiet retirement in the mountains behind Marbella.

London's gangsters went through a phenomenally successful period of jail escapes from the 1960s through to the early '80s. Their antics are worth recording because they provide further evidence of the old-fashioned criminal skills they clearly possessed.

On Tuesday, 15 December 1980, notorious London robbery gang members Jimmy Moody and Stan Thompson joined forces with IRA suspect Gerard Tuite to pull off one of the most daring escapes of all time from Brixton Jail in South London. At 2.45

a.m., all three men carefully put dummy figures made of clothing stuffed with newspapers under the covers of their beds. Moody and Thompson then both squeezed through holes that they had dug into Tuite's cell. Now the team were ready to punch a hole through the outside wall of Tuite's cell to make good their escape. They'd scheduled a further 30 minutes to ensure it was big enough.

At just before 3.15 a.m. the following day, Stan Thompson went face down into the hole through Tuite's outside wall. Tuite followed seconds later. Then it was Jimmy Moody's turn. He looked down at the hole and shook his head. 'It's too small, I can't do it,' he said. Tuite later recalled, 'So we literally tore him through the hole. I could hear the muscles tearing right off his back. He left a lot of flesh behind, but we got him through.'

Now Moody, Tuite and Thompson were on the roof of the next-door B-wing. An outside CCTV camera failed to spot them, thanks to another inmate shining a light in his cell at the moment they got on the roof. That diverted the camera from its regular route. The three men crept quietly along the flat roof going southwards alongside the ground adjacent to B-wing. They then moved along the end of Brixton's C-wing in a westerly direction, before turning towards the far corner of the prison where a 12-foot-high steel-mesh fence surrounded the 17-foot-high perimeter wall. They clambered over the fence to the top of the wall, which they crawled along until they reached a blank spot not covered by security TV cameras. Jimmy Moody had earlier carefully selected the time when a prison officer with an Alsatian was at the other side of the prison grounds.

Moody then threw a blanket over the 'Dannert' barbed wire on the top of the perimeter wall. A rope and grapnel was then dropped onto the ground outside the prison before the three inmates slid down from the wall. They left their bag of tools at the base of the wall as a calling card. Their pick-up vehicle was nowhere to be seen, so they walked down the hill towards the centre of Brixton before hailing a cab to freedom. Thompson was picked up a few days later after giving himself up, but Moody and Tuite stayed on their toes for years. Their escape was a massive slap in the face for the Thatcher government and led to the sacking of numerous prison officials.

Gerard Tuite is now a successful businessman in the Republic of Ireland, drives a Mercedes and lives in a luxurious detached house in a picturesque village 50 miles from Dublin with his wife and two children. He insists his days with 'the movement' are over. Stan Thompson, the master jail escaper, today lives east of London and works as a builder. His eyes light up whenever he talks about the Brixton breakout, and he says he'll never forget Jimmy Moody or the good times they spent together.

In the ganglands of London, certain names resonate for the sheer audacity of their stunning criminal enterprises. They're admired by new and old gangsters, they have the cozzers in their pockets and they live on the very edge. Meet Kenneth 'Kenny' Noye.

Noye was – and still is – one of the most powerful and richest criminals in Britain. A genius of the underworld, handling the proceeds of huge drug deals and legendary blaggings have helped make him tens of millions of pounds. He maintains a string of mistresses scattered around the globe, and he's always enjoyed a five-star lifestyle. He's also another member of that exclusive gentlemen gangsters' club – the Brinks-Mat robbery, the legendary job that links so many of the names in this book.

However, for much of the last 25 years Noye has been in prison, although, typically, being under lock and key hasn't stopped him from operating as one of London's top master criminals who's earned the respect of every gangster across the capital. Kenny Noye's emergence as a major player is part of recent criminal history; an account of his exploits gives a fascinating insight into the life of a criminal, post the Krays and the Richardsons.

Kenneth John Noye was born in Bexleyheath, Kent, on 24 May 1947. Without any smog and the inner city's concrete jungle of housing developments, Bexleyheath was the new face of southeast London. It had many of the area's appealing features but few of its bad habits. At first, Noye's parents found it strange, swapping their tiny terraced house in London's docklands for one of the square bungalows that dominated streets such as Jenton Avenue, where Noye was brought up. His father, Jim, was a fully trained communications engineer who'd served his country with the Navy during the Second World War. Before that he'd been a junior docker in Bermondsey.

Noye's mum, Edith, was a strong, blunt-speaking lady who took her young son under her wing from an early age, and worked three nights a week as manageress of the nearby Crayford dog track. Supporting the family was all that mattered in those days. There was no question of scrounging off the state – the Noye family didn't do things that way. They looked after their own.

Young Kenny Noye certainly proved to be quite a handful. At just three years old he broke his nose falling out of a tree in a neighbour's garden while pinching apples. By the time Noye was five he was adept at helping himself to cash from the till on trips to the corner shop with his mum, slipping behind the counter when no one was looking. He was only caught when his mum saw a ten-bob note (50 pence) sticking out of the top of his Wellington boots as they were walking out of the shop. Young Kenny was already boasting about what he'd do when he grew up. 'Earn lots of money,' he pledged to anyone who'd listen.

In the gritty dockland areas of southeast London, where Noye's father had grown up, petty thieves were still nicking tea chests off lorries and selling every commodity they could lay their hands on. Truck drivers were kidnapped and had their loads stolen, but usually no one was harmed. Everything was fair game in those days: fags, booze and clothing. Railway containers were raided at night, and their contents would end up on local street markets the next day.

Crime was an escape hatch for the unemployed, many of whom were part-time villains anyway. Then, in the early 1960s, armed robbery became the most lucrative form of income. In southeast London the status of blaggers in the local community put them on a par with film stars. At Bexleyheath Secondary Modern School, teenager Noye leaned on other school kids for protection money. A brief spell at a printing college followed, but that soon gave way to stealing cars and scooters and selling them on to other local villains.

Soon, young Kenny was making a lot of money handling stolen gear 'off the back of lorries' and even making a few bob off the cozzers at the same time by letting them in on a few secrets in exchange for some inside info on his rivals. Kenny called it back scratching: 'you scratch mine, I'll scratch yours'.

Noye married his teenage sweetheart, Brenda, and they had two sons, Brett and Kevin. They eventually moved out of the suburbs to the peace and quiet of West Kingsdown, a village in the Kent countryside; but it was still well within sawn-off shotgun range of his old southeast London haunts. That's when Noye decided to branch out and began fronting up cash for robberies and other crimes. The beauty of Noye's criminal career was that he rarely got his own hands dirty. He simply put up the finance for a job and then left it up to his team.

By the time Noye had turned 30 he was driving a Rolls-Royce, running a fleet of fancy women, and even had time to become a

Mason, in a cheeky bid to get closer to the police, judges and politicians who were also members. And Kenny Noye believed that being a Mason would certainly be good for his type of 'business'. Some police officers who were members of the west London Masons lodge that Noye joined were outraged by the presence of such a villain in their 'club'. But others saw it as an opportunity to utilise a good informant.

Then, on 10 October 1981, Noye appeared in Canterbury Crown Court for importation of a firearm, evasion of VAT, providing a counterfeit document after his arrest, making a false statement to the Customs and Excise Office, and breaking the conditions of an earlier suspended sentence. He was very lucky to get another suspended prison sentence plus a £2,500 fine. Many people still believe that Noye's 'friends' in the police helped him avoid a spell inside.

By this time Noye was under regular police surveillance. Raids with search warrants were even carried out on his home. A Crime Intelligence Branch report that I have seen stated that Noye was running a stolen motor vehicle parts ring, which also involved exporting lorry equipment to Syria. He was even rumoured to have supplied some of the heavy-lifting vehicles used to construct the Thames Barrier.

The ambitious Noye used the alias of Kenneth James when he wanted to travel incognito. He had a luxury flat in Broomfield Road, Bexleyheath, where neighbours spotted him in the company of various women. The police soon linked Noye to more than a dozen companies, and his list of 'associates' read like a *Who's Who* of the southeast London and Kent underworld. Besides his Rolls-Royce, Noye drove a Jeep and various Fords that he bought directly from Fords in Dagenham through a contact. Noye then sold them on for a fat profit.

One of Noye's former employees at his lorry yard in West Kingsdown told the police he was terrified of his one-time boss and stated that he'd 'suffered violence at the hands of Noye in the past'. Even in the early 1980s the police believed Noye was dabbling in the drugs trade. On one occasion they watched him pass over £10,000 in cash to an unnamed man in the Black Swan pub on the Mile End Road. They had no doubt it was drug money. The same informant also told the cozzers that Noye had handled the proceeds from the robbery in the Blackwall Tunnel.

The police report at the time stated, 'Noye allegedly puts up the money for organised crime. He is an associate of prominent London criminals. Noye travels to and from America and the Continent to allegedly change money.' The report also revealed that Noye even provided hundreds of thousands of stolen bricks for the construction of a housing estate called the Hollies, in Gravesend, Kent. But when the secret police report named an MP with whom Kenny 'had a business association', it made Noye's criminal CV look all the more impressive.

The report also featured Noye's full criminal record to that time:

14.12.66 Old Street Magistrates Court. Found on enclosed premises for unlawful purposes. Twelve Month conditional discharge and £2.20 costs.

20.6.67 Southeast London Q.S. Receiving stolen vehicles. Receiving stolen property. Found on enclosed promises for unlawful purpose. Borstal Training.

20.5.75 Marlborough Street Magistrates Court. Theft of sunglasses. Assault on police. Fined £50. Ordered to pay £15 costs. Also fined £15.

21.2.77 Croydon Crown Court. Handling stolen property (five cases). Possessing document with intent to deceive. Unlawful possession of a shotgun. [For all the charges, Noye was fined £2,100 and ordered to pay almost £8,000 in compensation plus costs. He also got a two-year suspended prison sentence.]

21.3.79 Malling Magistrates Court. Dishonestly abstracting electricity. Fined £250.

In 1982 Noye proved he had a soft side by showing the hand of kindness to a neighbour in distress. The Noyes offered West Kingsdown greengrocer Alan Cramer their sincere condolences when his 26-year-old son was killed in a car crash on nearby Death Hill. Mr Cramer was very touched by their concern: 'They sent me a nice letter with their condolences. It was one of the first we got. They said that if we needed any help, we only had to ask. They would help in any way they could, and they didn't mean money-wise. It was a nice thought.' Many years later Mr Cramer returned the Noyes' offer of kindness by staunchly sticking up for Kenny Noye following his arrest on major crime charges.

As Noye's criminal enterprises continued to expand so did his 'back scratching' with the Kent and southeast London police. He and a few other local faces occasionally collected 'reward money' for 'pointing the police in the right direction', which seemed to enable Noye to keep all his own illegal activities going unhindered.

Noye's ascendancy coincided with a complete overhaul of the old-school gangsters' biggest enemy – the Met's Flying Squad. Instead of dealing with all serious crimes, the Sweeney were ordered to tackle only armed robberies, with the officers forming a central robbery squad, run from a coordinating unit at Scotland Yard with four smaller groups dotted around London.

It was the Brinks-Mat job that really put Kenny Noye on the map – and gave him respect throughout the London underworld.

The Brinks-Mat robbery was already the stuff of legends. To nick enough gold to set up dozens of people financially for life was a gangster's dream come true. But the sheer size of the Brinks-Mat haul of gold bullion created a major headache for the villains still on the run. The gang needed a mechanism, or conduit, down which the gold could travel. It had to be smelted and sold to legitimate businesses in order to launder the cash before any of it could be shared around the robbers who hadn't been arrested.

Some months after the robbery, a unit of undercover police was ordered to hide out in the 20-acre garden of Hollywood Cottage, Noye's vast home in West Kingsdown, and see what he was up to. One night, Noye heard some movement in the bushes. He charged right in and struck out at a black-clad figure whom he later claimed he thought was an intruder. Noye used all his brute strength to smash his fists into the man over and over again. Then he pulled out a blade and began to plunge it into the body of undercover detective John Fordham.

In Hollywood Cottage, Brenda Noye rushed upstairs and grabbed a shotgun – one of at least half a dozen the couple kept in their bedroom cupboard. Loading the gun as she ran, Brenda, and her husband's fellow Brinks-Mat operative Brian Reader, headed down the drive in the direction of where they'd heard Noye shouting. Noye was standing over the masked figure, his Rottweilers growling. 'Who are you?' shouted Noye angrily. 'Who are you?'

Detective Fordham was still wearing his balaclava hood. Noye noticed the policeman's night-sight binoculars. He later claimed that he thought he was dealing with a rapist or a peeping tom. Noye

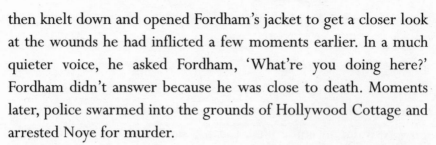

then knelt down and opened Fordham's jacket to get a closer look at the wounds he had inflicted a few moments earlier. In a much quieter voice, he asked Fordham, 'What're you doing here?' Fordham didn't answer because he was close to death. Moments later, police swarmed into the grounds of Hollywood Cottage and arrested Noye for murder.

Nearly a year on, Noye was acquitted of murdering Detective Fordham, but the long arm of the law finally brought him to justice when he was later jailed for nine years for his role in handling the gold bullion from the Brinks-Mat blagging.

Kenny Noye considered prison to be a den of vice. He watched inmates inject themselves with filthy needles. He heard the gossip about who were the 'girl-boys' and who'd just give blow jobs. None of it mattered to him because he had businesses to run. He was above the riffraff, and everyone knew it. He soon had his own 'employees' running around for him.

In 1987 – during a spell inside the relatively easy-going Swaleside Prison in Kent – Noye met a hyped-up drug peddler called Pat Tate, who told him all about a new designer drug called ecstasy that was just starting to take off in Britain. Pat Tate convinced Noye to invest £30,000 in one of his ecstasy deals. Many villains believe to this day that this was the first of millions of pounds of Brinks-Mat cash that helped flood Britain with ecstasy in the late 1980s and early '90s. (Tate, his partner Tony Tucker and another drug dealer called Craig Rolfe were later shot to death at point-blank range as they sat in their Range Rover in an Essex field.)

London underworld legend has it that Noye made £200,000 back from that original £30,000 investment. Drugs were undoubtedly where the really big profits could be made. Blaggings would soon be a thing of the past. Like all good operators, Kenny

Noye knew it was time to change direction. From inside the nick, Noye invested vast sums of his considerable fortune – estimated in the late 1980s at £10 million – in the drugs explosion.

Noye was released from prison in 1994 and immediately decided to embrace new technology by planning one of the most daring financial frauds of the 1990s. He teamed up with his old sparring partner, notorious south London villain John 'Little Legs' Lloyd, and they headed-up a gang that would eventually be dubbed the 'Hole-in-the-Wall Gang'.

They used their own contacts in prison to scout around for some technical recruits. The idea was to tap into the latest banking technology. It meant an army of corrupt communications engineers and computer experts had to be recruited to make vast numbers of cloned cashpoint cards. These would then be used to empty cash from thousands of bank accounts over a 24-hour period. If they pulled it off, it would throw the entire British banking system into total chaos.

Computer boffin Martin Grant was hired from inside Blantyre House open prison in Kent. He'd been jailed for attempting to murder his wife and child but in the slammer he'd studied for a degree in electronic communications. Grant was out on day release for work experience at a van hire business owned by Paul Kidd, another villain involved in the cashcard cloning scheme with Noye and Lloyd.

Noye and his Hole-in-the-Wall gang planned to enter British Telecom exchanges with their team of corrupt engineers to put telephone taps on the lines and memory boards. The info would then be transferred to the gang's computer. But unknown to the gang, computer nerd Martin Grant – who was completely out of his depth with this team of pros – was already feeding information about the card scam to the police. He'd confessed to a prison

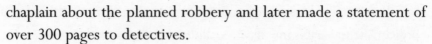
chaplain about the planned robbery and later made a statement of over 300 pages to detectives.

The audacious crime was abandoned, but the police then genuinely feared Noye and his mob of hardened criminals might decide to silence Grant, so they placed him in a safe house in the middle of the English countryside with gun-toting officers guarding him day and night. Grant's only form of transport was a police helicopter.

Later, Grant provided a fascinating insight into Kenny Noye and his old friend 'Little Legs' Lloyd: 'Noye and Lloyd were just names to me at first. They meant nothing. But people inside prison talked about them as if they were gods. Remember, I have seen the other side of Kenny Noye – not so much against me but against others who have mucked him about. Although he can be a very nice chap, he is quite capable of turning into an aggressor.' Grant said he attended one meeting with the gang where Noye and Lloyd produced prison paperwork on his record and family background, which clearly had been given to them by prison staff. Those details included the addresses of Grant's mother and brother.

In one chilling incident, Noye's associate Lloyd drove Grant to his mother's house in the Midlands, walked him through the front door and even introduced himself to Grant's mother, 'Just to let me know he knew where she lived,' Grant later explained. 'John Lloyd then phoned Kenny Noye to say he had met my mum. I was so scared.'

Grant added, 'Kenny Noye and Lloyd told stories about hijacking vehicles in the early days and what they did to people who crossed them.' Grant also said that they made continual references to other criminal associates in Spain and the United States.

And Grant revealed that Kenny Noye and Lloyd became very threatening towards him once they began to suspect that he might be grassing them up. 'One time they got a bunch of other villains to follow me back to prison to make sure I wasn't in touch with the police,' he said. Grant also recalled an incident when Noye and Lloyd almost came to blows after they had a problem with the computers they were using as part of the scam: 'I saw Noye lose his temper with Lloyd, and it wasn't a pleasant sight.'

The cops eventually made a move to arrest Noye but, typically, he'd been tipped off by a police contact and disappeared. However, Little Legs Lloyd and the rest of the Hole-in-the-Wall crew were pulled in, although none of them was foolish enough to point the finger at Noye, which meant there wasn't enough evidence for police to charge him.

In May 1996 Kenny Noye made the biggest mistake of his life of crime when he knifed to death motorist Stephen Cameron in a road-rage attack on the M25, just a few miles from his Kent home. Within hours of fleeing the scene, Noye was in a helicopter rising above the countryside just outside Bristol to begin a two-and-a-half-year spell on the run from the police. He was even dubbed 'Public Enemy Number One'.

Back on the ground, Kenny's brand new Land Rover Discovery, containing the knife he'd used to kill Stephen Cameron, was being driven in a bizarre three-car convoy to a scrap yard in Dartford, Kent, where it was crushed into a compressed box of jagged steel.

Noye's role in the road-rage killing focused a lot of unwelcome attention on the southeast London underworld. The police even started to wonder if Noye had been killed, because other gangsters didn't like the extra heat they were suffering during the frantic search for the fugitive.

In the late summer of 1996 Noye slipped quietly back into southeast London and began moving from safe house to safe house. His impressive network of informants and contacts meant that he was safer than in so-called unknown territory abroad. Such was his status in certain parts of Kent and southeast London that he could drink and live relatively openly without fear of being nicked.

Noye was also taking a leaf out of his old friend Little Legs Lloyd's book – he'd done exactly the same thing when he was a supposed fugitive in America following the Brinks-Mat robbery. The nearest the police ever really got to grabbing Noye was in early 1997 when an anonymous tipster said he was holed-up in a small terraced house in Catford. They swooped on the house with armed officers, but Kenny had long gone. At one stage Noye seemed to be deliberately making sure he was seen out in some of his old haunts, to let people know that, in his eyes, he'd done nothing wrong. He told anyone who would listen that he was innocent of the Cameron road-rage killing.

Then, in 1997, Noye moved to an isolated village in southern Spain but continued popping back and forth to London for important meetings, despite still being Britain's Public Enemy Number One. He even put up some money for a daring plot to spring another drug baron from inside Whitemoor Prison in Cambridgeshire. It involved smuggling in quantities of Semtex explosive, blasting a hole in the jail wall and then flying their man to freedom.

An inmate leaked the escape plans to prison bosses. Noye and a number of other gangsters had invested millions of pounds in this other drug baron's narcotics ring and needed him to be free in order to recoup their investment. It was a classic Kenny Noye-backed operation: the screw had been trapped into helping the gang because he'd been caught having sex with a woman who wasn't his wife. That same screw was already supplying many inmates with drugs inside Whitemoor. Prison authorities foiled the escape plan just a week before it was due to happen.

Noye's life on the run didn't stop him earning tens of millions of pounds in drug deals from his Spanish hideaway. He was so heavily involved in cannabis smuggling that he even visited Yardies in Jamaica while he was on the run. In Gibraltar, British police stumbled upon Noye without recognising him as Britain's most wanted man when he met up with a local drugs baron under surveillance by them.

In Spain, Noye bought a luxury yacht for £200,000 and chartered it out to drug smugglers. Noye even frequently smuggled his father, Brenda, and other relatives and friends to his home on the edge of the Atlantic, even though the police in Kent were supposed to be shadowing their every move. He wasn't even spotted when 20 Spanish police officers patrolled his neighbour's house when one of Spain's senior politicians spent the summer there.

Later, Noye's false passport was found to contain numerous stamps showing that he'd been a regular visitor to Jamaica and Morocco. In mid-June 1998, Kent police had a lucky break when they got a call from a long-time informant. He gave them the mobile phone number of another villain who was in regular contact with Noye.

British and Spanish police had Noye in their sights months before he was finally arrested – but no one could actually confirm his identity, because he'd dyed his hair blond and was using a false name and passport. Kent police immediately requested assistance from MI5 in London, who sanctioned round-the-clock surveillance of the target's phone from their Thames-side headquarters.

By the end of August 1998 Noye had been traced to his house in the tiny Spanish seaside village of Atlanterra, just south of the city of Cádiz. Days later he was arrested in a nearby restaurant by Spanish and Kent cozzers and slung in a jail in Cádiz. His brunette Moroccan girlfriend disappeared into thin air before the cops could find her. Noye's highly paid team of Spanish lawyers believed he stood a good chance of avoiding extradition. However, in March 1999, Madrid judges threw out all his appeals, and Noye was soon heading home to London to face justice.

On 20 May 1999, Noye was handcuffed and ordered out of his cell at Madrid's Valdemoro jail. He was then bundled into an anonymous white van and escorted by two plain Seat saloons out towards the city suburbs. Less than 30 minutes later Noye was handed over to three Kent policemen at Madrid Airport and flown to London's Gatwick Airport. Noye appeared before magistrates the following day in his old manor of Dartford to face the murder charges linked to the death of motorist Stephen Cameron. He was immediately taken to the most secure prison in London – Belmarsh – and placed in solitary confinement, at his own request.

Noye was rumoured to have persuaded prison officers inside Belmarsh to run errands for him, and it was claimed that he had a mobile phone with him at all times. He also let it be known that he was so confident he'd be acquitted of the murder of Stephen Cameron that he authorised James Stewart, a sidekick in Spain, to get his house ready for his return. He even paid thousands to his builder to do some last-minute modifications.

All the gossip and rumours surrounding the so-called road-rage killing of Stephen Cameron were finally put to rest when Noye walked into the No 2 court of the Old Bailey on Thursday, 30 March 2000 – nearly four years after the murder took place on the M25. Noye, now grey-haired and dressed in a grey cardigan and looking almost like an old man, sat hunched in the dock between three prison officers. His eyes panned the jury of eight women and four men from the moment he was led in by the three screws.

Before the case could proceed, Judge Lord Justice Latham ordered round-the-clock protection for each juror. He even told them, 'There are many people who have an interest in this case and its outcome. I have arranged for you to be provided with escorts that will, I am afraid, affect your daily life to some extent.' Noye claimed he was simply defending himself when he pulled a blade out from under the front seat of his car and knifed Cameron to death on the roundabout just off the M25. But the jury didn't believe him and found him guilty of murder by a verdict of 11–1.

Noye let out a deep gasp and held his head in his hands when he heard the jury's decision. Stephen Cameron's father leapt from his seat just feet away, hands aloft in celebration and shouted 'Yes!'. Then Lord Chief Justice Latham told Noye, 'The jury having found you guilty of murder, there is only one sentence I can impose and that is one of life imprisonment.' Noye looked unsteady on his feet as the three screws led him down the 21 steps from the dock to the cells below. A few minutes later he was taken back to Belmarsh in a van with its siren blaring.

Outside the court, Detective Superintendent Dennis McGookin, the Kent officer who led the two-year investigation, said, 'He's an evil man. He's been jailed for life, and that's where he should remain.'

After the verdict, the son of Detective Constable John Fordham, Noye's earlier 'victim', broke his family's 15-year silence on Kenny: 'You make your own tomorrows, and I think he has made his. You can't go on committing crimes. I am very pleased for the Cameron family, very pleased with the verdict. But it doesn't bring my dad back.'

In the hours following the jury's decision it emerged that Noye's defence, estimated to have cost between £500,000 and £1 million, had been funded by the taxpayer. He'd been granted legal aid because, on paper, he was not worth a penny. Meanwhile, Kenny Noye's criminal status as Public Enemy Number One would ensure

GANG WARS OF LONDON

he received the utmost respect from staff and inmates at whatever prison he ended up at. And there's no doubt Kenny's crime empire continues to expand – even from inside prison.

Kenny Noye was supposed to be one of the then Home Secretary Jack Straw's biggest targets in his bid to confiscate money and property from Britain's gangsters. But Noye is believed to still currently own at least six properties around the world worth at least £2 million – including a considerable amount of land in southern Spain, a timeshare holiday complex in Northern Cyprus, and two penthouse apartments in a nearby town on the island. His wife lives in a detached bungalow in Looe, Cornwall. Other family members live in a recently built, detached five-bedroom house in his old manor of West Kingsdown, Kent, and there's a semidetached house in nearby Bexleyheath.

In recent years Noye has also liquidated other assets, including a fitness club in Dartford for £150,000, the family home near Sevenoaks for £500,000 in 1998, an interest in a southeast London wine bar for £200,000, and an interest in two boutiques in southeast London for £300,000. Noye is also believed to have retained part, if not whole, ownership of some of his former homes, which were 'sold' for knockdown prices to criminal associates.

Meanwhile, Noye – the master manipulator – is currently still locked up in a top-security prison, no doubt plotting his next move. The key witness against Noye during the Cameron murder trial was gunned down by a hitman outside a shopping centre in Kent in the late summer of 2000. The murdered witness's wife told newspapers she did not believe her husband had told the truth during Kenny's Old Bailey trial. Shortly afterwards, Noye's legal team announced they were putting together a serious appeal against his murder conviction.

This certainly isn't the last we shall hear of Kenny Noye – Gangster Number One.

While Kenny Noye and a number of London's most feared faces like to keep understandably low profiles, the same cannot be said of their Number One Brief, Henry Milner. Since first representing Noye during the Brinks-Mat investigation, 'Mr Milner' – as all his clients call him – has earned himself the respect of everyone, from the most powerful faces to three of the suspects in the notorious Stephen Lawrence murder case. And Mr Milner does not fear the twilight world of gangland criminals, many of whom pay top dollar for his services. He's proud of how he's helped turn cases around.

Henry Milner's north London upbringing, Jewish boarding-school education in Oxfordshire and degree at the London School of Economics couldn't be further removed from gangsterdom. At weekends Milner retreats even further from the London underworld with three hobbies: Tottenham Hotspur football club, bridge and traditional American music.

Henry Milner's one-man business offers an exclusive service to just ten or twelve wealthy clients each year. His small office is squeezed between two jewellery shops in the middle of London's Hatton Garden. The lawyer's own office is panelled with dark oak and constantly filled with clouds of smoke from his ever-present, fat Cuban cigars. They sit on his desk in a walnut-veneer box, crafted in a prison workshop and sent to him by a grateful client.

Mr Milner's first big professional breakthrough as a brief came in 1978 when he represented one of London's best-known faces, who, as he later admitted, 'appeared at the Old Bailey as regularly as Frank Sinatra at the Albert Hall'. Milner's 'lovable rogue' was eventually acquitted of criminal charges in six successive court cases. That was when the word went out that Henry Milner was a brief to be trusted.

So, when the Brinks-Mat robbery came round in 1983, Milner received a windfall of clients. First through the door was main blagger Mickey McAvoy followed by the legendary Tony White. Then came Kenny Noye. The list went on and on.

Milner was once asked if there were any cases he wouldn't handle. He responded, 'That's a difficult question, because I do a lot of cases the public finds distasteful, like drugs. But I have never handled cases involving sexual offences on elderly people or young children.' He says that he's a born optimist: 'You've got to look confident even if you don't feel it. If you show weakness or fear, they will jump on it. Defendants are as shrewd as anything. They know whether you are on the ball.'

But even Mr Milner sometimes gets it wrong. On one occasion he represented an Iranian accused of possessing 100 kg of heroin. He was convinced that the case was hopeless and that he'd be doing well if his client went down for less than 18 years. He even begged the Iranian to plead guilty, but the client refused and was eventually acquitted, but Milner still can't quite understand why.

The lawyer insists he doesn't have a close relationship with any of his heavyweight clients, especially the superstar gangsters. He says he's never been out socialising with them, apart from having the occasional sandwich together at lunchtime. Milner also prides himself on always having complete control of a case. That means deciding which witnesses to call, influencing a counsel's closing speech and occasionally putting his foot down. He's also renowned for picking top barristers with a knack of winning.

Not surprisingly, Milner is well accustomed to the age-old question from many of his clients: 'What are my chances?' He always gives them the straightest possible answer, although he did recently admit to one journalist, 'You start with "hopeless", "very, very poor", "under 50 per cent", "evens" or "quite good". If you put

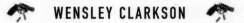

it above "good", you're in trouble if they're found guilty.' One of Milner's favourite responses to any question about his skill as a defence lawyer is, 'You can't guarantee anyone winning a case any more than love comes with a guarantee.'

Guarantee or no guarantee, it seems that Henry Milner will remain the brief's name on most gangsters' lips for a long time to come.

One of Kenny Noye's closest associates was south Londoner Keith Hedley, whose name appears in police surveillance logs of Noye at the time of the Brinks-Mat robbery. Hedley was a suspected money launderer and had a large home near Sevenoaks which was searched during the police inquiry into the massive robbery. All the police found was a sawn-off shotgun. In September 1996 Hedley was shot and fatally wounded by three men who tried to rob his luxury yacht in Corfu. He was 57.

Other smaller players on the London gangster scene include Brian Reader who fled abroad in the early 1980s while on trial for burglary after being named by a criminal supergrass called Mickey 'Skinny' Gervaise as a bank robber. Reader eventually returned to England and lived under a false name. He even became a regular visitor to Kenny Noye's Hollywood Cottage in West Kingsdown, and was present on the night John Fordham was killed by Noye. Cleared of assisting in Fordham's death, Reader was later convicted of handling Brinks-Mat gold. He is now 59 and keeps a low profile these days at a modest detached house ten miles from West Kingsdown.

Another South Londoner who allegedly had Brinks-mat connections was Micky Lawson, who was acquitted of handling the gold from the robbery. He made an out-of-court settlement with loss adjusters acting for Brinks-Mat. A close friend of Kenny Noye, Lawson used to run a Mercedes car dealership franchise and is now boss of a used-vehicle dealership in Dartford.

Others connected to the Brinks-Mat robbery who were not so lucky include Nicky Whiting, a car-dealer friend of Kenny Noye who was 43 at the time. In 1990 he disappeared from his office in West Kingsdown, just a stone's throw from where Noye had lived in the early to mid 1980s. Whiting's corpse was eventually found on Rainham Marshes in Essex. He'd been stabbed nine times and then shot twice with a 9 mm pistol. Noye and Whiting had even gone to school together. Whiting had bank accounts containing more than a million pounds when he died.

Barbara Harrold, from Igtham in Kent, was blown up in a bizarre parcel-bomb attack on her home in 1979. The chief suspect went on the run to Spain, where he recently died, still insisting he was innocent of any involvement in the death.

The most legendary participant in the Brinks-Mat robbery was criminal mastermind 'Mad' Mickey McAvoy. Only three people were ever actually jailed for taking part in the raid but it was McAvoy whom police considered the most important scalp. McAvoy, now 60, has always told close family and friends he never saw a shilling from Britain's biggest gold bullion raid. These days he resides in the suburbs of Kent, ofter jetting over to his villa on the Costa del Sol. McAvoy says he is a reformed character and even turned down a opportunity to be interviewed on a TV documentary about his most notorious crime, telling friends and family he wanted to forget the past. However, the makers of the two-part Channel 4 documentary did screen footage of a home video of McAvoy's 1986 prison wedding to second wife Kathy.

His former police pursuers have a sneaking respect for McAvoy, who was known as 'The General' because of his superb organisational skills. Others talk of a another side to McAvoy and allege that since his release from prison in 2001, he has been

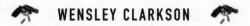

actively trying to track down the gold that was stolen but to no avail. But McAvoy knows he is still on the 'police watch list' so he's kept a low profile ever since.

Back in February 2001, detectives were still hunting for the missing Brinks-Mat gold and focused their search on an allotment and builders' yard on the south coast. The police raid, in Old London Road in Ore, Hastings, East Sussex, eventually yielded nothing. Kenny Noye was believed to have links with the area.

*   *   *

Knightsbridge, London's very own shopping centre to the rich and famous, had never seen anything like it and probably never will again. It was one of the most audacious robberies ever committed in criminal history and it has had a sinister knock-on effect ever since. But it all started one day in July 1987 when two men appeared in the Knightsbridge Safe Deposit Centre, next door to Harrods, the 'top people's department store', requesting a safe deposit box to rent. Once inside the vault the pair pulled out automatics and ordered the manager and two security guards onto the floor, where they were tied up.

The raiders then popped back up to the street-level door where they left a sign stating the Safe Deposit Centre was temporarily closed, at the same time letting in more accomplices who swarmed back inside with them. Minutes later they'd smashed open dozens of safe deposit boxes with contents estimated to be worth £40 million (in today's money about £70 million). Within an hour of the robbers' departure a security guard wriggled out of his handcuffs and raised the alarm.

It looked like the perfect crime until forensic investigators at the scene uncovered a barely visible fingerprint belonging to notorious Italian bank robber Valerio Viccei. On 12 August 1987, following intense police surveillance on Viccei and some of his accomplices, detectives launched a series of carefully planned raids. All were later convicted of the crime.

In 2002 Viccei's life ended in a hail of bullets in the Italian countryside after he'd shot at an Italian cop with his Magnum. Viccei was a criminal millionaire who lived by the gun and eventually died by the gun. Young, brilliant, smooth-talking, glamorous: Viccei had it all. He was labelled a criminal genius, a super-stud and a ruthless gunman. Before he died he even wrote his own bestselling memoirs.

Even the most legendary so-called kings of the underworld are not, it seems, immune from taking a bullet if they cross the wrong people. On 23 April 1990 no one took much notice of the young south Londoner with spiky, badly dyed blond hair sunning himself on a mini-roundabout close to the Urbanisation Montana in the hills behind the London gangsters' paradise of Marbella. A yellow mountain bike lay beside him as he sat on the grass verge. At midday, Great Train Robber Charlie Wilson's cousin Norman Radford and his wife – who'd been staying at Wilson's house, Chequers, up the street – were driving down to the shops when they spotted the youth. Radford didn't give the man a moment's thought until much later that day when he drove past him a second time on his way to Malaga Airport to fly back to the UK.

In the garden at Chequers, spring sunshine was beating down on the lawn and the swimming pool as a warm breeze blew gently through the pine woods that backed onto the property. Wilson lit the barbecue and then crouched down to pick some mint from one of his favourite flowerbeds for a very special dinner he was preparing for himself and his wife Pat to celebrate their 35th wedding anniversary.

Less than two miles away, another south Londoner was beginning his journey up towards the urbanisation in a white van, after calling his boss from a payphone on the N340 coastal road, known locally as the 'Road of Death' because it had claimed the lives of so many motorists and pedestrians over the years. The white van took a right up the hillside through the middle of two recently constructed blocks of flats.

The white-van driver passed a ten-bedroom hacienda on the left before reaching the mini-roundabout where his friend was waiting with his mountain bike under the shade of a big eucalyptus tree. The youth nodded as his friend parked the van just beyond the roundabout and got out. Then, separately, they walked up a quiet side street dotted with ornate street lamps and houses on one side and a huge empty plot of land on the other. They walked past No 7, a white house, then to No 9, then No 11. There was no No 13 on the next house, just the name, Chequers. They'd been there three times before over the previous few days, so they knew which was Wilson's house. Bougainvillea and carefully cultivated shrubbery covered much of the front of the property. They'd earlier checked out the garden wall at the rear and concluded that it was better to knock on the front door and then leave over the back wall.

Wilson, who was 58 at the time, was in the garden preparing the wedding anniversary meal when the doorbell rang. Pat answered it to find a pale-faced young man in a grey tracksuit on the doorstep. A baseball cap hid his eyes. With a distinct south London accent he told Pat he had a message for Wilson from a west London villain he knew. Pat told the young man to come in and put his bike in the porch. 'It might get nicked if you leave it outside,' she said pleasantly. The youth didn't respond, but placed the bike between the front door and Wilson's garden wall.

Later, Pat recalled what happened next: 'Charlie was busy outside cutting up tomatoes and cucumbers for a salad, so I called to him and he came in from the garden.' Wilson seemed to recognise the name given by the youth and immediately showed him out to the patio area next to the pool. For some inexplicable reason the legendary sixth sense which had helped keep Charlie Wilson one step ahead of his enemies for a lifetime failed to trigger any alarm bells. The two men continued across the patio of the house. Then Pat heard raised voices. She recalled, 'I remained inside. Charlie and this man must have been talking for at least five minutes. Perhaps he was telling Charlie about someone he knew back in London – giving him a message or something. He must have told Charlie something which caught his attention, otherwise they wouldn't have been together so long.'

Once the visitor had finished delivering the message he kicked Wilson in the testicles. As Wilson doubled over, struggling for breath, his nose was broken by a powerful follow-up karate chop. Then the messenger took a Smith and Wesson 9 mm revolver out from under his tracksuit top and fired at point-blank range. The first bullet pierced the carotid artery of Wilson's neck. The second entered Wilson's mouth and exited out of the back of his head. Boo-Boo the Alsatian, leaping to his master's aid, received a vicious kick in the chest that snapped his front leg and shoulder bone like twigs.

Back in the kitchen, Pat heard the two loud bangs. At first, she thought they'd come from some builders on a site behind the house. 'Then I heard Boo-Boo screaming. I came out and saw Charlie.' He was staggering towards the pool, blood spurting from his neck. His faithful dog lay wounded on the ground. Pat explained later, 'There was blood, blood, blood everywhere. He was desperately trying to stand up. He stared at me, but could not talk. Then he just pointed his finger to his open mouth. Blood was streaming from it.' In fact, Wilson was trying to point to the back wall, which the gunman had climbed to escape. 'As I looked at him struggling, everything went into slow motion,' said Pat. 'I couldn't do anything.'

Suddenly, that slow motion snapped back to real time and Pat screamed over the back wall to their neighbours, the Finches, to raise the alarm. When no one responded, Pat rushed in and telephoned their close friend, an architect called Marti Franco, who later recalled, 'She just said, "Shot Charlie. You come!"'

The shooter could easily have waited and turned his gun on Pat when she came running out into the garden, but instead he went straight over the back wall. The escape had been well planned because the killer knew precisely where to climb over. Along most of the length of the wall there was a 20-foot drop into a dry river-bed, tangled with thorny scrub and strewn in litter, but at the point he had chosen, just to the left of the barbecue, the earth was banked up on the other side to within six feet.

After jumping down from the wall the killer ran around to the front of the house and took the yellow mountain bike, which he then freewheeled down the hill to the mini-roundabout where his accomplice was waiting in the white van. They put the bike in the back of the van and drove off at a modest speed so as not to attract any attention.

Had this been a fully fledged mafia-style execution, Pat would almost certainly have been killed as well, since she was the only person who could identify the killer. But it was evident the shooter had strict orders that the argument was with Charlie and Pat was to be left out of it.

The two men drove back to the big roundabout and headed down towards Old Marbella and Avenida Cascada Camojan. Approximately six minutes after shooting dead one of Britain's most famous criminals, the two men parked their small white van next to a petrol station opposite the Hotel Don Pepe, took out the yellow mountain bike and went their separate ways. It was 5.45 p.m.

And so the spiral of violence continued: at 3 a.m. on 10 February 1996, Danny 'Scarface' Roff – recently released from prison at the age of 35 and suspected of being one of the two hitmen who killed Charlie Wilson – was in an upstairs bar at the Passport Club in New Cross, southeast London, when a gunman walked in and sprayed the crowded bar with bullets, smashing Roff's spine and hitting a girl of 16 in the arm. Miraculously, Scarface survived, but the incident raised serious questions about why Spanish police had never charged him with Wilson's murder. Scotland Yard had no doubt Roff was targeted to avenge Wilson's killing. One detective said after the attack, 'Roff knows who shot him, but he's too terrified to tell us.'

Then on a quiet Monday morning in March 1997, 'Scarface' Roff – released from jail yet again, this time after being inside for three months on remand – pulled into the driveway of his home in his dark-blue Mercedes. The front garden was littered with toys belonging to his two young sons. Scarface was about to heave his crippled frame over onto his wheelchair when a dirty, white Ford Escort van pulled up in the road and two masked gunmen opened fire, shooting him in the head and chest and leaving him sprawled on the tarmac. They sped off down the neat, tree-lined residential road in the van, its back doors flapping open. It was later found abandoned half a mile away.

Roff's wife Tina rushed out of the house after hearing the gunshots while dialling 999 on her mobile phone. Within minutes police had sealed off the area. An air ambulance landed in a street

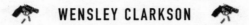

nearby and took Scarface to the Royal London Hospital in Whitechapel, East London, where surgeons fought, but ultimately failed, to save his life.

The other suspect in the Charlie Wilson hit is still alive, despite his alleged connections to the murder. He's currently on the run once again but continues to insist, through his family, that he is innocent of all involvement in Wilson's death. Detectives quickly announced that Scarface's death was linked to the feud started by Charlie Wilson's murder, which had already cost at least three other people their lives.

Charlie Wilson's murder had kicked off one of the deadliest feuds in British underworld history. At the centre of the struggle was the control of the drug routes to London from North Africa and South America. Police in the UK and Spain were watching the spread of cold-blooded violence with apprehension but seemed unwilling to do anything to prevent it. The experts at Scotland Yard's elite SO-11, the criminal intelligence branch, said they couldn't even predict who'd be the next victim.

Gordon Goody, Wilson's old train-robber pal, was far from convinced by the Spanish police's version of the events leading to Wilson's death. 'None of it makes much sense, none of it,' he said. 'Charlie would never have given no one no names. Never. And definitely not on the telephone. Christ, he thought his phone was hooked up [bugged]. Any case, you don't get chopped for giving out a name. You might get a good hiding, but that's about it.'

Ex-copper Sidney Wink – gunsmith and dealer – put a pistol to his head and pulled the trigger in August 1994, just as Met police were approaching. He was said to have supplied numerous guns to London criminals.

Donald Urquhart was shot dead in Marylebone High Street on 2 January 1993. The millionaire property tycoon and owner of a local golf club was on his way home when a man got off a nearby motorbike, pulled out a 32 mm pistol and shot him in the head.

Stephen Dalligan was shot six times in the Old Kent Road in 1990 by a man who rode up on a motorbike and started blasting away.

Josie Daly, 64, sharp as a knife and ten times more cunning, serviced punters as London's most powerful madam for almost 30 years. She lived in a seven-bedroom mansion called Bunty's Corner, named after her favourite Alsatian dog. She had a Rolls-Royce in the driveway, and her vice business had earned her more than £10 million.

Daly's palace in Crouch End, North London was her pride and joy. She even spent a fortune getting artists to paint pictures of her favourite pets onto the stained-glass window panes in her porch. Photos of her beloved Bunty, Bunty's brother Crunchy and Sammy-poo, an Alsatian–Dalmatian cross, dominated the walls of Daly's home. All three pets were buried in the garden with plaques and dog statues to mark their graves.

But there was another side to Josie Daly that was signified by the secure iron gate arrangement halfway down the hall of her house that could be slammed shut and locked in seconds. Good security was essential in Josie's game, because her team were in the habit of dropping off £10,000 in cash at the house at any time of the day or night.

Daly originally bought the house for cash, and the first thing she did was splash out tens of thousands of pounds on building a 12-foot-high, black-and-gold electronic fence around the whole property. In the driveway, her pristine white Rolls-Royce Corniche

was parked under a tarpaulin, to keep the dust off it. Daly also had a few other properties scattered around town including a hostel for her prostitutes, the Rose View Hotel in Muswell Hill, and a 60-bedroom flophouse which got so tatty she had to close it down. But its value had been going up at the rate of £5,000 a month, thanks to London's then property boom.

Despite her millions, Daly rarely left the capital. She hadn't had a holiday in more than 25 years. Daly believed she had a reputation to maintain, and before one court case she even produced a glossy press release professing her innocence. In it, she claimed that sickness had prevented her from stopping her 'massage parlours' providing more services than British Telecom.

But then Daly's fancy mansion sitting atop of Crouch End was a far cry from her humble roots in southern Ireland. Born in the village of Ardnageehy, County Cork, she was the youngest of eight children. Her parents, Jack and Eileen, ran a smallholding and struggled to feed their kids. Josie left school at the age of 15 with no qualifications. That's when she headed across the water to stay with a sister, Margaret, in the seaside town of Bournemouth, Dorset, and became a student nurse. Daly then had an affair with a handsome young local student doctor, and the couple had a daughter called Emelia Tawaih.

A few years later Daly moved to London where she trained in tissue studies at Paddington Technical College. A spell working at a clinic that treated baldness followed. Not long after that Daly fell into the London massage parlour 'industry'. She ended up running a sauna for a year before branching out on her own. She even claimed that she took a massage course along the way, which later helped her 'spot the women coming to work for the wrong reason'.

By the early 1980s she was making a small fortune. Then, in 1992, Daly suffered a massive heart attack and began taking a 'less active role' in the business, which now had three 'branches' – all in the Camden area. They were the Aqua Sauna, the Lanacombe Sauna and the Ishka Sauna. Daly briefly owned another establishment called the Thai Sauna before selling it on.

Girls worked in Daly's four brothels around the clock on 12-hour shifts and many hundreds of men visited her premises each six-day working week, seeking out some of Daly's renowned 'extras'. Josie took a minimum £10 cut from each and every one. However, the good old 'News of the Screws' exposed Daly's 'saucy' activities in 1992 in a splash article headlined 'Cops and Brothels', which revealed some of her most valuable customers were – police officers! The tabloid even uncovered the fact that Josie was employing a former CID chief to do her books. He'd fixed up two hookers for the newspaper's undercover investigator, who'd posed as a punter. Daly even boasted to one reporter disguised as a punter, 'The police need a massage, too, you know. I was even invited to a CID Christmas ball. I took a bottle of whisky and a bottle of brandy, but I didn't stay. It was too noisy for me.'

Daly only came unstuck when the police discovered that some of her premises – licensed as massage and sauna parlours by the local council in Camden – didn't even *have* a sauna. They also reckoned she'd been hiring girls smuggled into Britain by illegal-immigrant traffickers. The Met traced the ownership of the massage parlours to Daly's home in Crouch End. They watched staff pick up keys there every morning and saw that bags of cash were taken from the premises to her mansion several times a day. As Detective Inspector Paul Holmes said, 'She was a significant player in the London prostitution racket.'

When Daly was arrested in the summer of 1999 a lot of criminals expected her to blow the lid on some of her VIP client list, which included politicians and celebrities, as well as top

policemen. Instead, Daly took to her wheelchair, admitted three counts of controlling prostitution and avoided a spell in prison by claiming she was at death's door. Some of Daly's rich and powerful clients even sent bouquets of flowers to Harrow Crown Court, northwest London, where the case was heard. The court was told she had at least ten bank accounts, some showing balances of up to £90,000. Another £104,500 was found in a bedroom of her prized mansion. Daly was such a shrewd operator that she'd even openly declared a turnover of £250,000 to the tax man.

The court exercised its power to confiscate cash and assets amassed over the previous five years. Daly looked set to lose a figure as high as £7.5 million, based on £3 million that had been invested in property and £4.5 million that had passed through her bank accounts. But following a lengthy meeting between lawyers outside the court on the last day of her appearance the prosecution agreed to a figure of £2 million, largely because Daly had also paid all her VAT from her sex business. The judge even accepted that a third of her business was legitimate.

Daly told one keen young hack that she'd be celebrating her escape from a jail sentence with a glass of the best champagne. Throughout all this, Daly continued to describe her brothels as 'highly respectable places visited by doctors, lawyers and bankers'.

Some outrageous crimes committed in London barely get any attention, despite the vast amounts of money involved. Take the mugging of a 58-year-old messenger with money broker Sheppards. John Goddard was held up with a knife on a quiet City of London side street at 9.30 a.m. on 2 May 1990. The attacker fled with 301 Treasury bills and deposit certificates worth an astounding £292 million. Goddard was left dazed but otherwise unhurt. It's still not clear to this day if he knew the true value of what he was carrying.

A well-known south London criminal, Keith Cheeseman, was eventually arrested after a lengthy investigation by City of London police and the FBI. Cheeseman was sentenced to six-and-a-half-years in jail for his role in the robbery. Four other Britons were also charged with handling the bonds, although they were acquitted in unusual circumstances when no evidence was offered against them at the opening of their 1991 trials. A police informant eventually led detectives to all but two of the 301 bonds.

However, it was another aftermath to this crime which still puzzles police to this day: detectives eventually disclosed that the original mugging had been carried out by one Patrick Thomas, a petty thief from South London. He was found dead from a gunshot wound to the head in December 1991. Thomas was never actually charged with the robbery and no arrests were ever made in connection to this death, so draw your own conclusions.

John 'Little Legs' Lloyd is a legend in his own lifetime. And his fame in the London underworld doesn't just come from having allegedly been one of the original six Brinks-Mat bullion robbers who were never brought to justice. Kenny Noye even flogged Eastender Lloyd, now 64, one of his old houses in West Kingsdown, Kent. However, shortly after Noye was nicked for handling the gold from the Brinks-Mat bullion raid, Lloyd sensibly did a runner.

Police believed he'd gone to America, but Lloyd was, in fact, popping back and forth to his old London and Kent haunts completely un-bothered by the so-called worldwide manhunt in his name. He even boasted to one associate that he preferred flying back to London by British Airways ''cause they've got a better safety record than all the other airlines'. In the US, a Miami court ordered Lloyd, in his absence, to pay $400 million to Brinks-Mat insurers, but he never coughed up a penny in Florida.

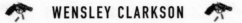

Little Legs – nicknamed because of his short, spindly legs – has been a prime mover in many of the best-known major crimes of the last 30 years. His personal fortune probably tops the £10 million mark, thanks to some shrewd investments of dirty money in a number of legitimate interests, including a transport business, and at one stage he also owned a car-hire business in Kent. He was a regular visitor to the infamous Peacock Gym in Canning Town as well as often dropping in to his beloved Lovatt pub in the East End for a swift pint.

While allegedly 'on the run' in the US, Little Legs even had his shorts specially tailored so they flattered his funny looking legs. He also splashed out a few thousand bucks on some surgery to correct his disfigured toes. Back in London a warrant was issued for Lloyd's arrest in connection with Brinks-Mat and a £10,000 reward was offered. Jean Savage, Lloyd's beloved common-law wife, received a five-year sentence for conspiracy in connection with the Brinks-Mat raid.

Then, in 1994, Little Legs Lloyd was named on the television crime show *America's Most Wanted*. A couple of weeks later Lloyd took the biggest gamble of his life by walking into Rochester Row Police Station with his solicitor to give himself up. The Crown Prosecution Service eventually ruled that there was insufficient evidence linking him to the Brinks-Mat job. The gamble had paid off. Less than a year later Lloyd reluctantly donated a five-figure sum to a consortium of insurance companies after he was fingered for his role in the notorious 1983 bullion robbery, even though there wasn't enough evidence to prosecute him in a court of law.

It was also Little Legs Lloyd who, as previously mentioned, hooked up with his old Brinks-Mat friend Kenneth Noye to form the 'Hole in the Wall gang' for that cash-card cloning scheme which they believed could net them as much as £100 million. It was only abandoned when their computer expert Martin Grant grassed them up to the police. Grant is still worried about Little Legs to this day, and says: 'I know he holds a grudge against me, and I'm very nervous about it.'

Little Legs was eventually given a five-year sentence for his part in the Hole-in-the-Wall scam. I recently paid his live-in partner a visit at their immaculate bungalow in West Kingsdown. Lloyd's lover was a charming woman, but her Rottweillers and seven-foot-high brick wall complete with electronically controlled gates were not so welcoming. After a ten minute conversation via her CCTV, I realised she wasn't going to let me in for a chat about Lloyd and his criminal enterprises. Lloyd was eventually released from prison and nothing has been heard of him since.

Combine the Kray Twins with the Richardsons and a sprinkling of the 'Guvnor' Lenny McLean, plus an IRA hitman thrown in for good measure, and you start to get an idea of Jimmy Moody's London underworld credentials. Moody's career spanned more than four decades and included run-ins with Jack Spot, Billy Hill, Mad Frankie Fraser, the Krays, the Richardsons and the Provisional IRA.

James Alfred Moody was a top enforcer for the Richardsons and became probably one of the most-feared gangsters ever to emerge from the London underworld – all before he reached the age of 30. And just like the Krays he even worshipped his dear old mum. Moody's first starring role came when he survived the legendary club battle at Mr Smith's in Catford in the early 1960s. Jimmy Moody ended up carrying the wounded, including Charlie Richardson and Frankie Fraser, out of the club before disappearing in a cloud of smoke. He was later acquitted of any involvement in the shootings.

Jimmy Moody's reputation then received another boost in 1968 when he was convicted of manslaughter after causing the death of a young merchant navy steward called William Day. Moody was sentenced to six years in prison, where he became a committed body builder, and on his release joined the notorious Chainsaw Gang which specialised in hijacking security vans.

Some people in the ganglands of London believed Jimmy Moody was already a contract killer at a time when this phrase was virtually unknown. But there's no doubting he was a vital member of the Richardsons' inner circle and then an armed robber with a fearsome reputation. Moody truly was a godfather, feared and respected by the London underworld.

In 1980 Moody was on the run from the law after yet another hijacking when he visited a relative's flat in Brixton and was nicked for a series of blaggings which involved a massive total of £930,000 in cash. Moody was then locked up in Brixton on remand. However, it was only after Moody had escaped and went on the lam – along with Thompson and Tuite – that his story took on legendary proportions. It turned out that Moody's cellmate, Tuite, had told him countless tales of brutality and torture inflicted by the British across the water. Moody even looked a touch Irish, with his heavy build, thick black eyebrows and bulldog neck, and his murderous skills were soon put to good use by the Provos.

It was then that Moody coined the chilling gangster phrase 'OBE' (One Behind the Ear). It went on to become the calling card used by many Belfast killers over the next 15 years. Meanwhile, Moody was renowned for professionally disposing of his victims' bodies, if that was part of the contract, or making sure that the hit occurred in a public place as a 'message' to others. Moody eventually survived on the run for more years than anyone else, with the exception of Ronnie Biggs.

By the late 1980s Jimmy Moody knew full well that he was in danger of overstaying his welcome on the Emerald Isle. The lure of the East End and all his old mates persuaded him to return to the Big Smoke. But the London he returned to was a very different place from the one he'd left ten years earlier. Huge drug deals – usually involving ecstasy and cocaine instead of armed robbery – were financing lavish lifestyles for many criminals. The stakes were higher, and so were the profits. Even a hardened soul like Jimmy Moody was disturbed by what he saw. He warned his own children to steer clear of drugs.

However, other people's deaths soon became his main source of income once again. In 1990 the police named him as the chief suspect in the 'plugging' of a member of a notorious south London criminal family. Moody never denied his involvement. Soon after, Moody told his ex-wife that he wanted to turn over a new leaf and retire from crime before it was too late, so he got himself a job humping beer barrels around at a pub near his latest hideout in the East End of London. But it didn't last long; he had to quit when an old face walked in and spotted him. By this time – the early 1990s – Jimmy Moody's list of enemies read like a *Who's Who* of criminal faces from both sides of the water. There was also the police, the RUC and the British security services. It was only a matter of time before someone's barrel pointed in his direction.

Moody was now known in the locality of his new East End home as 'Mick the Irishman'. The clock was still ticking away on his life until he was finally awarded his own 'OBE' on the night of 1 June 1993, while drinking at the bar of the Royal Hotel in Hackney – three bullets to the head and one to the back from a hitman special, a .38 revolver just like Moody's favourite weapon of choice. It was a cruel ending.

The fellow who shot Moody was in his early forties and wore a leather bomber jacket. The shooter even ordered his own pint of Foster's lager and put two coins down on the bar to pay for it

before making the hit. Then he turned towards Moody, opened fire and carried on blasting away as his target slumped to the floor. The killer escaped in a stolen Ford Fiesta.

In his book *Mad Frank*, Mad Frankie Fraser has another take on Jimmy Moody's demise:

> *He'd been in the area for ten years. He wasn't an out-and-out nightclubber, so he could have been there and very, very few people would know who he was. He's done quite a bit of bird, and now he took it as a personal thing to keep out. It was a personal challenge for him. He could be stubborn and obstinate, a good man but a loner. He'd be content to do his work and watch the telly knowing that every day was a winner. That's how he would look at it.*

Meanwhile, the mother of the one of Moody's most recent victims said, 'I'm glad Moody's dead. My family is overjoyed. The police rang to tell us this morning. He got it the way he gave it out. I'm glad he didn't die straight away. That man was evil, and I hope he rots in hell.'

Jimmy Moody pulled no punches. His life revolved around violence, black humour, the bizarre and the unemotional. But he was prepared to go beyond those traditional boundaries in order to make his name in the underworld. Murder was the recurring theme of Jimmy Moody's turbulent life; he admitted to at least a dozen. And if you live by the sword, you will eventually die by it . . .

The Brindle brothers – Dave, Tony, George and Patrick – were well known on their manor in southeast London but protecting their "turf" sometimes meant clashes with rival gangsters out to stake their own claims on the territory.

The Brindles and the Arifs were related by marriage but became sworn enemies after the Arifs' cousin, Abby Abdullah, shot their mate Stephen Dalligan seven times (as described earlier in this book). Some even suspected the Brindles of grassing-up Dennis and Mehmet Arif when the police swooped on them as they were trying to pull off a £1 million security van blagging in Reigate in 1991. The Arifs' conviction for that crime had been a huge nail in their coffin when it came to the pecking order in southeast London.

On the first day of August 1991, Dave Brindle wandered into the Queen Elizabeth, a pub frequented and run by the Daleys (enemies of the Brindles), and started mouthing off. He was given a beating by Jimmy Moody, on the run following his daring escape from Brixton Prison. Moody used a glass ashtray and a baseball bat during the attack. The clock was now ticking for the biggest showdown of all.

At 10.45 p.m. on Saturday, 3 August 1991, two strangers walked up to the saloon-bar door of The Bell pub in East Street, Walworth, knowing that Dave Brindle was inside supping a pint with his mates. The two men then sprayed the room with bullets from a revolver and an automatic. One civilian – Stanley Silk, 47 – was killed instantly. Barman John Plows, 36, defiantly threw a bar stool at the gunmen to protect his 15-year-old daughter. The stool hit one of the shooters in the chest, who then staggered back before turning and blasting the barman four times in the stomach and legs.

Meanwhile, Dave Brindle scrambled across the wooden floor before vaulting over the bar. As he turned his back, one of the gunmen fired a bull's-eye on his buttocks. The bullet passed through several internal organs and within seconds Dave Brindle was on the way to meet his maker. Moments earlier, his 21-year-old girlfriend Fiona – who was five months pregnant and had just set up home with him – had fled to the toilet when she heard the men calling Brindle's name.

At least ten bullets were fired in all. Some say the gunmen screamed out, 'This one's for Abby,' which could have been a bit of

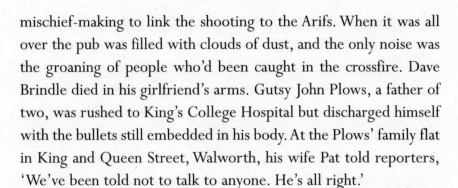

mischief-making to link the shooting to the Arifs. When it was all over the pub was filled with clouds of dust, and the only noise was the groaning of people who'd been caught in the crossfire. Dave Brindle died in his girlfriend's arms. Gutsy John Plows, a father of two, was rushed to King's College Hospital but discharged himself with the bullets still embedded in his body. At the Plows' family flat in King and Queen Street, Walworth, his wife Pat told reporters, 'We've been told not to talk to anyone. He's all right.'

Plows himself later explained, 'This was a gangland hit. They knew who they were after and had every intention of shooting it up. Everyone in the area knows who it was they wanted. There is a family which is like the mafia round here. They are bad, bad people. It's a tragedy because all the other people shot just happened to be in the wrong place at the wrong time.'

The Brindle brothers' mother, Grace, then 50, said after the Bell shooting, 'My boys wouldn't hurt a fly.' She told reporters that her 'lovely boys' cried when their pet budgie died and how they helped old ladies across the road. At the Brindles' house in nearby Penrose Street, a group of the firm's lieutenants stood guard shielding the family from unwanted callers.

In May 1992 Tony Brindle and his brother Patrick were acquitted at the Old Bailey of the betting shop murder of Abby Abdullah after it was argued that publication of their photo in *The Sun* made the identification of them unsafe. The tabloid had printed a picture of the Brindles before they'd been picked out in an identity parade. The Old Bailey erupted in cheers and laughter when the Brindle boys walked. Witnesses at the trial had been so scared they could only be identified by numbers instead of names. Some had even been allowed to give their evidence behind screens so they could not be spotted from the dock or public gallery.

The result smashed more than 12 months of hard work by the

police, who thought they were about to bring down one of the most powerful families in London. One witness – known only as 'No 5'– told the jury that he and his family had been subjected to weeks of threats since agreeing to give evidence and said, 'If I am going to die, I am going to die.' The inability to provide complete anonymity for another witness, No 37, proved too much for him to handle. In the witness box he refused to testify and told the jury he feared for his safety and that of his family if he did.

Commenting on the anonymity rulings, Judge Denison said, 'In my view, the fears of these witnesses are genuine. If they are to give evidence, they will require the protection of anonymity . . . If the wider interests of justice make it necessary for anonymity . . . then the interests of the defence must be subordinated to those wider interests.'

Naturally, the acquittal did little to calm the electric atmosphere out on the streets of the Brindles' manor of Walworth. 'You could cut through the tension with a flick knife,' said one old blagger from the area. The Brindles were so convinced they were targets that they had lookouts posted on street corners, and their boys cruised the manor in their BMWs and Mercedes making sure there were no strange faces on the territory.

In August 1994 two innocent men, Peter McCormack and John Ogden, were shot dead in Cavendish Road, Balham, southwest London. The police are convinced they were killed by mistake, because one of the men bore a striking resemblance to the Brindles' arch enemy, Pete Daley. A couple of days later, George, another of the Brindle brothers, was shot and injured while visiting his mum and dad's home in South London.

A scruffy van was parked just ten yards from 39-year-old Tony Brindle's £30,000 BMW in the driveway of his brand new home in

Christopher Close, part of a multi-million-pound redevelopment of private and housing association homes in the up-and-coming Docklands. As Brindle emerged from the front door at 11 a.m. on the morning of 20 September, 1995, the man in the van rolled down the driver's window, removed the wing mirror and opened fire, hitting his victim in the elbow, chest and thighs. But somehow Tony Brindle managed to scramble back towards his house. Shooter Michael Boyle then jumped out of his van with the intention of finishing off his target. At that moment, more than 20 armed police officers, who just happened to be carrying out a surveillance operation on Tony Brindle, swamped the area.

The police shouted a warning at the gunman to drop his weapon before returning fire. Boyle – aged 50 at the time – collapsed with wounds to the chest, arm and leg. As he was carried to a waiting air ambulance, medics watched in astonishment as wounded Tony Brindle – still able to walk despite his injuries – pulled open Boyle's oxygen mask and spat into his face while six squad cars and at least 25 officers, all wearing Kevlar bullet-proof vests and baseball caps, blocked off the street. Tony Brindle's wife Jane and young son Joey had witnessed the entire shooting from inside the house.

The Serious Crime Squad, supported by the Met's tactical-firearms unit SO-19, had been keeping an eye on Brindle and his mob ever since Tony and Patrick's acquittal of murdering the Arifs' cousin Abby Abdullah in a London betting shop in 1991. Incredibly, the entire 'hit' was caught on a police video camera, and the tape kept detectives entertained for months afterwards.

It even emerged that hitman Boyle was an INLA terrorist from across the Irish Sea who'd turned to freelance contract killing to make some extra money when the ceasefire in Northern Ireland had kicked in. Michael Boyle would have been paid £25,000 for killing Tony Brindle if he'd pulled it off. David Roads, Boyle's alleged armourer, was arrested soon after the attempted hit. In his lock-up in Lower Addiscombe Road, Croydon, South London, police found explosives, detonators, ammunition and weapons, including shotguns.

Following his arrest after the Tony Brindle shooting, Michael Boyle called Detective Inspector Steve Farley to his cell at Belmarsh high-security prison in southeast London and said the man who'd hired him on behalf of the Daleys was a notorious Irish gangster. He told Boyle that Tony Brindle was 'treading on a lot of toes' as he tried to expand his drugs cartel in southeast London. The London police later admitted that Irish police had told them that one of their most-feared hitmen, following orders from Pete Daley, was shadowing Tony Brindle with a view to killing him. Not surprisingly, Boyle later claimed the police had 'allowed' him to shoot Tony Brindle.

Boyle told London detectives that earlier that day he'd put on a blond wig, left a safe house in a stolen van and driven to Tony Brindle's home at Christopher Close, Rotherhithe. He said that he watched and waited for Tony for three hours, unaware that the police were watching him. Boyle's van had even been specially modified with the back window replaced by a Perspex sheet covered with a reflective film. The Met later insisted it didn't think Boyle would mount an attack until he got out of the van – but he'd fired from inside. They'd immediately sprung from their own 'British Gas' van parked across the street.

At Michael Boyle's trial, the jury were given round-the-clock protection, and the court was surrounded by machine-gun-toting special-branch officers. Boyle was told by Sir Lawrence Verney, the Recorder of London, that he was an 'extremely dangerous man', despite the disabilities caused by the shoot-out with the police. The court heard that Boyle had even been given the code name 'India 3' by the police. A camera mounted inside the police van monitored the entire operation, and one officer said on the tape 'India 3 is on the plot' when Boyle was spotted arriving on the scene. Then, addressing the hidden 'gasmen' by their call sign, the cozzer added, 'He is into you Trojan.'

In court, it was disclosed that the feud came about partly because of the drug-related turf war in southeast London. But then it was revealed that the police had decided Tony Brindle should not be told that Boyle was shadowing him. The Met insisted that it ignored the obvious threat of a pre-emptive strike on Brindle because they were gathering evidence against the Brindles at the time.

The judge recommended that Boyle should not be considered for release until he had served at least 15 years. Armourer David Roads, from Shirley, Croydon, was cleared of attempted murder and possession of firearms with intent to endanger life. But he was banged up for ten years after being convicted of possessing explosives and firearms without certificates.

In 1998 Tony Brindle was granted legal aid to sue the Met Police for £100,000, claiming that they allowed him to be shot by Michael Boyle while they stood back and watched. He claimed that they'd let hitman Boyle through their cordon of marksmen knowing full well that he'd take a deadly pop at his target.

Tony Brindle's writ stated:

Police were under a duty to ensure his safety. They knew there was a very high probability that Boyle, a man they knew to be armed and dangerous, would attempt to kill Brindle. But they failed to take any proper steps to prevent it.

It then emerged that Boyle had also been contracted to murder Brindle brothers Patrick and George before he was arrested for the

attempted hit on Tony. Brindle eventually lost his High Court damages action against the Met.

Meanwhile, little has been heard of the surviving Brindles since…

PART 4

1995–2007: MURDER, CYBERCRIME AND A BLOODY INVASION

The Adams brothers, part of the most notorious
gang in London in the 1990s

*'These foreigners don't give a fuck about anyone's lives. If you get in
their way, you're gonna get topped. Simple as that.'*

SOUTH LONDON CRIMINAL GORDON MCSHANE

THERE ARE SOME LONDON GANGLAND KILLINGS which really stand out on their own in terms of sheer brutality and cold-bloodedness. Take the night of 6 December 1995, when three east London gangsters were executed just off a deserted country track near the Essex village of Rettendon.

Pat Tate, Craig Rolfe and Anthony Tucker were feared, gun-toting, violent, drug dealers. Six-foot eight-inch 'Incredible Hulk' Tate was so off his head on drugs the whole time that only a few days earlier he'd wrecked a pizza parlour in a trivial dispute over what flavoured toppings he wanted. The pizza manager who Tate floored with a flurry of vicious punches later refused to press charges when he heard about the psycho's reputation.

Tate was clearly completely out of control, but his anger and aggression was used as a vicious tool when it came to the drugs trade. Tate, Tucker and Rolfe had, not surprisingly, first met in prison where they had joined forces with three other men called Michael Steele, Jack Whomes and Darren Nicholls. Steele was an old-school drugs smuggler with his own customised boat and a licence to fly light aircraft. He regularly 'ran' narcotics from Holland, Belgium and France to remote areas of Kent, Sussex and Essex. HM Customs & Excise knew all about Mick Steele's criminal habits but had nothing to pin on him. His loyal sidekick Jack Whomes worked alongside Steele constantly. The group's driver was Darren Nicholls, who'd been inside for handling fake money and dealing in cannabis.

Tate, Rolfe and Tucker organised the distribution of drugs, including cannabis, cocaine and ecstasy once they were smuggled into this country. But Tucker also ran a celebrity bodyguard firm providing bouncers for nightclubs and discos across London and Essex. As a result, Tucker and Rolfe controlled all the drug-dealing concessions in those clubs. Anyone stepping on their toes was soon warned off in vicious terms. Steele and Tucker couldn't resist showering their wives and girlfriends with designer clothing and jewellery as well as purchasing detached houses and luxury cars, and regularly took exotic holidays abroad.

Then one day Steele shipped in a consignment of un-smokable cannabis. Tucker and Tate demanded their money back and driver Nicholls was even ordered to dump the drugs in a lake near his home in Braintree, Essex. Steele went back to his original source but failed to get all his money back. Meanwhile, Tate's own drug consumption was going from bad to worse. He was by this time addicted to a lethal cocktail of cocaine and steroid pills which he took during his daily workouts. Add to this his hair-trigger temper and you have the perfect criminal psychopath.

When schoolgirl Leah Betts died in November 1995 after taking an ecstasy tablet during her eighteenth birthday party at her home in Latchingdon, Essex, her stepfather, Paul Betts, a former policeman, and his wife Janet launched a nationwide campaign to highlight the dangers of drug taking. This sparked a big clampdown on drug dealers by Essex Police, which in turn made life very difficult for Tate and Tucker's club dealers. Police even discovered that the pill swallowed by Leah was part of a batch of much stronger tablets Tucker had just received from a new supplier. So when Steele said he was picking up 30 kg of top grade Colombian cocaine with a street value of more than a £1 million from Holland, they all jumped at the chance of a big earner.

However, Tate and Tucker hatched a secret plan to cut Steele and his men out of the profits by hijacking the aircraft and stealing the drugs. They agreed that if Steele or his mob caused any problems they'd 'be seen to', and Tate and Rolfe had committed murder before when they 'whacked' a small-time drug dealer named Kevin Whittaker in November 1994.

But Steele had them well sussed out. The Colombian cocaine deal was all total fiction. Steele arranged for Tate, Rolfe and Tucker to meet him at a pub called the Halfway House near Rettendon on 6 December 1995, then take Rolfe's Range Rover to the field where he claimed he'd land the aircraft a few days later so they could finalise their plans. So at 6.30 p.m. driver Darren Nicholls drove Steele and Whomes to the pub where they were due to meet up. Steele walked to Craig Rolfe's Range Rover in the pub car park. Meanwhile, Nicholls dropped Whomes in a lane, which led to the field where the aircraft was supposed to land.

When Rolfe's Range Rover turned up he found the field barred by a gate so Steele got out to open it. A few yards away Whomes appeared and handed Steele a double-barrelled sawn-off. Jack Whomes then stepped out of the darkness, pressed the barrel against the back of driver Rolfe's headrest and let rip. His victim never moved a muscle. Both Rolfe's hands remained clutching tight on the steering wheel, his foot still on the brake.

With the blast ringing in Tony Tucker's ears, Whomes swiftly targeted Tucker in the back of the head by pumping out another round. By now Steele had his weapon trained on Tate, who unlike the others faced the full emotional horror of knowing precisely what was about to happen. He screamed and squeezed himself back into the corner of the car to try and avoid the inevitable. Steele fired both barrels into Tate's stomach. Whomes then shot Tate in the face and another to the stomach before pumping his weapon again and pressing the barrel up against the remains of Tucker's head and firing once more. He then did the same to Rolfe. Steele followed suit and shot Tate's corpse in the face before the stock of Steele's gun came away in his hands. Steele and Whomes burst into laughter while Steele ransacked the car for the parts of his broken gun. After being picked up, Whomes and Steele, still on an adrenalin high, told driver Nicholls that Pat Tate, the self-styled 'hard-man', had 'squealed like a baby' just before he was shot.

Mick Steele was quickly earmarked as a murder suspect by the police but there was no clear evidence to implicate him despite cellphone network records clearly showing that mobiles belonging to the victims, plus Steele, Whomes and driver Nicholls, had all logged onto a nearby satellite relay beacon from 6.45 to 7.10 p.m. on 6 December. But with no concrete evidence, the police investigation stalled.

Nicholls was arrested in May, 1996, for cannabis smuggling and spilt his guts to detectives after being told he'd be charged with being an accessory to the murders. During a five-month trial, defence lawyers for Steele and Whomes challenged star witness Nicholls. But carefully prepared alibis provided by Steele and Whomes fell apart under intense cross-examination. On 20 January 1998 a jury found the two men guilty and they were sentenced to a minimum of 15 years.

Dawn was still an hour away as eight black-clad figures armed with semiautomatics crept onto the roof of one of London's most exclusive apartment blocks in Victoria, Central London, in October 1998. Down on the street, another group of men was swarming through the back entrance to the building. Minutes later, SWAT teams of armed police burst in through the front door of Columbian cocaine cartel boss Luisa Bolivar's luxury flat just as the other group of men abseiled down from the roof. They'd been warned that Bolivar – known as 'La Patrona' (Lady Boss) – kept weapons on the premises and could well be accompanied by armed minders.

Luisa Bolivar earned millions and lived a life of luxury in London that included her £500-a-week apartment overlooking the Thames and a driver and limo to take her to £100-a-head restaurants and all

the best designer-clothes stores. She organised the supply of Columbia's finest cocaine to many of London's richest residents.

Luisa Boliv..'s transformation from the prim, naive teenager who arrived in London in 1978 to a manicured, sophisticated 37-year-old drug baroness perfectly reflects the power and influence that cocaine can bring in Britain's capital city. Back in the late 1970s she'd been a penniless cleaner who escaped Columbia because of its drugs and violence. She married a Briton, Frank Fleming, within a short time of arriving in London and told him she wanted to be a lawyer.

But within five years Luisa had risen through the ranks to become one of the most powerful Columbian cartel operators in Europe. Bolivar later married for a second time, this time to a London-based Columbian called John Diaz and had two children. She began her career with the Colombian cocaine cartels in the early 1990s when she was arrested for shoplifting in Tottenham. While awaiting trial she was recruited by another South American inmate to work as a 'mule' for one of the cocaine gangs from her home city of Cali, the cocaine centre of the world. She proved to be a very cool customer and was quickly promoted.

In 1994 Bolivar was arrested in possession of a cache of cocaine at Bogotá's El Dorado airport. Bolivar served just nine months in prison and her cocaine cartel bosses were so impressed she hadn't grassed them up that they paid out a bribe to secure an early release from her Colombian prison cell.

Bolivar was back in London within days, thanks to her British passport, gained through her first marriage, and soon she was dating a debonair cartel boss called Juan-Carlos Fernandez, who went by the dual nicknames of 'Snake Hips', because of his love of dancing, and 'Scarface', because of a knife attack he'd carried out years earlier on the streets of Cali. Bolivar's work for the Cali cartel also included the provision of safe houses across London for illegal immigrants. Luisa Bolivar remained one step ahead of the law by moving her henchmen and teams of couriers to different addresses on virtually a weekly basis.

On the surface, Bolivar seemed a highly respectable member of the tens of thousands of ever-growing official Columbian nationals living mostly in or near London's Elephant and Castle district in South London. It is believed that at least another 20,000 live in Britain illegally. Many arrive in London as tourists and then 'disappear'. Others – as Bolivar did 20 years ago – immediately seek out British men to marry.

By the summer of 1996 Bolivar had been promoted to recruiter and master smuggler for the Cali cartel. That meant she was now elevated to the title of La Patrona. Soon, Luisa was raking in around £50,000 a month. She bought at least three properties in London and splashed out £15,000 on a Harley-Davidson motorcycle as a birthday present for her lover. Bolivar – who stands just a shade over five feet when not in a pair of her favourite strappy platform shoes – then began throwing her money in the direction of a London plastic surgeon. She shelled out tens of thousands of quid on liposuction for her stomach and hips. Then she had the wrinkles removed from under her eyes, and she couldn't resist some breast enlargement.

So it was a hugely reconstructed drugs baroness known as La Patrona who found herself on Friday, 8 January 1998, at her favourite bar, the floating nightclub El Barco Latino, moored on the north side of the Thames near the Temple Tube station. At one table sat 16-year-old Jorge Castillo – nicknamed 'Little Egg' because of his shaven head – and several friends. Luisa was drinking at another table with her drugs baron Latin lover Juan-Carlos Fernandez.

A few minutes later a muscle-bound crony friend of Little Egg, called Yostin Ortiz, accused Fernandez of touching him up – the worst slight in the macho Latin-American underworld. A fight broke out and Little Egg stupidly ripped a £500 gold chain from Fernandez's neck and ran off. La Patrona was furious at Little Egg's 'disrespect' for her powerful gangster lover. Fernandez drew his finger across his throat, indicating that he wanted the boy killed. The next day Bolivar recruited 30-year-old hitman Hector Cedeno, who'd just arrived back in Britain after serving time for cocaine possession and Grievous Bodily Harm in New York. Cedeno had slipped into Britain after flying into France and catching the Eurostar to Waterloo Station. His documents weren't even checked.

La Patrona also called on 22-year-old Hernando Jaramillo, known as 'The Skunk' because he shaved his head except for a blonde streak running down the middle, resembling the tail of the animal. He had slipped into Britain pretending to be an asylum seeker. He would make sure that Little Egg was taught a lesson he'd never forget.

Luisa had the scars on her lover's throat photographed so that Little Egg could be shown the picture before his own throat was squeezed. Scarface watched in admiration as his curvy Latin mistress organised the hit. Then, just hours before the killing was scheduled to take place, he slipped quietly out of Britain on a flight to Madrid. Later, Cedeno and The Skunk turned up at a southeast London council flat where they knew Little Egg was staying. They asked him if he wanted to pop out with them to score some cocaine, which is the sort of thing that Colombian criminals do as frequently as the rest of us pop out for a pint. Little Egg was up for anything, so he didn't question their motives and skipped out to their waiting car, a borrowed Volkswagen Passat.

The three Columbians spun around the council estates of Lambeth and Brixton for more than an hour, knocking on the doors of drug dealers, none of whom were in. Then the Passat turned into

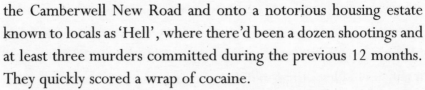

the Camberwell New Road and onto a notorious housing estate known to locals as 'Hell', where there'd been a dozen shootings and at least three murders committed during the previous 12 months. They quickly scored a wrap of cocaine.

Then they parked the car to share out the drugs. That's when ex-Columbian policeman Cedeno – reputed to have knocked off at least a dozen people back home in South America – leaned over from the back of the Passat and whipped a shoelace around the neck of Little Egg sitting in the front passenger seat. Cedeno wore white gloves as he expertly throttled the life out of the teenage thief. The Skunk watched coldly and even rang La Patrona on his mobile to see if she wanted to listen to the youth taking his last few breaths of life.

Seconds later, with the dead kid slumped on the passenger seat, the two killers drove off laughing. That's when The Skunk called Bolivar back to ask if she'd like Little Egg's ear or finger to prove that the job had been done. She told them to dump Little Egg somewhere her people could inspect the corpse. A few minutes later his five-feet-three-inch, seven-and-a-half-stone body was dropped in an industrial dustbin next to a children's playground.

That night, Bolivar's brother Diego was despatched to look at the body in the dumpster before giving the OK for the money to be paid. Meanwhile, Cedeno went home to his flat at Tyler House on the Stockwell Park Estate in South Lambeth. The Skunk, Jaramillo, lived in Union Road, Clapham, South London. The two hitmen then got a call from Diego to say that he would hand over the first instalment of £2,000 the following day at a local Tube station at one o'clock. Another £2,000 would be paid within a week. But the exchange took place right under the nose of the local police who were monitoring overhanging CCTV cameras for gangs of crackheads. The three Latinos were immediately arrested for suspected drug dealing after the suitcase was opened. Diego called his sister Luisa at a nearby police station to tell her what had happened. At that stage the police had no idea that they'd just caught a bunch of killers, red-handed.

Later that same day Little Egg's battered corpse was discovered, but the police still didn't know that they already had the guilty men locked up. It was only after some of the victim's family flew over for Little Egg's cremation service that the net started to close on La Patrona and her motley crew.

The Skunk openly bragged about his murderous habits in both London and back in Columbia, where he'd killed several street children, burning them out of the sewers where they lived. Word soon reached Luisa's kid brother Diego that other Columbians were saying he played a part in the topping of Little Egg. After a couple more days young Diego wilted under the pressure and confessed all to the local police.

That's when the police SWAT team abseiled into Bolivar's apartment as she was leaving the premises in Belgrave Mansions to take her daughter to school. In the apartment they found £20,000 hidden in her knicker drawer. La Patrona also turned out to be a 'mobile phoneaholic'. She had eight different mobiles and was adept at answering three phones at the same time. Her phone records made for very revealing reading.

La Patrona's eventual trial at the Old Bailey's No 1 Court on 11 October 1999 lasted five months. In the witness box, Bolivar cried whenever she was accused of any deadly deeds. But it didn't cut much ice with the jury. They deliberated over three days before reaching their unanimous 'guilty' verdicts. The trial cost the taxpayer £2 million, and Cedena and Jaramillo were ordered to be deported. After being sentenced to life for Little Egg's murder, Bolivar's lawyer later launched an unsuccessful appeal against her conviction.

Bolivar's little brother Diego joined a protected witness programme and still lives in fear that he'll be the next one to get garrotted. The police still want to speak to Snake Hips/Scarface Fernandez, who has since disappeared into thin air.

The downfall of London gangster John Palmer perfectly represents the opportunities that faced many so-called old-school criminals during the 1980s and '90s. This former Brinks-Mat gold-bullion smelter got an eight-year sentence in 2001 for two counts of timeshare fraud after he and his gang sold apartments in Tenerife to 16,000 couples from the UK and across Europe over an eight-year period. It was only thanks to the Yard's Operation Beryk, a seven-year investigation which took in four continents, that Palmer was brought to justice.

He'd first moved to Tenerife in 1985 following the Brinks-Mat job. Most of his victims were induced to buy on the spot in the resort, where Palmer and his gang artfully lured existing timeshare owners into buying a second time, by assuring them that Palmer's company would sell their old timeshare, providing them with a vast profit. Many were exploited by misleading sales talk, alcohol and other tricks – and nothing was ever paid back.

Numerous hard-working owners – including a lot of elderly people – found themselves stuck with a new timeshare they couldn't afford plus an old one that wouldn't sell at the prices promised by Palmer, who had interests in a total of 11 resorts, using a complex web of companies. Their vulnerability was undoubtedly increased by being on holiday far from home.

Meanwhile, the deadly criminal feuds which have peppered the streets of London down the years continued. Two masked men walked into the Beckton Arms in Canning Town, East London on 5

December 1999 and gunned down well-known faces Tommy Hole, 57, and Joey 'The Crow' Evans, 55, as they watched football. Hole had only just got out of prison for an armed robbery. It had been a busy Sunday afternoon, but police were surprised by the lack of witnesses. 'Loose lips sink ships' seems the most appropriate phrase to sum up that situation.

Many believe the killings were linked to a long-running feud involving Ronnie Knight, the notorious bank robber and ex-husband of actress Barbara Windsor. His brother David had been murdered in 1970 by a gangster called Alfredo Zomparelli. Four years later Zomparelli also met his maker. Knight was later acquitted after being accused of that killing, although Knight claims in his recently published memoirs that he asked a friend called Nicky Gerard to shoot Zomparelli.

Then in 1982 Gerard was murdered and Hole, the latest shooting victim, had been arrested and charged with the murder. He was later released when a key witness refused to testify against him. Police privately admitted that their hopes of catching the killer (or killers) were less than zero. To date, no one has ever been pulled for this audacious double murder.

Gun-toting Yardie gangsters who control London's multi-million-pound crack-cocaine market have become the most difficult and violent criminals faced by the capital's police over the past 15 years. In the drugs business, it's a cold, senseless world where honour and loyalty do not really exist.

So how did it all begin?

For many years, 'Back Yard' has been the description used by Jamaican-born Londoners to describe someone who shows up in the UK capital from Jamaica, and that's where the term 'Yardie' comes from. But these days Yardie describes virtually any criminal from a Jamaican, African or black gang. These cold-blooded gangsters initially feed off London's foreign communities, having arrived from Jamaica after being refused entry into more lucrative cities such as New York and Los Angeles. US immigration authorities have virtually banned all Jamaicans from their country in a bid to stamp out the Yardie menace in US cities.

Today's Yardies are bound together only by certain characteristics: they're aged 18 to 35, single and nearly always unmarried. These menacing street gangsters don't require legitimate employment, although many of them claim to be working in the music industry. Vast numbers of Yardies enter the UK on visitor visas before being provided with fake identities to help them 'disappear' into the community. They also adopt street names, making it even harder for police to identify them – even after they've been arrested.

Yet the full history of the Yardie menace goes back to the 1950s when the British Government encouraged immigration from the West Indies to fill job vacancies created by England's post-war economic boom. Afro-Caribbeans arrived in the UK hoping for a better life but many ended up with unskilled jobs, living in cheap housing in the inner-cities. When the big 1970s recession hit the UK, it was the Caribbeans who particularly struggled.

As had been happening in US cities since the early 1960s, virtual ghettos began to spring up in most cities, but particularly London. Soon, drug-related violence had become a virtual daily occurrence in the capital, not aided by angry confrontations between black youths and police. Into this tinderbox atmosphere, the Yardies thrived.

Take 1997 as a classic example: of 160 murders in London, 41 victims were black and 18 of those were shot in classic Yardie-style hits. To put this into perspective, the black population of London only comprises 8 per cent of the entire city. So it's particularly chilling to find that Yardie drugs and guns regularly spark a deadly cocktail when it comes to the killing of innocent bystanders. In 1991 for instance, a clubber called Mark Burnett was shot dead when he accidentally stepped on the toe of a short-tempered Yardie gangster. Police detained 270 clubbers that night but they all claimed not to have seen what happened, and the widespread publicity surrounding the murder simply served to helped boost the Yardies' killer image, ensuring no one would dare to cross them.

The Yardies even prefer to carry out these sorts of random killings in broad daylight by gunmen who don't bother hiding their faces in order to ensure that any witnesses are terrified. The Yardies' 'here today, gone tomorrow' culture helps fuel that climate of fear, even within other criminal gangs. Not surprisingly, the average life expectancy of a Yardie is only 35.

Yet ironically, numerous law-abiding Jamaicans arrived in London in the 1980s to get away from the Yardie violence on their own Caribbean island. Now many find themselves facing those same deadly gangsters on our streets. Harlesden, in northwest London, is probably the Yardie capital of the UK.

'A lot of the time it comes down to simple economics,' says British-born Ryan, 26, now retired from the Yardie crime scene having been involved in numerous robberies and shootings in Harlesden and nearby Willesden, where he grew up. 'You want to sell drugs, but you don't want to go to all the trouble of smuggling them into the country. It's much easier to find someone who has got the drugs, put a gun to their head and take them. Everyone does it. Most of the time it's OK, but every now and then you pick the wrong person, and that's when wars start. I've seen people get shot, I've lost good friends to it, but you just accept it – it's the way things are.'

In January 2000 Dean Samuels was stabbed to death in a mobile-phone shop by four black youths who fled the scene of the crime. Six months later Albert Lutterodt was found dead in Acton, West London, after neighbours reported hearing a volley of shots. A few weeks later drug dealer Dean Roberts was shot down in a hail of bullets fired from a MAC-10 machine gun.

Twenty-one people were murdered in London during 2001 in drug-related shootings, a slight rise on the year before. All the victims were black. There were 67 other attempted murders. Although the Yardie gangsters have previously concentrated their activity in five 'hot-spot' London boroughs, there were signs in 2002 that the violence was spreading all over the capital. When one man made a sarcastic remark about another man's hairstyle, he was shot dead. When entry to a nightclub was refused by a doorman, the man trying to enter returned and fired a gun randomly at other people waiting in the queue. Eight people were injured. There was a row between a DJ and a party-goer on New Year's Day, 2001. The gunman fired at the DJ, hitting him in the neck. The bullet then passed through a wall and hit another man. Both men died.

In June and July 1998 a posse of London Yardies were behind three barbaric murders, including the hitman-style execution of two young mothers. The Met linked the slayings after forensic tests revealed the victims were shot with the same 9 mm self-loading shooter. Mums Avril Johnson and Michelle Carby were shot in the head at their own homes. The bodies were discovered by their children.

The same Yardie firm rubbed out 34-year-old Patrick Ferguson at his home in Kingsbury, North London. The shooters were utterly ruthless, terrorising and sexually assaulting their victims in a deliberate attempt to send a deadly message to their criminal rivals.

The Met Police know certain murders being committed in London are as a direct result of feuds involving Yardie gangsters in downtown Kingston, or in Spanish Town, in Jamaica. It is a growing problem. Yardie turf wars have led to an escalation of gun violence and murders in London as Yardie gangs and home-grown British gangsters, modelling themselves on their Jamaican counterparts, battle to control the lucrative crack-cocaine trade. Firearm-related homicides in the capital continue to rise at an alarming rate. In the south London borough of Lambeth in 2001 there were 408 firearms incidents, including 105 in which shots where fired. In 2005 the figure was more than double the total four years earlier.

The semiautomatic pistol is the weapon of choice, but there is a worrying new trend of more frequent use of compact semiautomatic weapons, such as the Uzi – 'spray and pray' – and MAC-10. The Uzi earned its nickname because it fires at the rate of 1,250 rounds a minute. AK-47 and AR-15 automatic assault rifles have also found their way into the hands of hardened Yardies. A two-year Met study into gun violence in the period between 2002 and 2004 found that guns were fired in the capital 291 times. Chillingly, this includes 115 multiple discharges.

Jamaican criminals regularly fly in from Kingston, bringing with them their culture of violence. Bizarre as it may seem to outsiders, these killers can be role models for alienated youths living in London, who are tempted by the rewards of crime. Notorious Jamaican Yardie Donovan Bennett, alias 'Bulbie', the leader of a Spanish Town posse nicknamed the 'Clans Massive', is suspected of between 20 and 25 murders. He and his driver were killed in a gun battle in Jamaica in 2005. At the time of his death, Bennett's wealth was estimated at $100million. Two other wanted Yardie killers were recently stopped trying to enter Britain, one at Gatwick and another at Heathrow after arriving on a flight from Miami.

Detectives also say that Jamaican criminals wanted in London are making the trip the other way to Kingston. One police source in Jamaica said, 'They come over here to "chill out" when the heat is on in London. They arrive with lots of money and start flashing it around on expensive rental cars. They are an increasing problem.' One posse nicknamed the 'British Link' are a major Jamaican drug gang based in London who are said to be moving their operations to Kingston because of the level of police activity in Britain.

In Brixton there is an area known as 'Little Tivoli' – a reference to the Tivoli Gardens enclave in West Kingston, fanatically loyal to former Prime Minister Seaga's Jamaica Labour Party. Equally, there are parts of Harlesden rumoured to be named after areas loyal to the ruling Jamaican People's National Party. Witnesses in Yardie trials in London are regularly shot at and wounded by gunmen in cars on busy streets in both London and Kingston. To add to the picture of lawlessness, one Yardie suspected of murder in London was ambushed on a visit to Kingston and pursued down the street by gunmen firing from the back of a pick-up truck.

The profits from the drugs trade are easy to spot on the noisy streets of downtown Kingston. Among the battered cars and taxis that speed around the potholed roads are gleaming new sports-utility vehicles with blacked out windows, as well as the latest Mercedes and BMW saloons. Currently the favourite vehicle is the Ford F150, a massive luxury American pick-up, while the local German car dealership is said to be one of the city's most successful businesses.

For impoverished youngsters brought up in the slums, the attractions of such ostentatious wealth are obvious. Franklin Stephenson, 45, who was born and brought up amongst the violence said, 'There are boys in the ghetto who have nothing – no family and no chance of a job. The dons in Jamaican ghettos win favour and support among the communities by handing out money and gifts. Parents are given support for children's uniforms and schoolbooks. It is said that the children of the ghettos are among the best dressed in Kingston.'

There were yet more fatal shootings allegedly linked with the Yardies in London in 2002. Andy Balfour, 32, was shot eight times with a MAC-10. Earlier, BBC hip-hop disc jockey Tim Westwood was shot by a man on a motorbike who opened fire as he drove home from a gig in Kennington, South London.

Chief Inspector Leroy Logan, head of the Metropolitan Police's Black Police Association, has said that the black-on-black gun problem has been escalating for years, but because some sections of the black community, in particular, don't trust the police, many deaths have remained unsolved. This is reflected in the clear-up rate for murders. In London it's 80 per cent, but for murders in the black community it's half that figure.

Members of the foremost UK Garage group, So Solid Crew, have insisted their type of music is not a cause of the violence, although So Solid rapper Ashley 'Asher D' Walters has been convicted of gun possession. Walters pleaded 'self defence', saying he felt 'unsafe because of the attention brought by his new-found fame'.

Rumours that lorry loads of AK-47s are slipping into London crop up with alarming regularity. The guns are said to be smuggled in from ex-Soviet states. The Gun Control Network – a UK-based organisation that campaigns for better gun control – wants to see replica weapons taken off the streets, because they can easily be converted into real guns. They then end up in the wrong hands. In New York there are two cash-for-weapons schemes: one in which cops offer $1,000 for tip-offs; and another in which $100 is offered for guns to be handed in. The latter, although only offering a small incentive, has been effective. Murders are down to a 40-year low in New York.

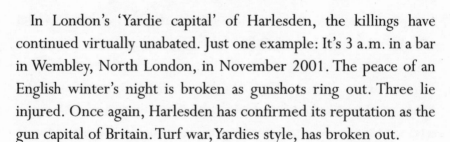

In London's 'Yardie capital' of Harlesden, the killings have continued virtually unabated. Just one example: It's 3 a.m. in a bar in Wembley, North London, in November 2001. The peace of an English winter's night is broken as gunshots ring out. Three lie injured. Once again, Harlesden has confirmed its reputation as the gun capital of Britain. Turf war, Yardies style, has broken out.

Drugs have undoubtedly sparked this virtual war on the streets of the UK capital. Conservative MP David Lidington once summed it up: 'From our enquiries, and the contact we have had with the community, we know there are many factors – such as gaining street credibility, and gaining respect within the community – that are the prompts for these terrible crimes.' The Met's Operation Trident was launched to try to reduce gun crime in London as a whole. But many critics say that the Met has failed to stem black-on-black violence because its information network is flawed. In other words, they have little or no informants amongst the Yardie gangs. John Brennan, a former detective sergeant in the Met, says intelligence is the key: 'For these particular criminals, it is imperative to utilise their friends, because it is a cultural thing that is very difficult to get into.'

It's not as if the Yardies and their imitators aren't hard to spot on the streets of London. 'When they go out on the town, they will dress to a T, drive their Merc and they'll have probably £10,000 in their pocket to buy the best bottle of champagne, and have the prettiest of women and the flashiest of jewellery,' says one former member.

Patrols by the Met's armed response vehicles have been increased, and there is a possibility that a gun amnesty might help remove some of the illegally held weapons, but for now the threat from the Yardie killers remains real and imminent. The Yardies have long since caught up with the Triads and other heavyweight criminal groups in London's gangland pecking order.

The Yardies' reputation for ruthless violence grows with each shooting. Yet back in the 1980s the Met was so desperate for inside information on them it even overlooked a series of violent crimes carried out by two Yardie informers, in exchange for intelligence given to Scotland Yard. While a Met informer, Green was involved in the UK's single-largest armed robbery, when 150 people were held up at a blues party in Nottingham. When these links were exposed, the Met completely pulled away from using such characters as informants.

Yardie involvement is now suspected in virtually every black-on-black murder in London. Commander Alan Brown, of Operation Trident, said there were 'clear links' to Jamaica in many gun murders: 'If we take someone out, there is an immediate struggle to take over the drug dealing of that particular gang.' Detectives estimated that until recently as much as four tonnes of cocaine was making its way into London through drug mules – mostly women – travelling from Jamaica on commercial flights to London each year.

In 1997 the leaders of 'Shower Posse' – one of America's biggest Yardie groups – were convicted and sentenced to numerous life sentences. They were called Shower Posse because they 'showered' their victims in bullets from their AK-47s. In addition, 26 other defendants were convicted on drug conspiracy and harbouring charges, receiving sentences ranging from two years to life.

Four remaining fugitives originally thought to be hiding in Jamaica and on the east coast of the United States are now believed to have joined gangs in Brent and Lambeth in London. It's also suspected that they've been travelling in and out of London with false papers ever since.

It was just after lunchtime on 6 March 1999 when a group of shoppers witnessed yet another Yardie execution on the streets of Brixton, South London. This time the victim was 36-year-old Jamaican-born Mervyn Sills, confronted on a busy road by a gun-toting Jamaican. Less than two months later – over in that Yardie hotbed of Harlesden – a man called Adrian Roberts was mowed down at a bail hostel. Then in 2001 came the shocking slayings of Laverne Forbes, 28, and her partner Patrick Smith, 31, in North London. The Yardies seemed un-bothered that they exposed the couple's seven-year-old daughter to the sight of both her parents being murdered.

Back in Harlesden a couple of days later, a gang of five armed men drew their car level with 51-year-old sound engineer Henry Lawes as he walked to his local newsagent. One witness later told how the vehicle's electric windows slowly went down and the gun barrels poked out. Lawes turned to flee as shots rang out and hit their target. As he struggled along the street two of the gunmen jumped out of the car and ran after him. They caught up with Lawes as he fell to the ground, pumped bullets into his body and then jumped back in the car and disappeared. A few days later a 21-year-old man was shot in the chest in a flat in another area of Harlesden. The day after, two more men were shot several times in the early hours of the morning as they sat in their car, also in Harlesden.

Back in Jamaica, on a strip of wasteland between Trench Town and Jones Town, a young boy with a revolver stuck into the belt of his shorts kicks a soccer ball around. Everton is a proud member of the Kool Kidz Krew, and he looks up to a senior gang member called Howie whose cousins live in England. Eventually, they'll all land in London.

The Yardies at their most extravagant and violent can be best summed up by the so-called 'Bling Bling Gang', whose luxurious lifestyles and obsession with designer labels eventually proved their downfall. They smuggled £50 million-worth of cocaine into London over a two-year period, and by converting it into addictive crack they boosted their profit to £3 million a week. The Bling Blings were eventually caught by the police and jailed for between five and 27 years.

They used mules from the tiny Caribbean island of St Martin – divided between French and Dutch authorities – to European cities Paris and Amsterdam. Then the drugs were transported to the UK by plane, ferry, bus and train. Favourite arrival points were the Waterloo Eurostar terminal and Victoria Coach Station, where gang members would be waiting to pick up their terrified smugglers.

Three mules – completely unaware of each other – were used for every flight as the gang accepted they might have to 'lose' one to customs or police. The Bling Blings homed in on drug addicts and poverty stricken single mothers as 'ideal mules'. Their families would be threatened with harm if they refused and then they'd be deliberately hooked on free cocaine. Other mules would take suitcases brimming with cash back to the Caribbean – often $100,000 (£57,000) at a time. Other funds were transferred electronically, including once when £1m was sent from London to Paris.

Gang ringleader, Ian 'Bowfoot' Dundas-Jones, 35, was already wanted for drug trafficking in Guadeloupe after escaping from prison. He was jailed for 27 years. Bernard 'Kofi' Clarke, 31, who got an 18-year sentence, was on the run from a jail in Guyana after attacking a prison officer. Clarke's lover, Lisa 'Sister' Bennett, 39, also got 18 years' jail. She specialised in cooking up the crack in a dingy East Ham house, a complete contrast to life at the family home in Romford, Essex.

The gang's nickname came from their penchant for flashy white leather sofas, designer clothes from Prada and Versace, Cartier and Rolex watches, and fabulous diamond jewellery. On one shopping trip, Clarke and Bennett splashed out £70,000 on jewellery, £50,000 on clothes, and £15,000 for a fitted kitchen – all in cash. Most of the gang were of French Guyanese descent and many 'reinvested' their ill-gotten gains on luxury villas and land back in the Caribbean.

When the ten-strong members were sentenced at Snaresbrook Crown Court, Judge Timothy King told them: 'You, and others like you, are a scourge upon decent, civilised society. You bear a heavy responsibility for the despair and ruination that you visit upon others.'

Up until the end of the 1990s the vast majority of victims of black-on-black violence were Jamaicans living in the UK illegally. Today, most are British, which makes the increase in the Yardie phenomenon even more disturbing. New posses of young guns, many of them teenagers and almost all of them under 25, have modelled themselves on the original Yardies and revel in high levels of brutality and cold-bloodedness. Feuds that would once have been solved by fists or knives are now always settled with a bullet.

Gang experts in London even believe there is now a pool of children as young as 11 and 12 who will be sucked into this menacing gang culture unless communities pull together to stop the criminals in their tracks.

In 2004 a 19-year-old youth was dragged from his car after a chase through West London, pistol-whipped about the head and shot in the leg. The following day a 20-year-old man was involved in a shooting rampage in London's West End. The front-line is all over town.

The Met has launched numerous operations since the late 1980s to try and quell the Yardie menace. The first probe on black-on-black crime, Operation Lucy, was closed down in 1989 after just two years. Many detectives believed it was never given a proper chance to work. Then in 1989, Prime Minister Margaret Thatcher encouraged the creation of the Crack Intelligence Co-Coordinating Unit. It, too, lasted only a few years after failing to provide high calibre intelligence which might have helped reduce violent gun crimes.

Then came Operation Dalehouse, which was based in Brixton. It only lasted until 1992 after a total of 274 arrests for serious crimes and hard drugs seizures topped the £1 million street value mark. But detectives needed to achieve ten times that amount to stand any chance of success.

In 2002, Operation Trident revealed disturbing levels of drugs-related gun crime with figures up 42 per cent on the previous year. Ten per cent of those incidents involved so-called 'drive-by' shootings. An advisory group attached to Trident tried to insist extra employment opportunities would end this menacing gun culture. But for the moment the number of killings and shootings continues to rise.

The main problem is that today, the Yardies seem virtually untouchable. Their power and influence is so far-reaching that they once even put a price on the head of London's most controversial gay rights campaigner, Peter Tatchell. He'd dared to criticise numerous Caribbean reggae artists whose lyrics, it was suggested, could help to encourage people to murder homosexuals. Tatchell's campaign led to cancelled concerts and cost performers, promoters and venues an estimated £2 million in Britain and the United States. Shortly afterwards, Tatchell's Outrage! organisation, based in southeast London, was contacted by a man called Rabid Monk who

told the gay rights veteran: 'I warn you if you go to protest at any large Rasta-based festivals you may not leave standing.'

Other groups of newly arrived immigrants threaten to destabilise London's underworld even further. Take the Russians. The mere mention of them strikes fear into the hearts of most 'old-school' British criminals. But then the Russians' background goes a long way towards explaining why they are so brutal. We're talking about 35 million people imprisoned between the mid 1960s and the 1980s in what was once the Soviet republic. Many inmates who were genuine criminals had tattoos – and the more crimes, the more tattoos. It's the ultimate way to show who's top of the pecking order. A prisoner with an unauthorised tattoo back in the bad old days of communism would be punished or killed by other inmates. According to Russian criminologist Arkady G. Bronnikov: 'Tattoos are like a passport, a biography, a uniform with medals. They reflect the convict's interests, his outlook on life, his world view.'

So into London's veritable powder keg of criminality came many of the thousands of Soviet citizens permitted to immigrate to the UK in the 1970s and 1980s. Many were hardened criminals, deliberately kicked out of the Soviet Union by the KGB, much like the way Cuban dictator Fidel Castro flooded Miami during the Mariel Boatlift of 1980.

By 1995 the Met became aware that a Russian-based mafia was emerging in London. Today, more than a dozen well-organised gangs have made the capital their home on a full-time basis. These villains come from all the former Soviet republics and specialise in extortion, prostitution, insurance and medical fraud, car theft, counterfeiting, credit card forgery, narcotics trafficking, fuel tax fraud, money laundering, and murder.

One Scotland Yard expert warned that organised crime by Russians in London is so rampant that there are real fears Russian gangsters on our streets could soon be dealing in nuclear weapons, which would be made available to terrorists or foreign agents. Russia's underworld hierarchy is carefully organised. Firstly there are 'pakhans' or bosses. Then come the 'authorities', the hard-men just beneath them who carry out their orders. Third in line are the 'men' – the grafters who run around for their bosses. Then come the 'outcasts'. There is no other way to describe them other than as slaves to those above them.

A pakhan usually controls four criminal cells through an intermediary called a 'brigadier'. That pakhan even employs two spies to watch over the action of the brigadier to ensure loyalty and see that he does not get too powerful. Most Russian street operators don't even know the identity of their so-called leaders, which helps avoid the problems faced by so many old-school London villains in the past – police informants.

There is a traditional code of conduct within this old style of organised crime in Russia which is called 'Vory v Zakone', or 'thieves in law'. If members break this so-called thieves' code, it can be punishable with death. The code includes forsaking blood relatives and even traditional marriage and children, although lovers are permitted. Russian criminals are even encouraged to have outside jobs as cover for their unlawful activities. They are expected to keep secret any information about the whereabouts of accomplices (e.g. hideouts, safe apartments, etc).

They are also encouraged to take the blame for another member's crime if it gives that person time to escape justice. Members are expected to carry out punishments if they have been agreed, however severe. But they are told not to gamble unless they have sufficient money to cover any losses. Helping train-up new recruits is obligated, as are having informants connected to other thieves. Keeping control under the influence of alcohol is considered essential, although they are discouraged from joining the military, which is interesting since many undoubtedly were called up.

So, Russian criminals in London are undoubtedly well organised and equipped with all the latest technology plus a superb counter-intelligence network. And since 2002 it's believed they have really stepped up their operations in the capital, even gaining a foothold in the London art world.

The notorious Armenian-Russian gangsters are into the cloned mobile-phone market which means they are stealing the electronic serial numbers of customers' mobiles and then programming them into computer chips. This then creates a duplicate or cloned telephone number. This illicit market has expanded greatly recently. Today there are several Armenian gangs in London with more than 150 members. And they are nasty pieces of work. They are renowned for kidnapping and threatening to kill victims and their families if protection money is not paid.

Money laundering is the key to the success of many Russian mobsters based in London. Organised crime gangs in the former Soviet Union wire-transfer vast amounts of cash from drugs and vice – ranging from thousands to millions of pounds-worth of currency – into this country from offshore bank accounts as far afield as the Cayman Islands and Finland. Smaller amounts of cash come from arms trading and the illegal importation of those art treasures mentioned earlier. Many experts believe the biggest victim is the Russian government itself, which has lost more than 1.5 trillion roubles (more than $1 billion) to mobsters using forged documents.

In London, these shady characters run import/export companies to handle all this illegal cash. Police sources say that the Russians have even forged alliances with Colombian drug barons to organise huge shipments of cocaine into Russian and other former Soviet bloc countries. The Met first got a sniff of this mammoth operation when 1.1 metric tons of cocaine was seized in St Petersburg in February 1993.

The Russian criminal groups are increasing in size on virtually a monthly basis. The Met also believes they are now using London as a base for global ventures, including currency exchange and stealing World Bank and IMF loans.

Despite leaving the running of the lower levels of the sex industry in London to the even more ruthless Albanians, the Russians are still heavily involved in dealing in people- smuggling, often for sexual purposes. It's believed the Moscow mafia are currently into the very lucrative trade of 'importing' pregnant Russian women into London adoption agencies. The handlers of these women are paid £10,000 for each pregnancy. Like most enterprises, this business seems to have first started across the Atlantic.

Meanwhile, Russian gangsters run their own highly specialised sex clubs in the capital. They supply young Russian, Ukrainian and Baltic prostitutes, many of whom are 'exported' to the UK by long-distance coach from their home towns. Many of them are held in near-slavery conditions and told in no uncertain terms that they cannot return home.

Russians gangsters undoubtedly prefer using the City of London to launder money, because once a legitimate bank account is opened it is seen as an international seal of approval. Even more important, London is deemed the most civilised and luxurious city in which to live. The gangsters adore the capital's high property prices because they provide another convenient way to launder money, as well as to live in an impressive home. Russian mobsters are also rather partial to sending their children through our much admired private education system.

The Russians are very adept at spreading their criminal tentacles. They've recently begun making bucket-loads of cash flogging counterfeit drugs on the internet. Sales of such drugs are booming as more and more people use the internet to self-diagnose and medicate their ailments. And they don't seem to mind that many of these so-called online prescription drugs could be laced with poisonous chemicals. Some provide pills containing mercury and motor-oil derivatives while others contain brick dust, because many of them are made in cement mixers.

Take the powerful fertility drug Clomid. It can be bought online and is then dispatched in a Jiffy bag with no usage directions. Yet it's a proven fact that over-use of the drug can cause fatal ovarian cancer. Fake versions of the impotency drug Viagra are also believed to have made some London-based Russian gangsters millions of pounds, because men prefer to order it online than face the embarrassment of visiting their GP for a prescription. The surge in demand has been seized on by the criminal gangs who also send out runners to tout them in pubs and clubs around the UK.

Back in Russia, some schoolgirls actually aspire to make large sums of cash by working as prostitutes, according to a poll. But then there are few other ways to make enough money to survive in their home country. However many come here seeking so-called 'straight work' only to be forced into a life of vice. Divorced Siberian housewife Nadia took a one-way ticket to London only to find herself being given no choice but to work in the world's so-called oldest profession. She said she had to do it to make enough money to feed her family back home. Today, pimps with links to the Russian mafia double as doormen at some of London's biggest and most expensive hotels in order to keep control of women like Nadia. It's a multi-million-pound service industry, according to those involved in London's seedy world of vice.

But it's hardly surprising, when you consider what's been happening in places like Moscow since the fall of communism. Ten years ago an entire Moscow police precinct was broken up when a vice ring run by officers was uncovered in the capital's Tverskaya Street area. Prostitution and police corruption go hand-in-hand as far as many of these characters are concerned.

In London, many Russian gangsters have found it hard to adjust to the fact that not all police officers will take a bribe and turn a blind eye. 'Back home in Moscow many cops were pimps but here it's not so easy but there is so much money swimming around London that it is the place for us to be,' said one Moscow-born entrepreneur, now living in Bayswater.

One Russian pimp called Alexii told me that Russian and Ukrainian women are now amongst the most valuable commodities in the sex trade in London. 'They are not as feeble as some of the other East European girls,' he explained.

In December 2004 a gang of Albanian pimps who tricked teenage girls into working in London brothels were jailed for a total of 63 years. The five men lured some of their victims to the UK by promising them bar work, before taking away their documents and forcing them to work around-the-clock in brothels. A disturbing recent example of this problem was a Lithuanian student, from the city of Siauliai, who was a virgin when she was sold into slavery after arriving in London expecting to work as a cleaner. The innocent teenager was paid just £40 to lose her virginity to a stranger the morning after she arrived in the capital. A trial at Southwark Crown Court later heard how the girl was forced to have sex with hundreds of customers, earning the gang who'd bought her tens of thousands of pounds. A prosecutor at the court said her situation was: 'As close to being a slave as it is possible to be in a Western country'.

It's also a little-known fact that many London language schools are used as a cover by traffickers bringing women 'slaves' into the UK. This is how it works: an Eastern European 'student' applies to join a course at the school and is sent an enrolment form. She then takes it to the British Embassy in her home country to apply for a visa. On arrival in London she's met by traffickers and disappears into thin air.

In 2003 the Met's Vice Unit provided protection for an Eastern European girl called Alenka who'd been forced to work as a prostitute at the age of 15. She'd sought sanctuary at a youth project in East London before being persuaded to give evidence against her persecutors. But then Alenka – who'd been bullied and beaten by her pimp for months – absconded to Holland and disappeared. Her pimp was eventually convicted of burglary.

The vice trade is not just run by men: more and more women are managing brothels and hostess clubs where innocent young women are forced to have sex with strangers. As one police source explained: 'In many ways the women gangsters are tougher than the men because they are not using these girls as sex objects for themselves. These women are purely in it for the money. It's horrible.' Joint operations between police, immigration and foreign police forces have helped bring a number of such women to justice in recent years.

In the financial year 2004/05, the Met's special vice squad seized £2.5 million in cash and assets from brothel owners and porn peddlers.

Operation Pentameter was launched across London by the Met in 2004 to counter the effect of people-smuggling for the sex trade. It was intended to build on the success of the Met's previous operation, Maxim, which from 2000 onwards targeted organised criminal gangs trading in all forms of modern-day slavery. The Met joined forces with Immigration, Customs and women's advocacy groups to expose the tip of this vast prostitution iceberg.

Police investigations utilised Interpol to uncover a number of networks suspected of trafficking women into Heathrow Airport from countries as far as apart as Moldavia and Malaysia. In February 2005 Pentameter helped save 44 women and two girls from the clutches of a vice gang. Most of the women – mainly from Eastern Europe and the Balkans, as well as Thailand, China and Brazil – were aged between 18 and 22, but there were also two teenagers aged 17 and 15. Their alleged pimps were charged with offences including kidnapping, false imprisonment, controlling prostitution and rape. A month later more than 50 officers from Operation Pentameter carried out a series of dawn raids at seven addresses in London, the West Midlands and Hertfordshire, arresting 12 people.

One of the most shocking aspects of London's booming vice 'business' is how violence is used as a commodity to strike fear into women forced into this evil trade. A classic example is that of a woman in Lewisham, South London, who jumped from a second-floor window to escape her violent pimp. The woman was discovered unconscious and naked from the waist down. She'd suffered a broken elbow, broken teeth and numerous cuts and bruises. A police search of the property uncovered her assailant hiding in a cupboard. Later, detectives discovered another woman had made similar charges against the pimp but they'd been dropped because of lack of evidence. His earlier victim said she'd also jumped out of the same second-floor window to escape.

Today, it's reckoned that more than 6,000 women are working as prostitutes in brothels, saunas and massage parlours across London. Three quarters of them are foreign, with many smuggled into the country from Eastern Europe and Asia as sex slaves. Nearly 800 brothels are now operating in the capital, plus more than 60 supposedly legitimate lap-dancing clubs where some dancers are rumoured to be offering sex to clients. Each London borough has an average of 19 sites where sex can be bought, with on average between four and eight women working at each location. London's off-street sex industry is largely ignored in most discussions of prostitution, yet the women working in it are vulnerable to being exploited by violent and abusive pimps and traffickers.

In 2005 the Met's Clubs and Vice Unit took 300 girls and women, including ten children, out of brothels. Only 19 per cent were British, the rest were from Eastern Europe (25 per cent), Southeast Asia (13 per cent), Western Europe (12 per cent) and all over Africa (2 per cent).

The victims are frequently forced to live in terrible conditions, sleeping on floors, and are then farmed out and moved around the capital. Women can be sold between brothels for up to £10,000 and may be sold on four or five times. Some are also advertised on the internet, which police believe is fuelling demand for trafficking.

London's Heathrow, Gatwick and Stansted airports are busy locations, not just for travellers, but also for sex-slave auctions. One such takes place regularly outside a coffee shop in the arrivals hall at Gatwick Airport. The victims – most of whom are duped into believing that they are going to 'normal' jobs as dancers, au pairs or housekeepers – are coerced into prostitution, with London as a prime destination because it's a place where demand is constant, prices high and immigration controls are perceived to be lax.

In 2005 two failed asylum-seekers from Moldova were jailed for bringing almost 600 women into Britain illegally. They were Gavril Dulghieru, 36, who was sentenced to nine years, and his wife Tamara, jailed for five. The girls were forced to work as prostitutes to pay the couple's £300-a-day rent and repay the alleged £20,000 cost of getting them to Britain. They were said to have used cloned credit cards and stolen and bogus passports in one of Britain's biggest trafficking operations.

But it is the Albanian connection to the sex slaves of London that continues to be viewed with the greatest concern by the Met. In most desperately poor Albanian villages, donkeys stacked high with firewood crawl along potholed streets, but nowadays there are also bizarre sightings of gleaming Audis, Mercedes and even the odd Lamborghini, all undoubtedly bought with the proceeds of crime, a lot of it in London.

The Republic of Albania in the Balkan peninsula of Southern Europe is a small nation with a population of just three million spread over 10,362 square miles. Albania is impoverished, underdeveloped and politically unstable, and it is run in many ways through rampant corruption and a virulent criminality. One-third of the inhabitants earn the equivalent of two dollars a day, forcing many to seek employment elsewhere. No wonder Albanian criminal gangs constitute one of the highest crime-generating elements at international level. They are organised into clans, with rigid internal rules, rigorous punishments for any betrayal, and a chilling talent for entrepreneurship.

The Albanians now have cells in Europe and South America, where they liaise with Colombian cocaine traffickers, and in cities like New York and London. They often recruit Albanian women on the basis that they will provide them with a better life abroad, but once at their destinations, they are sold to the highest bidder.

A secret Home Office briefing admitted that the 'tightening grip' of Albanian gangs on the London vice trade was 'changing the landscape' of the capital's sex industry. A Save the Children study in March 2003 stated that thousands of Albanian girls as young as 14 were being abducted from their families and sent overseas to work as prostitutes.

The Met believes 90 per cent of the women know they will be working as prostitutes when they leave Albania but a spokesman rejected the idea that they were working independently, saying: 'What they believe is that once they have paid their debt bond, they will be able to make significant money for themselves. The reality is completely different. At its most benign, it is ruthless exploitation, and at its most malevolent it is rape on a daily basis.'

The cold-blooded conquest of Soho, Britain's best-known red-light district, by the Albanian mafia seems to virtually represent a 'white slave trade' in impoverished young women. Over the past decade violent Albanian criminals have taken control of 75 per cent of prostitution in Soho. It is London's sex-tourism honey-pot, and the Albanians are now raking in tens of millions of pounds each year. It's almost as if an endless stream of women is available, and so far the Albanians' takeover has been a relatively bloodless coup.

Once in Britain, the Albanians snatch back the girls' bogus

papers and use them to bring others into the country. The victims do not officially exist and are powerless to resist. Some girls controlled by Albanian pimps charge as little as £30 for sex and on average are expected to 'sleep' with between 20 and 30 clients a day. The National Criminal Intelligence Service (NCIS) is particularly worried about the Albanians because already numerous blood feuds have been being fought out on London's streets. Albanians are even suspected of sending money home to the Kosovo Liberation Army.

A top government official in Albania has admitted that organised criminal gangs from his country were specifically targeting Britain – and especially London – to traffick women and children for the sex trade. The head of the country's anti-trafficking unit, Colonel Avni Jashallari, said the London-connection had been sparked by a huge clampdown in recent years on the traditional route between Albania and Italy via the Ionian and Adriatic seas. In the summer of 2002 the police seized 40 boats that carried women and children, effectively shutting down these avenues.

In a seedy hotel room in Earls Court, West London, a young nurse who fled her home in Serbia in 2005 fears for her life after escaping from evil Albanian pimps. She'd been smuggled across the Adriatic to Italy in a speedboat and then spent several days concealed in the back of a lorry with an Albanian girl. When the truck finally stopped and the doors opened, she was bundled into a blue car where two men were waiting for her. She thought she was in Germany until she saw a traffic sign for London. She was then locked in a basement flat until next morning when an Albanian told her it would cost another £7,000 to get her from London to Germany. He then told her she'd have to have sex with men for money. She was beaten until she agreed and made her escape a few weeks later.

In 2001 a 23-year-old Albanian woman escaped from a flat in Bayswater, Central London, after claiming her pimp, Shemsi Gjika, 35, had regularly abused her physically. The woman said Gjika had duped her into travelling to London where she'd believed she would work as a waitress. A family friend had introduced her to Gjika and another Albanian, Fatmir Gashi, 27, who arranged a false Greek passport for her. Two days after arriving at Heathrow she was set to work as a prostitute in a Soho flat. When she eventually escaped, police offered her protection and a safe house in return for testifying against her captor. Gjika has now been convicted of living on immoral earnings. Police are still looking for Gashi, who disappeared soon after his arrest.

Another tragically familiar case is that of a 15-year-old Romanian girl, smuggled into Britain via Brussels and Ostend on a hovercraft in July 2001. She was met at Victoria Station and taken to a flat in northwest London. A day later, an Albanian gangster called Mustapha Kadiu, 31, arrived and made the girl, later known in court as Miss X, phone saunas and massage parlours to find work as a prostitute. Kadiu threatened to kill her if she failed to earn between £400 and £500 a day, charging £30 for straight sex. After three months of sexual slavery in London the girl escaped and went to the police. In December 2004 Kadiu was arrested and convicted of rape, indecent assault and of living off immoral earnings, and sentenced to ten years in prison.

Yet despite all these disturbing cases, London has fewer than 20 officers based at Charing Cross police station who deal specifically with human trafficking. As Balkans countries continue their entry into the EU, many in London say this will be an open invitation to more vice criminals to invade the city.

The story of a 15-year-old schoolgirl called Ilena from Romania sums up the sheer brutality that awaits many innocent girls when they arrive in Britain's capital city. Ilena was told she owed a man called Stanislav £3,000 for bringing her to London and was made to earn thousands of pounds every week for her pimp. She was nearly killed by the pimp when he thought she was trying to keep all the money from her customers and in the end she went to police after hearing that Stanislav had put a £10,000 bounty on her head. Stanislav fled the UK when he heard that Met detectives were looking for him and Ilena has been allowed to stay in London where she now works as a cleaner.

Sadly, it seems there is no escape for London's sex workers from the full brunt of the capital's criminals. In 2005 three men were jailed for life after murdering a male prostitute at his flat in London. The gang had also been robbing female prostitutes for months. Twenty-nine-year-old Londoner Darren Johnson viewed prostitutes as easy pickings. He assumed they'd be too ashamed of their occupation, or too worried by the consequences, to report the attacks to the police.

In June 2004, Johnson, a hard-up clothing salesman from Battersea, South London, recruited two other men – Muhammed Nduka, 26, from Camberwell, and a 25-year-old who cannot be named for legal reasons – to join his robbery team. Trawling through the adult services adverts in *Loot* and *Exchange & Mart* he spotted potential victims and rang them, claiming to be a prospective client. He'd then arrive at their home and trick or force his way in, together with an accomplice. Once inside, Johnson and his gang used a terrifying amount of violence on their victims to rob them of small amounts of cash, mobile phones, jewellery and credit cards.

The gang's first three victims – all women – had flats in the

Regent's Park, Paddington and Fulham areas of London. But on 15 July 2004 they changed tack and picked out a 32-year-old male masseur called Niphan Trikhana, from Thailand, who operated out of a flat in Cranley Place, South Kensington. He ended up being stabbed seven times and strangled with a ligature. He also had his little finger cut off. Mr Trikhana's body was only discovered by his landlord a week later.

When police checked calls to all the gang's victims, a couple of mobile phone numbers kept cropping up. One of them belonged to Johnson, and soon the evidence against him was piling up, with several female victims giving evidence about their ordeal at the hands of the gang. At their eventual court appearance, the jury found them guilty. Johnson, who'd been acquitted in 2000 of murdering a man in South London, was jailed for life and told he would have to serve a minimum of 35 years behind bars. Nduka was given a minimum tariff of 22 years, and the third man told he must serve 25 years.

Millions of pounds change hands every week within London's vice trade. But it's the so-called 'high class' brothels in Central London which are the biggest money-spinners. Take notorious madam Ann O'Brien. In any other business she would have been one of those fearsome captains of industry. Her bizarre story begins in a mud hut in Kenya, where a girl called Ann Wamboi was born in the early 1970s. Dropping out of school and then selling vegetables on her mother's market stall was clearly not enough for her. Soon she set up her own second-hand clothes stall.

Ann's family saved the cash to buy her a one-way plane ticket to Europe in 1995 and she settled in London and was married to a man called Patrick O'Brien, enabling her to stay in the UK. Within months Ann changed her name to Nancy and began operating as a hooker in Central London brothels. By 1997 she could afford to splash out £200,000 on a hairdressing salon called Dreamgirl Creations, in Kilburn, northwest London. She spent another £150,000 redecorating it.

And so the money kept pouring in for Ann. In May 2001 she paid a £487,000 cash deposit for a five-bedroom house in Mayfair and immediately bought whips, chains and other sex toys before recruiting dozens of beautiful women and girls to work round-the-clock at an average of £150 a time. It was later claimed Ann was raking in £12,000 a week in profit, which would have meant she was banking more than £500,000 a year. The local vice squad eventually sent in a team of undercover officers to gather evidence before raiding the Mayfair house and closing it down.

Ann O'Brien told officers she ran a legitimate escort service and had no idea the girls were providing 'other services' on her premises. In May 2005, O'Brien was convicted and ordered to carry out 180 hours of community service. The Metropolitan Police's Clubs & Vice Financial Investigation Unit believes O'Brien made £2,169,710 from her life of vice, but once her properties were sold off and everything else deducted, £602,915 was left over. O'Brien did not contest the confiscation order.

The sheer scale of some vice rings in London has stunned the police. When detectives raided a six-bedroom brothel near Hyde Park in March 2005, they discovered 13 Malaysian women aged between 19 and 25 working as sex slaves. A monthly rental of £6,000 was being paid for the upmarket town house. Brothels run by the same gang in Paddington, Soho and Golders Green were also raided. The suspected Vietnamese ringleader of the racket and his girlfriend were among 12 people detained during the raids. Chief Supt Ian Dyson, head of London's Metropolitan Police Clubs and

Vice special unit, said afterwards: 'We believe we have successfully dismantled the British end of a suspected trafficking network.'

Carlos Pires, a truly evil man, and his girlfriend, 'imported' Brazilian women ranging in age from 18 to 25 into London by promising them work as nannies, maids and dancers once they had 'paid off' the cost of their transportation to the UK, usually between £7,500 and £9,000. On arrival the women's passports and travel documents were confiscated by Pires, so they could not escape, and they were forced to sleep with 10 to 15 men in 12-hour sessions, six to seven days a week. They were permitted to keep £50–£60 after charging a minimum of £250 for sex. Each woman was also made to pay £350–£450 a week for accommodation and expenses. The Met eventually traced the backgrounds of 100 women who'd travelled from remote villages in Brazil to London over a five-year period.

The vice invasion of the capital is typified by the case of a Lithuanian man who was arrested in 2005 for shipping 55 Russian women into the UK. He used a car import/export business for cover and was eventually sentenced to five years in prison.

And it was summed up by Chief Superintendent Simon Humphreys, Commander of the Met's Clubs and Vice Unit, formed in 1975 after the police corruption scandals of the 1960s: 'Prostitution has become acceptable throughout the British Isles.'

London's long-standing and notorious Chinese Triad gangs run their brothels on regimental rules, keeping ten women in each house and only allowing them out with a minder. Their services are advertised through escort agencies, at the back of magazines and on cards found in central London telephone boxes.

In 2004 a 'chain' of six Triad-run brothels were raided by police who rescued ten women from Malaysia, Hong Kong and Thailand. They'd been working 12–14 hour shifts for the Triads, seven days a week. As is so often the case, the women had their identification papers confiscated so they couldn't escape, got only a small percentage of the client's fee, and then the gangsters deducted air-fares, rent and meals.

Then there is the scourge of prostitution and the most disturbing section of London's illicit vice 'industry': the kidnapping, imprisonment and sexual exploitation of children. These innocent youngsters are looked upon as prized possessions by evil pimps who know they can charge perverts money for the victims' so-called 'services'. Usually the children are locked up in squalid bedsits, often denied access to food or a toilet.

This sick and twisted demand for sex with underage children has, it seems, been further fuelled by the plague of child sex tourism, which is prevalent in some Far East holiday destinations, including Thailand. Those British tourists experiencing it return to the UK with an insatiable appetite for regular sexual relations with children, which has encouraged this repulsive market to grow dramatically in recent years.

Now the authorities in Thailand are being specially trained by the Met Police in special one-week sessions during which they learn how to deal with victims of such abuse and compare notes on who the most likely offenders will be. Eventually it's hoped the 'supply route' can be cut off to completely stem the flow of children being smuggled into London. The Met also recently launched similar training schemes in Sri Lanka, India, Pakistan and Nepal on how to deal with both victims and offenders.

Almost as disturbing is the increase in child porn internet sites financed by hard-nosed gangsters who look upon the lucrative cybersex market as an easy way to make millions, even if the images shown include underage children. Today, more and more gangs are employing computer experts to help them gain access to this lucrative market.

And, it seems, there are many sick and twisted individuals out there prepared to spend money on such sites. Take rock star Gary Glitter, charged with child pornography offences after indecent images were found on his home computer when he took it to be repaired.

There are even gangs specifically targeting the child pornography market in London. These criminals are often child porn addicts themselves, running their own sick and twisted paedophile websites. Seven British men who peddled child pornography on the internet were jailed for between 12 and 30 months each in 1999. Their paedophile ring – called The Wonderland Club – was smashed by Operation Cathedral, the largest international operation to be coordinated by the National Crime Squad in London.

Earlier – on 2 September 1998 – 107 arrests in connection with similar gangs were made across the UK, Australia, Austria, Belgium, Finland, France, Germany, Italy, Norway, Portugal, Sweden and the United States. But under laws at the time, the men only faced a maximum of three years in jail. However those sentences were doubled following the scandal that erupted about the Wonderland case.

All of the children involved were under the age of 16 and in one case the child was only three months old. More than 1,263 children were featured in the pictures – but only 17 were ever identified – six in the UK, seven in the United States, one in Portugal, one in Chile, and one in Argentina. Club members 'paid' an entry 'fee' of

10,000 indecent images. Authorities traced the internet paedophiles after discovering that a child abuser had broadcast live images on the internet to a paedophile ring in California, in May 1996.

It is predicted that the internet will eventually completely take over from those traditional 'shop windows' for sexual services such as telephone boxes and contact magazines. In 2005 a German millionaire based in London was arrested for running an international hooker business on the net. Prostitutes flew between London, New York and Hong Kong, and were paid £1,000 an hour or £6,000 for a night. Clients were predominantly wealthy Asian businessmen, and the women's fees were paid straight into offshore bank accounts.

London is such a popular base for such 'escort services' that it is now considered the sex centre of Western Europe. 'London is renowned for providing straight, gay and bisexual services with all sorts of perverted extras thrown in,' explained one Met vice detective. A surf of the web soon lists literally hundreds of internet sex services, all based in London. These businesses – renowned for low outgoings and high returns – are often financed by London-based gangsters reinvesting the proceeds of massive drug deals

But apart from the internet, there are plans to install pornography computer sex kiosks which will give access to internet porn in pubs and clubs across the country.

Away from the sordid, disturbing world of the illicit sex trade, other criminal 'businesses' are also earning gangsters a fortune. Fake IDs have facilitated the people-smuggling market into London and the rest of the UK. The Met openly admits that passport 'factories' are now operating under franchises in much the same way as Burger King franchises.

A classic example of this came in 2004 when police uncovered such a business turning out fake passports and credit cards, as well as IDs. They found a total of 1,335 fake passports and ID cards and 2,000 credit cards at a house in Croydon, on the southern edge of London, owned by a Romanian couple, who were jailed for a minimum nine-year term.

But even in the new century it seems some old fashioned criminality still flourishes: a gang of middle-aged London armed robbers snatched £340,000 from security guards refilling cash machines at banks. Known as the 'Old Blaggers', the gang were eventually caught after police used listening devices to trap the men, who were heard boasting about heists dating back ten years.

They pleaded guilty to conspiracy to rob six banks and building societies between 1 January 1999 and 31 August 2004. Three of them pleaded guilty to conspiracy to possess firearms with criminal intent and one admitted possession of a prohibited weapon and 17 ecstasy tablets. The London court heard that the raids were meticulously planned and often involved breaking into the banks before the cash machines were due to be filled. Ringleader Stephen Howard, 50, got 22 years. His 'lieutenant', Stephen Dickson, 53, was sentenced to 16 years, while firearms provider Paul Johnson, 45, got 12 years. The gang's locksmith Richard Hall, 54, was sentenced to 11 years.

However, for others it seems that being connected to London's so-called old-school gangsters remains a very risky preoccupation. Known criminal John Marshall, 34, was found shot dead in his black Range Rover in Sydenham, South London, just after the disappearance of road-rage killer and master criminal Kenny Noye following the M25 murder in 1996. Marshall, a friend of Noye, also knew drug dealer Pat Tate, shot dead in a Range Rover in the Essex countryside in 1996.

The increasing spate of armed incidents in London has highlighted a disturbing trend. Armed street robberies shot up from 435 to 667 in 2001 – an increase of 53 per cent. The overall statistics show that there were 45,255 street robberies and snatches in 2005 compared with 32,497 in 2000. The market for stolen mobile phones has obviously greatly contributed to these figures.

There are genuine fears that street robberies and gun crime are overlapping as young gangs of muggers graduate from knives to firearms. Some believe the dramatic increases were sparked by shortages of inner city police officers, diverted to protect terrorist targets in the wake of 11 September attacks in America.

Yet following the Dunblane massacre in 1996 – in which 16 school-children were killed by a lone gunman – the government hoped to nip Britain's burgeoning firearms culture in the bud with an outright ban on handguns. Although all privately owned handguns in Britain are now officially illegal, the tightened rules had the opposite effect in London's ganglands. No one knows how many illegal firearms there are in the capital, although estimates range from between 40,000 to 250,000. Whatever the true figure, it is growing daily.

The Met Police already have armed response vehicles, equipped and ready to attend the scene of a robbery or siege at a few minutes' notice. But rank and file officers are still against carrying guns on the beat. Many believe it would be counter-productive, inviting more criminals to arm themselves with even more deadly weaponry. As already mentioned, the growth in gun murders in London is mainly a result of so-called revenge killings among drug gangs.

There are actually more shootings in the fashionable West End of London than in so-called ghetto boroughs such as Lambeth, Hackney and Brent. At least two people a day are now robbed at gunpoint in London. More and more armed robbers target all-

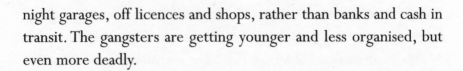

night garages, off licences and shops, rather than banks and cash in transit. The gangsters are getting younger and less organised, but even more deadly.

In November 2001, the curse of the Brinks-Mat robbery struck again with the murder of Brian Perry outside his South London office. At Perry's home in Brasted, Kent, his family refused to talk about the killing but everyone presumed it was linked to Britain's most notorious robbery. Perry, 63, from South London, served a nine-year jail term for handling stolen goods from the 1983 gold bullion heist. Then living in Biggin Hill, Kent, he was supposed to look after the interests on the outside of the two jailed Brinks-Mat gang members, Mickey McAvoy and Brian Robinson, but had set about feathering his own nest.

A few days after Perry's murder, a police sniffer dog found the revolver used in the killing in a dustbin in Ilford, to the east of London, where one of two men later accused of the murder was allegedly spotted. When they appeared at the Old Bailey in April 2006 they were cleared of the murder of Perry after the prosecution offered no further evidence.

It's clear that certain murders in London are undoubtedly deliberate, paid-for hits. Another example is the case of south Londoner Alan 'Big Al' Decabral, shot dead just seconds after he'd heaved his 20-stone frame into the passenger seat of his son's 2-door Peugeot with great difficulty on a quiet afternoon in October 2000. Decabral was more used to driving around in his own vintage Jag, once owned by Reggie Kray. But as he was checking the time on his gold Rolex, a man holding a gun equipped with a silencer pulled alongside him in the car park of a Halfords store, near Ashford, in Kent.

Decabral didn't even have time to plead for his life as two shots rang out and his vast, blubbery body slumped against the dashboard. Terrified shoppers fled in terror. Welcome to Kent – seemingly the epitome of lush, peaceful English countryside. But lurking amongst the unprepossessing villages are many of the biggest names in the London underworld. This corner of England has been privately labelled The Wild West by police because a lawless society exists behind the high walls of many of the county's most valuable properties. They are multi-millionaires who describe themselves as 'businessmen' and 'property developers' but many of them only deal strictly in cash. Alan Decabral – who lived in the quiet village of Pluckley – was just one of numerous villains who've turned the countryside communities of Kent into the criminal badlands of Britain.

One of London's most psychopathic killers is alleged hitman Gary Nelson. He shot dead a man who 'disrespected' him and a police officer who came on the scene by chance in October 1993. But it wasn't until 12 years later that Nelson, 36, was found guilty of the murders of security guard William 'Kwame' Danso and PC Patrick Dunne in Cato Road, Clapham, South London. Nelson, suspected to be involved in other killings, was already serving life after police found his 'hitman's kit' in 2003. Sentencing him to life, Mr Justice Wilkie recommended Nelson serve at least 35 years.

Nelson was just 24 when he killed Ghanaian-born Danso because the bouncer had refused him entry to a nightclub and then intervened in a row involving a friend of Nelson's at the mobile phone shop where Danso also worked as a security guard. That night Nelson and two others, armed with a Browning 9mm semiautomatic and an Italian-made Tanfoglio self-loading pistol, went to Danso's flat and mowed down the father-of-four in a hail of bullets.

By coincidence, PC Dunne, 44, a former maths teacher who'd joined the police only four years previously, arrived on his bicycle to deal with a minor domestic dispute at a house opposite. Hearing gunfire, PC Dunne, dubbed locally as 'Dixon of Dock Green' for his friendly manner, rushed into the street where Nelson, still carrying the Tanfoglio, fired a single shot into his chest, killing him instantly. Witnesses heard the trio laugh and fire a celebratory shot in the air as they walked to a waiting car.

Nelson was charged with the murders five weeks later, but the case was dropped due to lack of evidence. A group of women went on a bizarre, middle-of-the-night expedition to retrieve the murder weapons, buried in Wandsworth cemetery near where Nelson lived at that time. They couldn't find them, but five months later police dug them up, guided by anonymous phone calls from one of the women and lipstick crosses on the gravestones.

There was still not enough evidence to charge Nelson. But he continued to inspire fear in all who knew him, even from his prison cell after he was arrested for opening fire on a man who overtook his car in a road-rage incident. In 1994, Nelson ran naked from his cell, lunging at prison officers with a broom handle. He once managed to break free from a straitjacket, and intimidated some of the country's most hardened criminals into handing over phone credits so he could ring his many girlfriends.

His background is chilling. Nicknamed 'Tyson', Gary Nelson shared the controversial American boxer's physique and hair-trigger temper. He was completely infatuated with guns and even called his Browning 9mm semiautomatic pistol 'my special thing'. With a violent record stretching back to his early teens, and links to one of London's most infamous crime families, he accumulated a fortune which he spent on a luxury apartment, top-of-the-range cars and designer clothes. The jury in his trial was allowed to hear details of his previous convictions, including the road-rage incident. 'He was a hitman but also he was so much more than that,' explained one Scotland Yard detective. 'Hitmen are at the bottom of the criminal food chain, taking the orders. Nelson was at the very top, giving them. He killed whoever he wanted or arranged to have them killed.'

Released from jail in 1999 after that earlier offence, Nelson was soon back in the south London criminal underworld. In January 2003, in an investigation not connected to Cato Road, police bugged his new apartment in Woolwich, southeast London, and heard him racking his gun. Officers burst in to find a Browning 9mm, complete with laser sight and silencer, and he was subsequently sentenced to life for possession of firearms. The police were amazed to see 30 pairs of trainers, all arranged on the bedroom floor with exactly the same distance between each pair, while in the wardrobe hung rows of designer suits and coordinated shirts and ties.

The Cato Road case was officially reopened in 2001, partly because of pressure from the Dunne family, and a BBC-TV *Crimewatch* appeal brought forward a former fellow inmate in Wormwood Scrubs who testified that Nelson told him in 1994: 'I shot that copper, the one on the bike.'

Sandra Francis, the woman whose Christian faith prompted her to alert police to the guns all those years earlier, was also traced and agreed to give evidence. Detectives travelled to Ghana and tracked down Eugene Djaba, manager of the shop where Danso had worked. Djaba had fled after jumping bail in 1996 and was convicted in his absence of a £3 million cigarette fraud. In a highly unusual move, he testified via video link about seeing Nelson pull a gun – which he later identified as the Tanfoglio – from his jacket the day before the murders and threaten to put a 'bullet in the belly' of another man.

There was no definitive forensic evidence and Nelson was never picked out at an identity parade. But Richard Horwell QC, prosecuting, built his case on 13 'planks' of circumstantial evidence, which, he argued, placed Nelson in Cato Road and the Tanfoglio in his hand. DCI Richardson described Nelson's attitude during police interviews as 'nonchalant', but as Mr Horwell told the jury: 'Arrogance and notions of invincibility sometimes go before a fall.'

London hitmen, it seems, come in all shapes and sizes. Mohammed Mustafa, 26, and Edward Allimadi, 25, aided gunman Daniel Turvey, 22, when he targeted two friends as they walked home from a nightclub in April, 2004. Twenty-five-year-old Sudanese student Galadin Hamza was shot dead in the street and his friend, fellow student Abdel Aziz Abdelaziz, was shot through the left thigh but managed to run for his life after they were followed by the three men in Earl's Court. In June the following year, Turvey was convicted at the Old Bailey of the murder and the attempted murder of Abdelaziz, and jailed for life.

The other pair were each sentenced to life for murder, and must serve a minimum of 30 years before being considered for parole. They were also jailed for 20 years for the attempted murder. Judge Stephen Kramer QC told them: 'Though none of you two pulled the trigger, you are each as culpable.' Although the true motive for the murder is not known, detectives believed Turvey was summoned to the scene to carry out the shootings.

So, it's clear there's no shortage of work for a good hitman on the violent streets of modern-day London; in fact the number of shootists has reached epidemic proportions. Twenty years ago, if you wanted someone bumped off there was only a small crew of

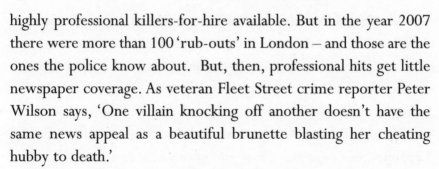

highly professional killers-for-hire available. But in the year 2007 there were more than 100 'rub-outs' in London – and those are the ones the police know about. But, then, professional hits get little newspaper coverage. As veteran Fleet Street crime reporter Peter Wilson says, 'One villain knocking off another doesn't have the same news appeal as a beautiful brunette blasting her cheating hubby to death.'

Hitmen themselves revel in the low-key nature of their business. Says one, 'The less publicity the better. The papers don't seem that interested in most hits.' Even the police play down such crimes. As one detective explains, 'We take the attitude that every time there's a hit it means one less villain on the streets – and that can't be a bad thing.'

But now, even the Met's finest admit the situation has got completely out of control. They've set up a special squad to crack down on these so-called criminal renegades. David Veness, Assistant Commissioner in charge of specialist operations, admits: 'We have a genuine fear that there is a greater capacity for criminals to gain access to individuals willing to kill for money. There is clear evidence that there are small groups for whom this is the main form of criminal activity.' That's copspeak for: 'It's a big problem.'

The bottom line is that life's a lot cheaper in the 21st century than it was when sawn-off shotgun-toting armed robbers swaggered across pavements taking pot shots at The Sweeney, as the plain clothes boys crouched behind their Ford Granadas. These days small-time hoods are prepared to knock off other villains, cheating lovers and work rivals. Some of the real pros are in danger of being put out of business.

Take south London hitman 'Lenny'. He's been in 'the business' for 12 years, lives in a nice, comfortable three-bedroom bungalow in the Kent countryside – and no one other than his dear old mum and wife and kids knows his real identity. That's the way he intends to keep it. 'The fellows who hire me don't give a toss who I am. But I've got their respect. I do the job clean and simple with no fuckin' aggro,' explained Lenny.

Lenny reckons the hired hand who popped London millionaire-gangster-turned-police-informant Pete McNeil, alias James Lawton, on 10 February 1998, didn't put a foot wrong. Coke-and-hooker addict McNeil, 40, was targeted at point-blank range outside his very respectable, commuter-belt redbrick, modern detached home on the Bow Field housing estate in the twee Hampshire village of Hook.

The victim had been proudly telling people there was 'a bullet out there with my name on it' from the moment he turned supergrass after he was nicked for involvement in a $70 million cocaine heist. The drugs ring had links with an American branch of the mafia in Detroit, not to mention a number of Medellin men from Colombia. So when McNeil finally got the bullet on his own doorstep at 8.01 p.m, as a pot of pasta simmered on the stove, there wasn't a lot of grieving.

The list of suspects was longer than Peter Crouch's arm. There were criminal associates he'd double crossed, ripped-off call girls, pissed-off coke dealers, and even some poor mug who bought a second-hand car off McNeil and discovered it had been nicked.

Final word on the hitman culture has to go to my man Lenny, renowned as one of the most feared shootists on the streets of southeast England. 'The rules of the game are changing every day. My basic price is twenty grand, unless I'm being asked to take out a big-time face who's got a lot of protection. I always get paid in full, in advance, in cash. How else could I handle it, take a cheque? There are other unwritten clauses that go into every hit contract.

If I get nicked, the geezer commissioning the hit takes care of all my legal costs plus my bail if I manage to get it. He'd also make sure I was comfortable in the nick, that my missus was comfortable at home, as well as doing everything to try to get me out. Finally, when I finish my bird, he would have a bundle of cash waiting for me. This is done to guarantee silence. As long as all obligations are taken care of, I'm not going to say a word to no one. I'm certainly not going to land anyone in the shit. They'd soon finish me off.'

But Lenny says it's not the risk of being caught for his crimes that bothers him. 'There are other so-called pros out there popping people for five grand apiece. But you get what you pay for and these cut-price operators all get caught in the end and then they start singing. Let's face it, a granny in Blackpool who wants shot of her old man after thirty years of abuse is going to end up hiring a fucking amateur or an undercover cozzer.

'There's too many wideboys makin' out they can carry out hits for two-and-six. All they do is make problems for blokes like me.' But Lenny reckons he has the answer. 'I'm planning to retire soon. Buy myself a nice little villa on the Costa Del Sol and start relaxing and enjoying my life.'

He pauses and slowly nods his head. 'If I live that long ...'

So murder has become a boom business in London, where more than a third of all killings are contract jobs organised by criminal gangs. Don't forget that, of the 200-plus known gangs in the capital, over half have violent intentions. Then there are the two- thirds who deal in more than one illegal trade besides drugs. Until recently the Met tended to target single crime gangs, mainly those dealing in drug trafficking. But the emphasis today is on the networks or 'corporations' behind a vast range of different criminal 'industries', many of which have already been mentioned in this book.

The Special Branch – after 100 years in the front line against terrorism and political crime – have now linked up with mainstream Yard detectives to investigate gang-related crimes, ranging from drug smuggling to protection rackets to people smuggling. Highly trained specialist surveillance teams have had notable successes, including the tracking of an IRA gang trying to blow up London's electricity supply stations. Gangs such as the Yardies, the Russian mafia and the Albanians quietly run their powerful empires with the minimum of public exposure and virtually no public profile, which makes police infiltration even more difficult.

Traditional, old-school London families still dabble in protection rackets, bootlegging and some extortion, but they seem mainly to concentrate on drugs and illegal importation of cheap and/or fake cigarettes from abroad. Today, rather than an organised, experienced team of villains, most bank and cash van robberies are carried out by young loners, often armed with weapons which are frequently incapable of actually firing.

However, it is true to say that longer prison terms and the risk of forfeiture of the criminals' cash and property mean a lot gangsters are moving away from high-risk, high-profit activities such as drug smuggling to areas which offer high profit with the risk of far shorter prison terms, such as fraud and people smuggling.

But it's so-called 'cross border' crime throughout Europe that is turning so many London criminals into millionaires. Europol, the European Union's police office, has warned that trafficking in arms, drugs and people is on the increase, as well as counterfeiting and money-laundering rackets. The main gang activity in London remains drug trafficking, even though narcotics have drastically reduced in price. All the principal routes, each operated by different gangs, have also provided routes for illegal immigration, alcohol and tobacco smuggling, plus sex-slave trafficking. In the Nordic and Baltic region, Russian-speaking gangs naturally dominate, while the Dutch, the British and the Belgians rule the Atlantic area. And it is through these corridors that more than 100,000 women and children are trafficked across EU borders.

The strong mob connections to money laundering in London are hardly surprising considering its key strategic position as a global financial centre. More than £1.3 billion of cash was secretly siphoned through City of London banks during one recent financial scandal. Even Barclays Bank (entirely innocently) handled more than $170 million of funds, most of it looted from the Nigerian treasury by the military regime of the late dictator, General Sani Abacha.

Financial institutions in the City of London are vulnerable to money laundering, as a result of globalisation and the ease of funds transfers from the capital. In 2002, London was said by some of the world's most successful criminals to be the cocaine capital of the world, with financial institutions indirectly fuelling the market of 'Charlie' through their staff's excessive use of the drug. Now there's quite an irony in that.

Incredibly, even certain wildlife products have been turned into currency to barter for drugs and to launder drug traffic money in London's underworld. Smuggled birds from Australia have been exchanged for heroin. In April 2002 the UK government created the National Wildlife Crime Intelligence Unit, but few believe it will end trafficking in wildlife connected to drugs.

London-organised gangs now threaten to undermine conservation groups working and spending millions to save the world's endangered species. Live snakes stuffed with condoms full

of cocaine are shipped across borders; venomous snakes even guard contraband, while live snails packed with heroin are regularly airlifted into the UK.

Those vast amounts of cash floating around London have helped encourage foreign gangs to begin operating here. And it is often illegal arms which are the cornerstones of these operations. Powerful criminal faces such as a notorious London-based Russian drug lord are said to possess guns and rockets. AK-47 machine pistols are essential fashion accessories, just like Gucci handbags for the wives. Underworld armourers operate leaseback schemes for guns to the smaller firms. Typically, a 'piece' can be rented for a day at £250, or bought for £500. Ominously, at least two of the best-known armourers in the London underworld have been ex-policemen.

Once upon a time, guns were only ever used to commit the most serious offences, but police now say many small-time crooks such as burglars and low-level drug dealers always 'pack a piece'. They even arm themselves with CS gas, supposedly for personal defence.

During one bloody day in North London, police received calls from two separate hospital casualty departments about young men with gunshot wounds. It was soon established that both were shot during the same incident earlier that same day, but had fled the scene to seek treatment separately to try to lessen the risk of capture. Reports of shots being fired or cars found riddled with bullets are increasingly common. Initiatives aimed at reducing the number of shootings have been set up in crime 'hotspots' such as Hackney, Westminster, Lewisham and Brent.

Britain's tighter gun laws since the Dunblane shooting tragedy seem to have failed completely. Now there is a race against time to stop the UK from becoming as trigger-happy as the US. Police in the capital have even been confronted by automatic-machine-gun-toting youngsters on mountain bikes. Mark Lee, 22, of Islington, North London, was jailed for five years after admitting being in possession of one of only two of Croatian-made Agram 2000 submachine guns so far seized by British police. Southwark Crown Court heard that officers from Operation Trident's Anti-Drugs and Guns team raided his flat in Bletchley Court, Wenlock Street, Islington, on 17 March 2005 and saw him hurl the weapon – which can fire 750 rounds a minute – from a fourth-floor balcony. The firearm had most probably found its way into the UK after being originally used by troops and militia in the war in former Yugoslavia.

Lee, a convicted heroin dealer, insisted he'd been handed the weapon at 2 a.m. that morning and was looking after it for a mate. Lee eventually pleaded guilty to three firearms offences, including possession of the gun with intent to endanger life, and possession of the silencer and the bullets. The court was told that police would not make an application to destroy the weapon, but would instead use it for training purposes.

No wonder the Met continually fears an outbreak of gun war between immigrant and black drug gangs in London. Turkish gangs are already fighting among themselves, but the threat from Albanian, Asian, Southeast Asian, Chinese, and Jamaican/black London armed gangs remains as deadly as ever.

But where do all these weapons come from?

A mock-Tudor, five-bedroom house in a quiet residential area of the London suburbs. Hardly what you'd imagine a makeshift 'gun factory' to look like. Yet the alarming increase in replica guns being restored to full working order and used by criminals across the capital has turned this into a boom time for such places. Southeast Regional Crime Squad officers and a tactical firearms unit discovered one fully converted and one partly converted gun at this particular location. Special customized ammunition was also being produced on the premises.

The so-called 'gun factory' gang had even worked out how to replace the solid barrel of a replica gun with a hollow one. Unlike deactivated guns – real firearms which have had holes drilled through their barrels and the firing pins removed – replicas are considered completely safe and are sold by mail-order firms to gun enthusiasts and collectors. The gang also knew how to convert blank ammunition – available without a licence to anyone over the age of 17 – into lethal live rounds. Police believed that dozens of converted replicas may have been sold on, at £25 each, to London criminals in the six months the house was under surveillance. Compare those prices to deactivated weapons which cost up to £300 and sell on for up to £1,000, once altered.

Meanwhile, London's criminal gangs continue their search for new weapons. Ironically, opportunities to buy real weapons have declined with the legitimate trade in recession. Hence the interest in replicas. Elsewhere in London other replica weapons seized have included 'fake' Israeli Uzi submachine-guns and AK-47 assault rifles.

And other, less traditional weapons are now being used by gangsters on London's streets: there has been a steady increase in the number of incidents in which dogs have been used as 'weapons of choice' by criminals. During one horrific assault on a man by two men and their dogs, the victim lost three fingers. The Met is convinced that dogs are also being used to intimidate as well as cause harm.

In June 2005, south London police launched Operation Cruise Lambeth – a massive drive to combat a 44 per cent rise in firearms offences. Police seized everything from a .44 Magnum to body armour, Samurai swords, a Beretta 9 millimetre – standard issue of the US Marines – Glock machine pistols and Smith & Wessons.

Many illegal arms smugglers prefer compact weapons because they have a high profit ratio. Handguns are usually pretty cheap in their source country but can be sold with a healthy mark-up. In London, real Uzi submachine guns costing £600 to £800 are amongst the most available, although they can go for even more cash out on the streets. There are even at least four copies of the Uzi produced in four other countries.

There is also a limited business in stolen military weapons. Once deactivated, so-called 'repair guns' are often traded by collectors, which can lead to them being modernised and going out on the criminal market place. 'Factories' all over London and the Home Counties are churning out decommissioned guns, often stolen from private collectors and sold at trade fairs and through the classified ads of specialist magazines. Usually, they've been reactivated by re-boring the barrels and replacing the firing pin.

Then there are the 'cloning' or 'off-ticket sale' dealers, who operate in a similar way to car ringers. Stolen firearms 'disappear' by being given the identity of an older decommissioned weapon, which aren't recorded under present laws. In 2005 ex-Special Constable Tony Mitchell was jailed for eight years for supplying criminals with hundreds of guns. He specialised in Mac 10's at £1,100 apiece. Mitchell used his engineering skills to reactivate guns from products bought via mail-order catalogues. One was traced to a 1997 street murder in Brixton, South London, and another was used in the shooting of a police officer by a youth in Manchester's Moss Side.

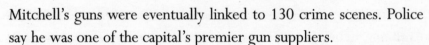

Mitchell's guns were eventually linked to 130 crime scenes. Police say he was one of the capital's premier gun suppliers.

MI6 has no idea how many packages of guns get into this country, but they are aware of larger consignments being brought across the Atlantic by private yachts and dropped into the sea, often near the Kent and Sussex coast. The bundles are usually fitted with remote-controlled flotation tanks and beacons whose signals can be picked up by global positioning systems.

The tentacles of London's underworld reach far and wide. Crime bosses know that the more influence they can have on certain parts of society, the more chance they have of holding onto power. Britain's Labour Party has recently conceded that while published figures show the bulk of the really big donations to their funds, the largest section of their annual income is from small, undeclared, donations under £5,000 to main party political offices.

Now a question mark hangs over the role played by some of London's major league gangsters in the ascendancy of Labour. There is absolutely no suggestion that Labour encouraged these criminals to make donations, but a number of London villains obviously believed such donations might give them some 'leverage'.

Key members of one notorious London based family were recorded during a secret police sting operation, talking about how they'd made donations to the Labour coffers just before the party's landslide election victory in 1997.

The Met later announced it had heard members of the gang talking about donations of between £2,000 and £3,000.

And other London crime bosses claim to have greased the palms of New Labour. By a strange coincidence, Michael Michael – a

notorious London gangster – boasted about his donations to New Labour before he was jailed for six years in December 2001. Michael became a supergrass for the Met after years of operating alongside some of Britain's most notorious criminals. He named more than 100 accomplices in his vast drug and money laundering enterprises, and in return, his sentence was drastically cut from its original 24 years.

Michael told investigators he could pick up the phone and get whatever he needed, including planning applications from a couple of 'tame' local Labour council bosses in North and Central London, where he ran dozens of massage parlours. Michael organised extensive money laundering operations to handle the tens of millions of pounds that came flooding into his coffers from drug deals. He even had his own bureau de change to help 'clean up' the massive sums of cash, and boasted of having a senior Metropolitan Police detective in his pocket, whom he paid £10,000 a week.

Michael's alleged boss, multi-millionaire Mickey Green – known as the Scarlet Pimpernel of Crime and mentioned earlier – had also boasted to associates that his 'Labour connections' helped him get off major drug smuggling charges in Spain. The charges were dropped late in 2001 when Customs officers said they'd lost confidence in Michael's evidence after another defendant in his trial was cleared.

Master criminal Kenny Noye – currently serving life for murdering a motorist during a road-rage incident in 1996 – also claims to have donated thousands of pounds to local Labour officials on his favourite manor in southeast London. In the early Eighties, Noye boasted he had a Labour MP in southeast London 'in his pocket'. This fellow would even stand up in the House of Commons and ask questions relating to requests Noye had made to him.

When that MP died, Noye began looking around for new friends in high places. By the mid-1990s he'd started nurturing a couple of up-and-coming local politicians in southeast London and claimed to have made his last donation to the Labour Party in 1995, just a year before he committed murder. Noye also claimed to have a couple of judges and some senior Masons in his pocket.

Then yet another of Labour's 'dodgy donors' found himself at the centre of an international money-laundering investigation. Wealthy businessman Uri David's Swiss bank account was frozen following an inquiry to track down billions of pounds looted by Nigeria's former military dictatorship. Many believe this 'tradition' goes back to the Harold Wilson years in the Sixties and Seventies, when villains were falling over backwards to bung a bit of cash in Labour's coffers.

Meanwhile, in May 2003 the curse of the Brinks-Mat robbery returned once again to haunt the London underworld. At 5 a.m. on a warm, early spring morning, one of South London's best known old-school villains, George Francis, 63, associate of the Krays and the Great Train Robbery gang, was shot dead in his green Rover 75, registration number LX02 RBV. He'd just pulled up outside his courier business, known as 'Signed, Sealed and Delivered,' in Lynton Road, SE1, shortly before 5 a.m. The killer was believed to have lain in wait until the car came into view. Francis – who'd once been questioned by police about handling some of the £26 million Brinks-Mat gold bullion – died from bullet wounds to the head and chest.

Police soon established that a man – described as white, wearing trainers, jeans and a hooded top – broke into Francis's yard the previous night at about midnight and tampered with the CCTV camera to make sure they would not record the following morning's events. Detective Inspector Damian Allain told reporters at the time: 'It is possible that that individual did not know why he had been asked to interfere with the CCTV camera and so I would appeal to him to come forward and speak to police.'

Seventeen months earlier, Brian Perry, also 63 and also linked to the Brinks-Mat raid, had been shot dead in almost identical circumstances as he arrived for work at his minicab office just a few hundred yards from where Francis was killed (see previous reference).

Georgie Francis had been a wealthy scrap metal dealer and pub landlord with a substantial house in Kent and he'd been linked by police many times to the London underworld. In 1981 he was cleared of involvement in a £2.5 million cannabis smuggling operation, in which a customs officer was shot dead. Two years later he survived after a hitman burst into his pub near Hever Castle, in Kent.

On the fringes of the underworld, with a string of convictions for theft and violence, George Francis first rose to criminal prominence in late 1979 when he became part of a group of armed robbers who decided to move into drug trafficking. Specially converted containers were sent to a shoe factory in Pakistan where millions of pounds of cannabis was hidden by legitimate goods and shipped back to the UK. The first four runs went like clockwork. Francis and other members of the gang began living the good life, buying cars, jewellery and making a show of lighting their cigars with £20 notes in south London pubs.

But when the fifth drug consignment arrived, customs officers were watching. Gang member Lennie 'Teddy Bear' Watkins, driving a lorry containing £2.5 million-worth of cannabis, spotted the surveillance team, prompting Customs Investigator Peter Bennett to move in to make the arrest. Watkins shot Bennett dead.

Watkins was sentenced to life and the rest of the gang were put on trial. The first jury failed to reach a verdict, resulting in a retrial that led to Francis's acquittal. While Francis walked free, several other members of the gang, faced with the same evidence, had pleaded guilty.

However, in August 1990 Francis was found guilty of being involved in smuggling £1 million-worth of cocaine aboard a private yacht. He was sentenced to 16 years. Released in 1999, he started his courier firm and moved into a mansion in Bromley. There is little evidence that he was actively involved in crime at the time of his death.

The murder of George Francis was just another in that long list of killings and shootings linked to Brinks-Mat, Britain's biggest armed robbery. Francis's murder was the ninth in a 20-year saga of betrayal, double-dealing and death in the hunt for the proceeds of Britain's biggest-ever robbery.

Some of those earlier 'Brinks-Mat victims' included Hatton Garden jeweller Solly Nahome, who'd helped melt down hundreds of gold bars on behalf of the Brinks-Mat gang. In December 1998 he was shot dead outside his home in North London. All the other killings with bizarre connections to Brinks-Mat have been covered in more detail elsewhere in this book.

Joe Wilkins, one of the old school of London criminals, is still remembered to this day. He loved playing everyone off against each other: the cops, other mobsters, even poor old Joe Public. They all provided an income to slippery Joe. When one of Scotland Yard's most disastrous sting operations came crashing down, leaving London's police with a £25 million bill after a court case against a suspected money-laundering gang collapsed in the summer of 2003, guess who was being blamed? Old Joe Wilkins.

He undoubtedly played a pivotal role in the operation, despite being an escaped convict, sometime fraudster, Soho vice king, and friend to many of London and Spain's most notorious gangsters. Scotland Yard detectives even set up a money-laundering operation to entrap drugs and tobacco smugglers based in Spain and Gibraltar, using Joe Wilkins to introduce them to the so-called 'major players'.

This particular bizarre tale kicked off in 1992 when Joe went on the run from a low-security prison in East Anglia where he was serving ten years for drugs smuggling. Like so many others, he turned up a few months later on the 'Costa del Sex 'n' Crime'. Then he got tapped up by undercover detectives who wanted his help setting up the sting.

Wilkins was encouraged to introduce UK detectives posing as dodgy businessmen to major villains operating in Spain and Gibraltar. They were lured into 'investing' their dirty money in a laundering scheme that was really a police 'front'. It turned into a five-year operation that snared dozens of London criminals 'washing' money from drugs, tobacco and vice smuggling rackets.

At six-feet three-inches tall, Joe Wilkins was a handsome, larger-than-life character, who favoured Michael Caine-style specs and was married for a time to the glamorous dancer Pearl Read, who later modelled in her bra, at the age of 56, as part of Age Concern's 1998 advertising poster campaign. In 1972, Wilkins had been at the centre of the Soho porn wars and was once shot at in his office by a rival gangster. He took two bullets in the chest, but survived. Then in August 1987, customs officers intercepted a fishing boat called **Danny Boy** off the Sussex coast. On board were 30 sacks of Moroccan hashish, worth £1.5 million. Joe Wilkins and several other men were nicked. And that's how he ended up being back in the slammer for ten years.

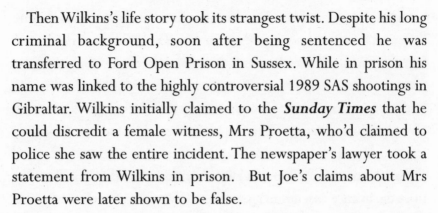

Then Wilkins's life story took its strangest twist. Despite his long criminal background, soon after being sentenced he was transferred to Ford Open Prison in Sussex. While in prison his name was linked to the highly controversial 1989 SAS shootings in Gibraltar. Wilkins initially claimed to the *Sunday Times* that he could discredit a female witness, Mrs Proetta, who'd claimed to police she saw the entire incident. The newspaper's lawyer took a statement from Wilkins in prison. But Joe's claims about Mrs Proetta were later shown to be false.

In the summer of 1991 Wilkins escaped from Ford by literally walking off the premises, only to be rearrested and taken to another low-security prison, Highpoint. In January 1992 he was allowed out on an unaccompanied visit to his dentist in London and fled to Spain. Wilkins was soon living openly in a villa in Estepona, slap-bang in the middle of the Costa world of drug-smuggling and money laundering.

It is alleged that in the early 1990s the Foreign Office had become concerned over allegations that senior politicians in Gibraltar were involved with lucrative drug and tobacco smuggling operations. Wilkins was said to have helped with a top-secret operation, making introductions and identifying leading smugglers. The Met set up Operation Cotton, a money-laundering front to reel in well-known criminals. A senior undercover officer even went to Spain to meet Joe Wilkins, who introduced the detective to various people, which eventually led to bureau de change outlets in Gibraltar. It's alleged they were used for money laundering through what appeared to be a Mayfair-based financial services company, but which in reality was the front for the police sting.

But at the Southwark Crown Court trial in the summer of 2003, Judge George Bathurst Norman described the operation as 'massively illegal' because British law does not allow entrapment.

Charges against all the defendants were eventually dropped. Later, Wilkins became persona non grata with the highly paranoid (and fast depleting) British criminal fraternity in Spain. However he remained on the Costa until his death in early 2005. At least it finally put an end to those numerous questions being asked about why Joe Wilkins had not been extradited or deported from Spain.

In the late spring of 2006 it was revealed that more than half of the most dangerous foreign criminals in London had been released by mistake by the Home Office and now could not be found. More than 1,000 foreign criminals, including killers, rapists, child abusers and gang members, had been released into the community. Prime Minister of the day, Tony Blair, promised 'automatic deportation' in future for jailed foreigners. But Blair's 'get tough' pledge fell apart when it emerged that he was talking about 'a presumption' that foreign prisoners would be deported, rather than guarantee that it would happen in every case.

Overcrowding in London's jails hasn't been helped by a huge increase in foreigners sentenced for crimes committed in this country. This has gone up by more than 150 per cent over the past decade, which has stretched prison staff to the absolute limit. An estimated one in every eight prisoners in England and Wales is now a foreign citizen, and they come from 165 countries. In Wormwood Scrubs, West London, more than half of the 1,200 inmates are foreign – more than at any other prison in the country.

The war on crime in London is an uphill struggle. The Met Police have had a tough time implementing the wishes of the Assets Recovery Agency, although in June, 2005, they did manage to freeze £9 million of assets of a London criminal. The ARA contended that property and other assets held by the man had been

273

acquired as a result of unlawful conduct linked to a classic 'carousel fraud', a form of VAT scam. The Agency claimed that 99 per cent of the business conducted by the man's company, of which he is a director, involved fraudulent trades. Assets frozen by the ARA included a £1.2 million property in Knightsbridge, a £1.8 million villa in Marbella, Spain, and two large plots of land at the Emirates Hills Golf Club in Dubai.

In East London on 3 September 2005, police raided two houses which doubled up as sophisticated 'factories' producing equipment used to capture the details of credit and debit cards being used in cash machines around the country. Officers from the Dedicated Cheque and Plastic Crime Unit (DCPCU) liaised with Forest Gate Police following the arrest of five men and one woman, plus four males and a female at a separate location in Beckton. All the suspects were charged with conspiracy to defraud.

Equipment found at the Forest Gate house would have enabled the suspects to capture electronic information stored on a card after use at a cash machine. There were also numerous laptops and personal computers, together with counterfeit cards and thousands of compromised card numbers. The criminals were then targeting cash machines at supermarkets and petrol stations, which were under less supervision than automated telling machines at bank branches.

The creation of the DCPCU to handle card fraud has helped to reduce losses after a record high of £160.4 million in 2001. The banking industry and ATM suppliers have also become far more diligent. These days, most ATMs are positioned in well-lit locations and CCTV cameras scan the area to deter fraudulent activity. But with a dummy card and the cloned PIN code, a victim's bank account can still be emptied.

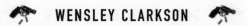

Levels of sophistication are increasing all the time when it comes to these sorts of scams. In October 2003 a London gang stole thousands of pounds from cash machines using a hi-tech trick that left bank users unaware they'd even been robbed. The thieves used micro-scanners and cameras on specific hole-in-the-wall machines. This allowed them to clone cards and record PIN codes without having to be anywhere near the cash machine.

The revival of so-called 'long firm' frauds in London is causing major headaches for the Met Police. This is when criminals set up a business dealing in items with a rapid turnover. Business is swiftly built up and lines of credit established with suppliers. In fact all this credit is gained quickly so they can be disposed of quickly for cash. The fraudsters then disappear without paying for the goods before there is time for creditors to be alerted. It's something that has been around since the days of the Krays and the Richardsons, but with the advent of the internet it has made an underworld comeback.

Internet gambling threatens to change the entire face of crime in London. A special Met police unit has been formed to investigate illegal gambling websites, many of which are run by London-based gangs. Organised criminals are using the net to set up illegal, 'virtual reality' casinos. By 2007 gamblers had spent around £12 billion in virtual casinos using their credit cards to place bets, and a large percentage of that was to fraudulent sites. Gamblers giving their credit card details are often putting themselves at financial risk and there is no guarantee that online games such as roulette and blackjack are actually being played fairly on some of these sites.

Criminal gangs in London often operate these illegal gambling sites in order to launder the proceeds of drugs. All this online

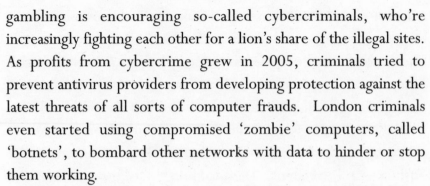

gambling is encouraging so-called cybercriminals, who're increasingly fighting each other for a lion's share of the illegal sites. As profits from cybercrime grew in 2005, criminals tried to prevent antivirus providers from developing protection against the latest threats of all sorts of computer frauds. London criminals even started using compromised 'zombie' computers, called 'botnets', to bombard other networks with data to hinder or stop them working.

At least 30 per cent of the spam or junk e-mail travelling the net comes from hijacked computers infected by viruses. However, these latest waves of computer virus attacks are not the work of geeky teens but well organised gangs of virus writers. In London, the lure of big bucks and the excitement of developing something new that could earn them a name in the cybercriminal community are motivating people to become virus writers.

'The money is coming from the spammers and we are seeing evidence that they are starting to employ the best breed of virus writers to help them,' said Mr Paul Wood, chief analyst at an internet security firm.

These cybercriminals can even avoid detection by using antivirus software and they routinely include on their sites a code that will either disable antivirus updating mechanisms on infected machines or remove antivirus software completely. Experts recently reported a five-fold increase in the amount of malicious software designed to steal financial information. Another trick is to send thousands of false requests for information to websites in a bid to paralyse them and halt trading. While an attack is under way, it can make it impossible for the public to access the sites.

A classic example of this was when a completely legal online betting site was attacked by criminals who bombarded their site and then threatened to e-mail child pornography under its name, unless it paid 7,000 euros (£4,863). London computer crime investigators have called it a 'sinister development'. The blackmailing e-mail sent to the London-based gambling site came from an internet address in Serbia. It read: 'You have time until 5 p.m. your local time. I will now start an attack for one hour. This will be 1/20 of the power I can do.'

It went on to demand that the money be paid into a specific offshore bank account. The gambling site never made the payment and eventually repelled the computer attack but it was a chilling insight of how cyber crime could well develop over the next few years.

Cyber gangsters – many of whom are believed to be aged between 16 and 26 – are almost like street gangs and seem to give adolescents a sense of belonging and help improve their self-esteem. Many of these cyber gangs have flooded into London from the former Soviet Union, where a high number of technically sophisticated but out-of-work programmers are based. These gangsters can earn millions by dropping viruses and trojans onto computers of unsuspecting home users, siphoning money from online bank accounts, trading stolen identities, distributing porn, and blackmailing firms.

More than 90 per cent of malicious codes now circulating around the internet are designed for criminal gain. The total amount of financial losses worldwide resulting from cybercrime exceeded $411 billion at the end of 2006. 'There's a lot of money on the internet,' says one expert. 'And it's very easy to develop a trojan or web page that looks like a bank's website.'

Corporations in London are believed to be losing billions through illegal hackers contracted by rival businesses stealing vital data including customer lists, contracts, marketing strategy and finances. Few complain to the police in case the publicity undermines their stock value. Many of these so-called 'black hat hackers' often get away with their crime and some are even hired by their targets to trace other intruders and beef up security. The cost of dealing with such attacks between 2005 and 2006 by disinfecting computers, investigating who has committed crimes and securing networks and machines was £195 million in London alone.

Cyber gangsters create a 'zombie army' – a network of thousands of compromised computers – a lucrative asset that they can hire out to illegal spammers and criminal gangs wanting to extort money from companies facing similar attacks to those mentioned above. In July 2005 the UK's National Hi-Tech Crime Unit, working with its Russian Ministry of Internal Affairs equivalent, Division K, smashed a gang from St Petersburg and southwest Russia responsible for extorting thousands of pounds from UK online companies reliant on their website availability. The gang had demanded between $10,000 and $40,000 to stop their computer attacks.

Meanwhile, there are still crimes committed by London villains that owe more to the so-called 'good old days' of cops 'n' robbers more than 30 years ago. Take the Millennium Dome raid on 8 November 2000, which seemed to show that London's criminals were more than capable of going back to basics, even though they did ultimately fail to steal £200 million-worth of diamonds on display at the controversial tourist attraction in South London. With a powerboat standing by on the Thames as their means of escape, the robbers smashed their way into the Dome with a JCB digger before setting off smoke bombs and ammonia gas in the Dome's diamond vault as they donned gas masks and protective clothing.

The gang members, from London and Kent, were also armed

with tools and automatic guns. Later it was claimed the diamond collection was virtually priceless and any effort to sell any of the pieces would probably have failed because they were so well known. However, the Met Police were watching the gang's every move after mounting a surveillance operation following an earlier tip-off from an informant. As the police swarmed into the Dome and arrested all the would-be robbers, fellow officers arrested the man in the boat. Another member of the gang, thought to be monitoring police radio frequencies, was detained on the north shore of the Thames opposite the Dome.

On Monday, 18 February 2002, the Old Bailey heard that the audacious plot had been months in the planning, but so too had a Flying Squad operation, code-named Magician. It was the biggest surveillance operation in the squad's history, and the judge in the case later made a special point of commending the way it was carried out.

Four men were convicted of conspiracy to rob, and another was convicted of conspiracy to steal. They were jailed for a total of 71 years. A sixth man was later jailed for four years after pleading guilty to conspiracy to steal.

The police work that led to the Dome convictions was aptly summed up by one detective: 'The operation was in the finest traditions of the world-famous Flying Squad.' There's no doubt it brought the squad back into the forefront of the fight against organised crime after many years in the wilderness.

The squad, renamed SCD7, now has a female commander as part of its new image, and informants are referred to as 'human covert intelligence sources'. But suspicions of corruption resurfaced after allegations by former Met commissioner Sir Paul Condon that 'bent coppers' still existed in the squad. It was claimed that some detectives still regularly went into partnership with criminals. In 2001 three Flying Squad detectives were each jailed for seven years after a police informant was 'sprung' from prison to take part in a robbery with the tacit approval of those officers.

The glamour of the Dome Robbery (even though it was a failure) sparked a professional comeback for armed blaggers, although the 'good old days' when they'd charge across a pavement brandishing sawn-offs belonged to a bygone era. In February 2002 two robbers got away with £4.6 million in dollars and other currencies stolen from Heathrow Airport despite supposedly intense security following the 9/11 terrorist attacks. The cash was en route to New York from Bahrain on two British Airways flights. The men hijacked a British Airways van containing the cash, forced the driver out of the vehicle, threw him to the ground and bound his wrists. The two-man team then transferred cash boxes containing the currency into another similar looking British Airways van before driving out of the airport undetected. However, thanks to inside information the two men were later caught and jailed.

Then in May 2004 a white Transit van containing a gang of robbers rammed through the shutters of the Swiss Port Cargo warehouse on the outer perimeter of Heathrow. The bandits emerged brandishing at least one firearm and other weapons, including knives and cudgels. They planned to steal a large quantity of precious metal – said in one report to be gold bullion – and banknotes worth a total of £40 million, which had just been delivered to the warehouse.

But within seconds of the raid, Flying Squad officers – backed up by a team from the Met's specialist SO19 firearms unit – fired baton rounds at the van and instantly disabled it. Six men were arrested, while two others escaped after hijacking another van and

forcing the driver to take them out of the airport towards Stanwell, West London. The van and its driver were later safely recovered. The Met operation, code-named Cartwright, successfully thwarted the robbers who were on the verge of pulling off an even bigger haul than the notorious Brinks-Mat gang in 1983.

During the first couple of years of the new millennium, 'carjackings' also came into vogue. Stolen luxury vehicles – especially 4x4s – had a roaring market all over the rest of Europe and the Middle East as well as certain parts of Africa, and it was undoubtedly gangs of criminals 'stealing to order' who were behind this rash of new crimes.

Twenty-five-year-old estate agent Tim Robinson was stabbed to death in South London in front of his fiancée as he parked his car outside his home. His two teenage assailants were only after his £30,000 Audi. There is absolutely no doubt they were working on behalf of a gang of car 'handlers' who'd ship the car abroad within hours of the theft.

A few days later, in Dulwich, South London, a woman was violently pushed out of her BMW sports car at night. In another incident, a mother got out of her £45,000 four-wheel drive car for to drop off a letter, only to turn and see two thieves driving away with her screaming children inside. The children were released a short distance away, but neither the car nor the offenders were ever traced.

Meanwhile, back on the drugs scene, 34 people, mainly from Colombia, were jailed in London in 2001 after police smashed a highly organised Colombian cocaine importation and money laundering ring – the biggest ever uncovered in the UK. The arrests affected the Class A drugs trade to such an extent that it led to a reduction in the quality of cocaine available on the streets of London.

But despite this impressive work by police, there is no doubt the Colombian cartels have made huge inroads into London's cocaine trade over the past 20 years. It's only when actual arrests are made that any hint of the sheer scale of their operations come to the surface. In 2003 the Met decided that instead of going for seizures of drugs and money seizures they'd concentrate on those responsible for the distribution.

As a result, that same year 12 men were arrested after police smashed a multi-million pound drugs ring following raids by more than 100 officers on 19 addresses in London and Kent. The operation was the result of a two-year probe into a Colombian cartel supplying two London-based gangs of criminals. They'd trafficked 530 kg of cocaine with an estimated street value of £60 million across London since 1998. Seizures made in other raids included 233 kg of cocaine, 50 kg of heroin, 7 kg of amphetamines, 20 kg of cannabis plus £233,500 in cash and two semiautomatic handguns.

The cocaine came from Columbia via Jamaica and then into mainland Spain and through Europe before reaching London. Although three drug gangs had effectively been taken off the streets, it was likely the cartels would soon find other people to replace them. The Met hailed another 'breakthrough' with the conviction of another Columbian gang that had smuggled at least 38 million pounds-worth of cocaine into Britain in 2005. In all, 48 people – 34 in the UK and 14 in Columbia – were sentenced to a total of nearly 400 years in prison following court appearances.

Turkish, Bulgarian and Kosovan Albanian gangsters are rumoured to have linked up with Czech couriers to supply London-based drug dealers with new, even more potent supplies of heroin. Police and customs officers are powerless to act against many of the gang leaders, who remain back home in places such as Turkey. A classic example is gangster Gungor Tekin, who played football with the Turkish clubs Galatassaray and Fenerbahche, and later in Canada, well before the enormous explosion in soccer wages. Following retirement, Tekin set up a business exporting London 'black cabs' to Turkey and also dabbled unsuccessfully in the property market. Then Turkish gangsters in North London suggested to Tekin that heroin was a simple way to recoup his losses, so in 2000 he set himself up in a flat off the Edgware Road, in the heart of Central London.

Tekin employed a young Turk called Mustafa Mus as his driver and translator and linked up with a third man, Yucel Konakli, who lived in the London Turkish heartlands of Haringey, North London. Tekin flew regularly between Turkey and Northern Cyprus where he dealt with at least one of the six main crime organisations running the heroin trade there. Eventually he set up a 70 kilogram smuggling operation which he believed would earn his gang in excess of £6 million. However one of contacts brought Tekin to the attention of Customs and Excise investigators, who put him under surveillance.

They observed as Tekin hired a Czech man called Jan Jisl to drive the vehicle with Tekin's heroin across Europe. Jisl travelled with his wife and child to give the impression he was on a family shopping holiday. When Jisl disembarked at the Kent port of Ramsgate in a Czech-registered minibus, his every move was being watched by the UK Customs Investigators.

Jisl eventually met his Turkish contacts at a nearby Travel Lodge hotel, on the M2 motorway in Kent, still unaware he was being shadowed. They were all eventually arrested in London by detectives later that night. In 2005, at Kingston Crown Court, Tekin was jailed for 23 years, Konakli for 18, Jisl for 16 and Mus for 11.

Another driver from Jisl's home town in Czechoslovakia was also arrested in 2005 and jailed for 25 years. That area of the Czech republic has become a centre for exiled Kosovan Albanians who provide the heroin connection from Turkey. Kosovan Albanians regularly rent houses in villages outside Prague for their deliveries from Turkey. Couriers then take the drugs on to Germany, Belgium, Spain, and the Netherlands before arriving in London.

In another example of international gangster cooperation, London-based Turkish drug traffickers now use Bulgarian-organised crime gangs to protect their shipments en route through Europe to the capital. There has been a vast increase in the use of containers to smuggle heroin following the seizures of lorries with Turkish origins.

Naturally, this virtually nonstop influx of heavy drugs into the capital has many disturbing knock-on effects. The Met estimates that London's foreign gangs are carrying out a kidnap every day. These gangs regularly use violence and torture to extract ransoms connected to drug deals. London police even have their own specialist kidnap unit – the only one in the UK – which works on nearly 100 'live kidnaps' each year. However, in most cases detectives only got to hear about the snatches after money is exchanged and the victim freed.

Police say that many of London's foreign gangs are a law unto themselves when it comes to the business of kidnapping. And it's not always big money that's handed over, either. In 2005 Lithuanian criminals snatched one of their fellow countrymen from a London pub, beat him senseless and then used his mobile phone to demand a £200 ransom from his family. When detectives eventually traced the victim he was so badly beaten he had to spend weeks on a life support machine before recovering.

Officers from the Met's kidnap unit are on standby 24 hours a day and have an impressive 100 per cent success rate in recovering victims alive. But prosecuting the gangs is much harder and the prosecution rate for kidnap is just 20 per cent.

Christmas Eve 2003: a gun-wielding African-Caribbean gang seized another African-Caribbean man in his mid-20s in East London, in connection with drug debt. The kidnappers tortured the victim, pistol whipped him and burned his back with a steam iron and then demanded £10,000 to £15,000 cash from his family. Police eventually rescued the victim, but the gang were never prosecuted because the victim refused to give evidence against them.

Over in Southall, West London, in March 2005, a man and a woman pulled up in a car beside an 11-year-old boy walking home from school to ask directions. They forced the boy into the car, took him to a nearby house and contacted his family to demand £40,000.

The boy was locked in a squalid room strewn with rotting rubbish for 26 hours and then threatened with death as he pleaded down the phone with his father for the money. He was only freed after police arrested one of the kidnappers who revealed where the boy was being held. Although physically unharmed, the youngster still suffers panic attacks and nightmares. Three men – Ravideep Singh Babu, 24, Amerjit Singh Dhariwar, 30, Gurnham Singh Dhanoa, 22, and a 20-year-old woman, Ayisha Zahoor Choudrey, were eventually jailed for kidnap, false imprisonment and blackmail.

There's a small, but growing number of kidnappings of wealthy people, purely for financial gain. Just before midnight on 20 February 2005 the family of a 50-year-old millionaire Asian businessman received a phone call saying he'd been kidnapped and demanding £500,000 for his release. It transpired the victim had been grabbed as he parked his car in East Ham, East London, and bundled into the back of a Range Rover. He was bound and gagged, transferred to a Transit van and taken to an industrial estate in Essex. His wrists and ankles were tied with tape, his arms pinned to his body and tape put over his eyes and mouth. Police eventually rescued the victim, and Danny Gibney, 31, from Essex, was arrested at the scene and later jailed for seven years for kidnap and false imprisonment.

In another recent case, a London man was targeted after he bragged about the profit he and his brother had made on a property sale. He was lured into buying a quantity of drugs at a railway station on the evening,, but was instead forced into a white van. The victim was tied up and threatened with torture by men who used the aliases of *Reservoir Dogs* characters Mr White, Mr Blue and Mr Black. He later said he was taken to an address in East London while the kidnappers made threatening phone calls to his family.

The family called police while negotiating to pay tens of thousands of pounds for the man's release. When they later dropped off the cash in a bin in East London, police waited and watched until a man collected the money. He was then followed. The victim was eventually dumped, still blindfolded, many miles away. He had bruises all over his body, a burn on his arm from a lighter and sore wrists caused by shackles. Police later stormed a flat opposite the cash drop-off point where they found a woman counting the money. She leapt from the window but was caught nearby.

The excessive use of firearms on the streets of London in recent years has provoked a deadly response from the police on occasions. In Edgware, northwest London, in April 2005, Azelle Rodney, 24, of West London, a passenger in the rear seat of a car, died when police opened fire on the car. The vehicle had been under surveillance by the Met as a result of intelligence which suggested the driver and passengers were in possession of firearms. Three loaded and fully operational guns were later recovered from the car. An investigation followed but the Crown Prosecution Service said there was insufficient evidence to prosecute the police. The two other men in the car with Rodney later admitted firearms offences.

The so-called 'Turkish gangs' (actually a generic term, because many are Cypriot or Kurdish) have embraced London's new criminal habits. Although drugs remain their number one activity, the Turkish gangs cleverly use the same smuggling and distribution networks to move large numbers of illegal immigrants and stolen vehicles. Profits are laundered though complex financial transactions, often via Turkish and Cypriot banks.

In 2002 open warfare feuding between the Turkish gangs, who were London's main heroin suppliers, ended in deadly consequences in the 'Battle of Green Lanes' in North London, at 6 p.m. on 9 November. Forty men armed with guns, knives and baseball bats clashed outside the Dostlar Lokal Club. By the time police arrived, 21 men had been injured, and 43-year-old Alisan Dogan, an innocent bystander, was fatally stabbed. And it all stemmed from problems within the Turkish and Kurdish gangs who control the majority of the heroin importation to the UK.

Tensions first began when teenagers trying to withdraw their gang membership were threatened with death if they dared leave. Then the battle proper kicked off when local entrepreneurs, tired of extortion by local criminals, attacked a gang that had beaten a store owner who refused to pay for protection. Police later found an AK-47 assault rifle, five automatic pistols and a large amount of ammunition linked to the gangs when they raided properties following the street battle. Ironically, the murder of that innocent man in the 'Battle of Green Lanes' triggered a new alliance of interests between the Kurdish and Turkish communities and the police.

The death and mayhem on Green Lanes also sparked a chain reaction which eventually ended the reign of London's heroin godfather, Abdullah Baybasin. The 45-year-old, who lived in Edgware, North London, was jailed for 22 years in 2005 after pleading guilty to charges of conspiracy to blackmail and to pervert the course of justice. He was also convicted of conspiracy to supply heroin. Woolwich Crown Court heard that he used a gang to racketeer, import drugs and instil fear into London's Kurdish community. Detective Chief Inspector Robin Plummer, of the National Crime Squad, said after the case: 'Threats were made with firearms, they'd quite often go with armoured machetes, baseball bats and smash premises up. People were kidnapped against their will, brought to premises, then the threats were made.'

The Baybasin family had been building a London-based network since the late 1990s capable of facilitating the majority of heroin trafficked into Britain.

In 2001 younger brother Abdullah took over the family drugs empire after elder brother Husseyin Baybasin was arrested in the Netherlands and jailed for 20 years for his organised crime activities, including conspiracy to murder and drug smuggling. The sentence was raised to life when he appealed. Despite the fact that Abdullah was confined to a wheelchair, the Baybasin clan's reputation ensured few people from within their own community were willing to openly challenge their activities.

In early 2003 Abdullah Baybasin's operational HQ at the back of

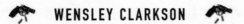

a shop on Green Lanes was fitted with hidden cameras and microphones. Surveillance revealed beatings of their own members to enforce ruthless discipline, the making of petrol bombs to intimidate businesses, and Abdullah Baybasin holding court like a London version of Don Corleone.

Ecstasy is the drug of choice for hundreds of thousands of Londoners every weekend. 'E' was introduced into Britain 20 years ago as the ultimate party drug. But the price of has plunged so dramatically in recent years that pills now cost between 40p and 70p compared with £6 to £7. Prices have been slashed because production is now a sophisticated, worldwide business worth billions of pounds.

According to a United Nations report, 125 tonnes of ecstasy is sold every year and the ecstasy and amphetamines market combined is reckoned to be worth in the region of $65 billion a year. As a result, London's gangsters have stepped up their own supply and it's even estimated that there are numerous ecstasy factories capable of producing up to a million tablets of the drug each week.

The Triads (see below) have virtually cornered the market in the production of the raw materials needed to make ecstasy in London. They've used China's burgeoning trade relationships with the rest of the world to distribute the required chemicals across the globe. The only chemical companies in the world still producing E's most important single component, PMK, are all in China, where they are officially registered as producing perfume. Triad gangs in London run front companies which buy the chemical and ship it to ecstasy factories across the globe, providing profits of up to 3,000 per cent. An ecstasy lab turning out thousands of pills each week can be constructed inside an average sized toilet for about £4,000.

That conveniently brings us back to the Triads, who've spent the past 30 years turning one small district of London's West End – the so-called 'Golden Mile' in Soho's Chinatown – into their own special territory. There's lots of mythical stuff around about these gangsters suggesting they started as a resistance movement to China's Manchu emperors more than 400 years ago. In fact they developed much more recently than that when the Japanese invaded several major Chinese cities during World War Two. The Triads thrived by working for the Japanese, who brought them together under an association called the 'Hing Ah Kee Kwan' (Asia Flourishing Organisation). They were even used to help police the streets of Hong Kong, especially to prevent anti-Japanese activity.

They were first named Triads by the ruling British in Hong Kong because of the triangular shape of the emblem of the Chinese 'secret society' – said to symbolise the unity between Heaven, Earth, and Man. But since the end of the last world war, menacing groups of criminals have sprung up under the Triad banner. The Triad gangs, whose language and family history ties them to their ancestors' villages in mainland China, are known specifically as 'Snakeheads'.

In London at the start of the 20th century the first area to be known as Chinatown was located on the banks of the Thames, in the Limehouse district. The Chinese residents served the Chinese sailors who arrived in the docks, and the area was notorious for its (legal) opium dens and slum housing. Then in 1934 much of the old housing was demolished leaving just a small number of elderly Chinese still living in the area.

Following the Second World War, Chinese food became so popular that there was a flood of immigrants from Hong Kong, which led to large numbers of Chinese restaurants being opened all over London and, eventually, the rest of the UK. In the 1960s the present Chinatown began to emerge in Soho off Shaftesbury Avenue, with Gerrard Street as the main thoroughfare.

Today, London's Triads are regularly also linked to local youth gangs as well as the infiltration of business and government organisations. Seven major organisations exist under the Triad umbrella. They are: the Sun Yee On Triad, the Wo Group, the 14K Triad, the Luen Group, the Big Circle Gang, the United Bamboo Gang, and the Four Seas Gang. The Sun Yee On has at least 56,000 members worldwide, including 1,000 in London. The capital's Triads are heavily involved in illegal immigration which has become an alternative to drug trafficking because it provides multi-billion dollar profits without the same severe penalties if caught.

The roundabout trip from China to the United States or Europe can take as long as two years, and the Triads charge up to £20,000. Flying directly into Britain with sophisticated, forged documents can cost as much as £32,000. The Snakehead gangs from the Chinese mainland make vast profits by using rundown cargo vessels where 'passengers' are forced to live for months in overcrowded squalor.

London's Triad gangs sometimes even arrange transportation of illegals through their own travel agencies, which schedule connection routes depending on where in China that person is coming from. Those London groups are frequently connected to other Triads based in Taiwan, which boasts the most-feared section of Chinese organised crime, rumoured to be in total control of transportation networks by air or sea.

But life certainly comes cheap as far as the Triads are concerned. When they hit rival gang members it usually goes unreported – and unsolved – because of their mafia-style secrecy and the fears of victims and witnesses. They rake in vast profits from protection rackets on restaurants and businesses, prostitution, fraud, illegal immigration and illicit gambling. They also rely on home-grown killers to strike fear into the community.

Take the classic case of Triad hitman Wai Hen Cheung – known as 'George' in the badlands of Soho – who was specially initiated into the Triads to kill people. George had his finger pricked so as to bleed into into a glass of wine before he was accepted by the clan. Then he joined a gun club in Chingford, Essex, to learn how to handle lethal weapons. He was even sent off to a job in a Chinese takeaway on the Channel island of Guernsey so that his face wouldn't be known around Soho while he was training for his first hit. George later shot Hong Kong businessman Ying Kit Lam, 31, in a contract job intended to punish him and deter others from crossing the deadly Triads. But Lam lived, although he was crippled for life, and George the Triad-trained hitman was sent down for life in 2000.

So, violence is always bubbling just beneath the surface when it comes to the Triads. In the summer of 2006 a man was shot dead in a crowded bar in London's Chinatown, sparking fears of a new Triad war. The victim, Chinese and in his late thirties, was drinking with two friends in the BRB bar in Gerrard Street when a gunman walked in and shot him twice at point-blank range. The killer then calmly strolled back into the mingling crowds outside.

Just a few yards from that shooting, a man had been hacked to death by a gang with machetes five years earlier, in 2001. Experts presume these brutal attacks are part of a gang battle for control of the restaurant trade, gambling dens and smuggling rackets in the West End. Tensions in the area are riding high as the home-grown Triads, who've controlled Chinatown for decades, increasingly clash with rival Snakehead gangs from mainland China who are appearing in the capital with alarming regularity. It seems they've woken up to the potential of Chinatown's protection rackets. These gangs are heavily armed and have a penchant for torturing rivals and holding them prisoner in Britain until their families in China pay ransoms.

Another shooting in Chinatown came amid claims by police that Snakehead gangs had smuggled a total of 200,000 illegal immigrants into Britain over the last ten years. The Met genuinely fears that London could go the same way as New York's Chinatown, where the Snakeheads carried out a bloody takeover of territory previously run by the Triads in the late 1990s.

On 18 June 2000, port officials at Dover discovered the bodies of 54 London-bound Chinese men and four Chinese women in a sealed lorry driven by Dutchman Perry Wacker. The jury at Maidstone Crown Court in the subsequent trial of Wacker – who was sentenced to 14 years for manslaughter and conspiracy to smuggle immigrants into the UK – heard how customs officials were confronted by a 'sea of motionless bodies' when they opened the back of the lorry during a random check.

Only two immigrants survived the five-hour sea journey from Belgium to the UK after Wacker, from Rotterdam, closed the only air vent on the side of the container to avoid detection. Co-accused Ying Guo, of South Woodford, Essex, was jailed for six years for conspiring to smuggle illegal immigrants into Britain. People-trafficking is the 21st century version of the slave trade.

Organised immigration crime in London has been tackled through Operation Maxim – set up as the Met's response to the deaths of those London-bound Chinese migrants in 2000. Maxim is a joint effort by the Metropolitan Police, UK Immigration Service, UK Passport Service and the Crown Prosecution Service.

In the summer of 2006 there was further, chilling evidence of just how high the stakes are for those foreigners willing to risk all to be smuggled into Britain. Two immigrants died of heat exhaustion when they hid in the tiny compartment of a lorry travelling from Europe to London. The pair were found by the side of the A12 road in Essex in June, 2006, and were among five Asians who'd been driven across Europe in scorching temperatures during the summer heatwave. A third man survived, but as one Albanian criminal later told me: 'He won't say a word because he knows the gangs will come after him if he informs the police.'

The Met openly admits that London-based criminal gangs trading in people and fake IDs are now 'out of control'. In November 2003, five men who first started helping illegal immigrants into the UK in 1990 were given stiff jail sentences. This particular smuggling operation was based in the Punjab state of India, and the gang promised illegal immigrants a new life in the West for up to £8,000. They even provided them with fake passports with which to fly to the UK. At one stage the smugglers brought up to ten people into the country each week and, over 13 years, brought thousands to the UK. English lessons were provided – as well as free legal representation if they were unlucky enough to get caught. Ringleader Sarwan Deo, from East London, received the longest sentence of seven-and-a-half years, but was reckoned by police to have made millions of pounds from the operation.

More and more of these smuggling rackets have emerged from within London's foreign communities. In 2005 police arrested 19 people following dawn raids in London and Lincolnshire as part of a crackdown on the alleged smuggling of Turkish Kurds into the UK. Eight of the suspects were eventually charged with aiding people-smuggling. The Operation – called Bluesky – involved officers from six European countries working closely with the Met.

The network allegedly smuggled people into Britain in groups of up to 20 a time, hidden in cars, vans, lorries and aircraft.

Those smuggled in from the Kurdish areas of Turkey paid between £3,000 and £5,000 and faced months of travelling before being passed on to gang members in several European countries. Often staying in safe houses before being smuggled into the UK in cramped conditions, many of them found low-paid, black-market menial jobs in North London's Turkish community. The racket earned its ringleaders millions of pounds, much of which was reinvested in cafés, snooker halls and nightclubs.

The face of London's crime culture changed drastically following the 9/11 terrorist attacks in America. The capital even became known as 'Londonistan' because of its prime location as a base for both home-grown and foreign radical extremists. Rumours abounded that London's mosques were frequented by talent-spotters and recruiters looking for sympathetic Muslims prepared to take up arms.

It's certainly true that London is seen as an 'important target' for terror gangs because of Britain's close links to the US-led Iraqi campaign and the war on terrorism in Afghanistan, combined with the capital's role as a melting pot of different religions and languages. But for whatever reasons, the Met is convinced Islamic militant groups are raising millions of pounds for terrorism through credit card fraud.

London's 7/7 bombings in 2005 seemed to be a classic example of London's links to extremism, although intelligence services were insisting in the weeks before the attacks that there was no group capable of bombing the capital in such a devastating manner.

So when Al Qaeda-linked suicide bombers blew up three London underground trains and a bus, killing more than 50 people, it caused reverberations throughout the nation. Some London-born Muslims have also travelled to the Middle East to undertake bombings in Iraq and Israel. Meanwhile London, with its large Arab population, has become the natural home for these terrorists.

In May 2002, Faraj Farj Hassan, the suspected leader of an Islamic terrorist cell with links to Italy, was arrested in Harrow, West London, where he'd taken refuge with a relative who had political asylum. Hassan, 23, was arrested for immigration offences and held in Belmarsh high security prison until his extradition to Italy. Then in April 2004 London's pivotal role in the world of terrorism was reinforced when 29-year-old Somali-born Cabdullah Ciise was arrested in Milan days after arriving from London where he'd fled to escape Italian investigators months earlier. The Italians suspected him of financing a terror cell involved in the car bomb attack on Israeli tourists in Mombasa, Kenya, in November 2002. According to Italian court documents, Ciise transferred money from Great Britain to Somalia through Dubai.

In November 2004 an Algerian-born British national from West London was arrested after travelling to Poland. He was the subject of an Algerian arrest warrant alleging his involvement in a terrorist group, believed to have been involved in a rocket attack against the Baghdad hotel where Paul Wolfowitz, the American deputy Secretary of Defence, was staying at the time.

Twenty North Africans were arrested in London in 2004 on suspicion of planning a terrorist attack. It later emerged that ten of them were asylum seekers, which sparked an urgent review of 3,000 other Algerian asylum cases, especially when it was discovered that many of them had gone missing. Were they in terrorist sleeper cells waiting to hit targets in the UK? It is believed that the Algerian Armed Islamic Group (GIA) has cleverly exploited the UK's asylum system to set up self-financed London-based terrorist networks.

One GIA member, Ahmad Ressam, was arrested with £5,000 on him after being connected to a planned bombing attack on Los Angeles Airport in 2000. A GIA-inspired bombing campaign in Paris, also in 2000, is believed to have been planned from the Finsbury Park mosque in North London. Weapons and bomb-making equipment was hidden in Belgium.

Terrorists use forged documents and give false asylum stories to pass themselves off as genuine asylum seekers. Once in London they are absorbed into a world of informal housing and forged documents. A terrorist can have his photograph put into a stolen British passport for as little as £500.

When police raided the infamous Finsbury Park mosque in North London in 2002 they found dozens of forged and stolen French and Belgian ID cards. These would have enabled anyone to travel to and from Britain. The French version, using technology 50 years out of date, is said to be simple to duplicate. More than two million British passports had been issued overseas in the past six years.

On 20 July 2005 – just a couple of weeks after the 7/7 outrage in the capital – the Met uncovered another plot to set off bombs on three underground trains and a bus. The bombs' detonators fired, but didn't trigger the explosives. There were no serious casualties. The following day a man ignored police warnings to stop and was shot dead in a South London Tube station. He was said to have appeared to have been of south Asian appearance. Yet two days later the man was identified as a Brazilian citizen completely innocent of any involvement in terrorism. A victim of our times.

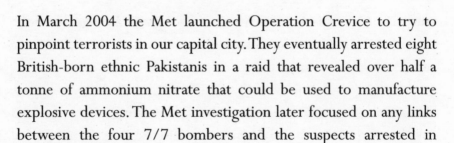

In March 2004 the Met launched Operation Crevice to try to pinpoint terrorists in our capital city. They eventually arrested eight British-born ethnic Pakistanis in a raid that revealed over half a tonne of ammonium nitrate that could be used to manufacture explosive devices. The Met investigation later focused on any links between the four 7/7 bombers and the suspects arrested in Operation Crevice.

Since the 9/11 attacks, a security dragnet in Pakistan yielded the arrest of over 800 suspected al-Qaeda associates. Many of them had relatives and friends based in London, which has led security experts to presume that many terrorists remain at liberty on the streets of the capital.

The Met and intelligence services have hundreds of London terror suspects logged on their database following domestic and foreign investigations. The London 7/7 suicide bombers were all subjects of this country, which suggests that terrorists live and work in our midst. They are not necessarily foreign fanatics sent here to cause death and destruction. They are British citizens.

But equally, London criminals whose families originally come from Islam nations are not necessarily all terrorists. Many are simply 'in it for the money'. The Met says that Somali gangsters are 'an acknowledged criminal presence' in the capital. They dominate the Southall area of West London and have even in recent years spread into suburban areas of the Thames Valley. Like so many immigrant gangsters, most of their victims are their fellow countrymen.

Much of the latest Somali gang activity centres on the narcotic Qat, a drug that is legal in the UK but illegal in the US. So-called Qat Wars between Somali gangsters have ended in violent clashes on the capital's streets. When four Somalis were arrested over the shooting of a policewoman in Yorkshire in 2005, it was of no surprise to London detectives, who'd been warning about the Somali gangs' menace for years and how they were 'branching out' into robberies.

One of the biggest computer scams of recent years was originated by Nigerians. This online fraud – dubbed the 419 scam – demanded advance fees for lottery wins and bank details so that large sums of prize money could be shared. The 419 scam is named after the Nigerian penal code section criminalising it, and usually involves the recipient being told by e-mail that they've won a prize or a lottery, and their bank account details are needed to help claim the money from Nigeria. Naturally, the victim has to first send some money and the details of his account to pay for the paperwork before the prize is released.

One man who was tricked out of his entire savings by a 419 scam in the Czech Republic burst into the Nigerian Embassy in Prague and shot dead a diplomat after realising that he'd been conned. Many other victims, embarrassed by their gullibility and humiliation, don't even report the crime to the authorities. Others, having lost so much themselves, become 'part of the gang' in a bid to get back their stolen money.

Today, many of the Nigerian gangs perpetrating the 419 fraud are based in London and they are also behind a myriad of other con tricks which all involve requests to help move large sums of money with the promise of a substantial share of the cash in return. A similar scam, originally known as the 'Spanish Prisoner Letter', was first carried out in the 16th century via ordinary postal mail.

Greed is a timeless emotion and that is exactly what these scams rely on.

Meanwhile, other Nigerian gangsters are involved in credit card fraud, bank fraud, cheque 'kiting', various types of insurance fraud, entitlement fraud, false identification, passport and visa fraud, marriage fraud to obtain British citizenship, vehicle thefts, the counterfeiting of currency, and the counterfeiting of corporate cheques. These criminals, of various nationalities, are costing Londoners, and citizens of other countries around the world, tens of millions of pounds each year, as well as organising the importation of a significant amount of the heroin used in the UK, and much of the cocaine smuggled to Europe, Asia and Africa.

In London in September 2004, Nigeria's former Bayelsa State Governor, Chief Diepreye Alamieyeseigha, was arrested by the Met on suspicion of running a vast money-laundering operation, which had links to the notorious 419 scam. While undergoing trial in London he jumped bail and returned to Nigeria under mysterious circumstances to assume his position as governor. But he soon faced a major political crisis at home, leading to his impeachment by the State House of Assembly and he was subsequently arrested by the police to face trial in Nigeria for massive looting of the state treasury.

Nigerian criminals based in London regularly use drug couriers from West Africa. A clampdown on drug smuggling in the Caribbean has shifted a lot of the narcotics activity to the African continent and there are currently more than 100 Nigerian women in British prisons accused of working as drug mules. They're paid up to £5,000 to smuggle in four kg of cocaine, but face sentences of as much as 20 years in a British jail. In May 2006, Mary Kofi, from Ghana, flew into London's Heathrow Airport on a flight from her home country. In her stomach were 61 packs of cocaine. She was found collapsed outside St Helier Hospital, in Sutton, Surrey, hours after arriving in this country and died just one hour later.

Latin American drug barons have now targeted West Africa as

prime territory for their criminal enterprises because of poor security and the low cost of labour.

Globalisation of the world's economic and information infrastructure has helped create a new, organised gangster elite in London. Many villains are covering their tracks with a vast array of legal businesses established as a front for their trans-national underworld activities. Even the term 'organised crime' is rapidly being replaced by 'organised global crime.' The Met believes that terrorists already turn to criminals to provide forged documents, smuggled weapons and clandestine travel assistance.

Fraud is big business in London. Throughout London there are people looking to make a quick and easy buck out of the misfortune of others. It is estimated that London is suffering about £3 billion a year in losses through fraud and other forms of economic crime and criminal gangs are infiltrating the banking industry. The City of London Police have blamed temporary workers for this increase in banking fraud. These gangs can be organised groups targeting tax credits in Ealing or card cloners in Peckham, eBay fraudsters in Tottenham or tax dodgers in Southwark.

Hundreds of thousands of Londoners are also finding themselves out of pocket when they discover counterfeit money in their wallet. But how does this fake money make its way hot off the presses of organised criminal gangs and into the pockets of the capital's law-abiding citizens?

One sophisticated counterfeit money gang was based in a bar called TPA (Tin Pan Alley) owned by Jimmy Fraser, nephew of notorious gangland enforcer 'Mad' Frankie Fraser, whose criminal record has already been mentioned here earlier. Jimmy Fraser boasted to one undercover reporter: 'You can name what you want printed. I can show you the birth certificates I've got.' He also claimed he could easily get hold of fake £5 notes and just about anything else required. Fraser got his fake notes through a printer in Scotland and then distributed them to customers as change at the TPA bar, and through other criminal connections in London's West End.

According to the Met, there are at least five major money counterfeiting printing operations in London at any one time. Hidden high security features on banknotes ensure that most counterfeit cash is not good enough to fool banks, but it is usually only circulated through small businesses and once the note has been accepted, the job is done. But the Bank of England has always insisted there is no compensation for anyone who discovers they have a fake banknote.

London's foreign embassies are believed to house a vast range of diplomat criminals. Between 1999 and 2004 more than 100 serious crimes were committed by embassy staff. This included an alleged murderer in the Colombian embassy, plus rape, indecent assaults and even child abuse by other nation's diplomats. Other embassy staff are believed to have strong links to crime syndicates.

In the capital, the downgrading of cannabis in January 2004 drastically reduced arrests for cocaine and heroin dealing by almost 20 per cent. Senior police officers and government ministers had pledged they'd make the fight against such hard drugs a priority.

The drugs centre of London is probably Brixton, which has seen a dramatic explosion in the numbers of dealers out on the street instead of hiding down darkened alleyways as they once did. Today many of these gangsters openly try to out-score their rivals by boasting about the strength of the cannabis on offer.

Public apathy towards cannabis has helped breed an up-and-coming new generation of relatively young London drug barons who've become immensely rich by importing high-quality cannabis direct from South Africa where the local product – known as dagga – is so cheap that they enjoy profit margins as high as 4,000 per cent, more profit than even with cocaine and heroin. In Britain, high quality 'skunk' cannabis goes for £3,500 a kilo. In South Africa, the same product sells for £20 a kilo, even less if bought in bulk.

During the summer of 2005, five out of ten drug smugglers arrested in the capital were South African. Marius 'Mars' Le Roux, 39, who bought a yacht, a beach house in Durban and several properties in London before being arrested by the Met in 2006 is a classic example. In September 2006 he was convicted of drugs offences and sentenced to 14 years in prison. He'd arrived in the UK on a year's tourist visa in 1994. Then he created a new identity to avoid deportation by using the birth certificate of a dead baby – similar to the plot of Frederick Forsyth's *The Day of the Jackal*. Le Roux even collected a jobseekers allowance while building up his multi-million pound drugs empire. As Judge Roger Chapple told Le Roux at the end of his trial: 'You made a huge profit through dealing in misery.'

The potential for vast profit from South African cannabis was highlighted in another 2005 case when five members of a gang led by unemployed 24-year-old Robert Beal were jailed for varying terms totalling 30 years. Beal was arrested at a north London flat along with two South African accomplices, businessmen Aaron Reichlin, 53, and 40-year-old Katiso Molefe, when police carried out a search in connection with a robbery. They found 25,000 ecstasy pills, 5.2 kg of cannabis and a cache of firearms, including a submachine gun and two semiautomatic pistols. Officers also

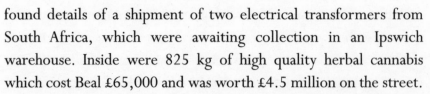

found details of a shipment of two electrical transformers from South Africa, which were awaiting collection in an Ipswich warehouse. Inside were 825 kg of high quality herbal cannabis which cost Beal £65,000 and was worth £4.5 million on the street.

So-called 'grow yer own' gangs have become the other new boys on the block and they're managing to make large profits out of cannabis they are producing themselves. As one dealer told me: 'It's easy to run in any property with a loft, which is warm and well insulated. The equipment costs no more than a few hundred pounds and it can then provide a steady stream of income across the entire year.' Some gangs have dozens of low-cost housing properties across the capital which double as cannabis 'factories'. A couple of years back, eight people were arrested in a police raid on a cannabis factory in a terraced house in Woolwich, southeast London. More than 800 plants were found in six rooms during the dawn raid – but it was a rare success for the boys in blue.

Fearful of possible booby traps, armed Met officers smashed through the door of a house in Stevenage, Hertfordshire, during a raid to discover a hydroponics factory with more than 300 cannabis plants, worth £60,000, which covered every inch of floor space in the bedrooms, lounge and kitchen. They were being harvested for sale as potent, high-grade herbal cannabis known as 'skunk', which many believe is as addictive as heroin or cocaine. This particular drug factory was run by a Vietnamese gang and police only discovered it after a tip-off.

So the Met's ongoing mission to tackle the menace of drugs in the capital continues. In the autumn of 2005 £4 million-worth of cannabis was found during one raid by police. Later that same day officers seized 2.2 million pounds-worth of heroin in North London, where they discovered 44 plastic-wrapped blocks. The dealers undoubtedly helped trigger many other crimes, because addicts steal to fuel their habit. A recent Home Office report revealed the impact of heroin on London's communities, reporting one kilogram of heroin can be linked to £220,000 worth of property stolen and 220 victims of burglary or theft.

A week after those police raids, two kg of cocaine was seized from a house in South London. Two people were later arrested and charged with possession with intent to supply. Later that same week, officers also recovered 1.5 tonnes of cannabis in Dagenham and three more people were arrested.

In the summer of 2005, 40 kg of cannabis resin with an estimated street value of £1 million was seized near Folkestone when police carried out an armed search of a lorry which had just arrived on a cross channel ferry from France. A 46-year-old man from Cricklewood, northwest London and a 55-year-old man from Germany later appeared in court and were given heavy jail sentences after being found guilty of possession of 500 kg of cannabis, with intent to supply.

Not even computer games and movies are exempt from the activities of London's criminals. Over the past couple of years more and more gangs – often of Asian origin – have been copying films and games onto DVDs and selling them through market stalls. It's a business said to be worth £25 million a year. One Met operation in 2006 saw the arrest and conviction of more than a dozen movie counterfeiters who'd had teams of runners secretly and illegally copying new movies within days of their cinema releases.

Identity theft is another fast-growing crime, costing the country £1.3 billion every year. In 2002 a court confiscated £200,000 from

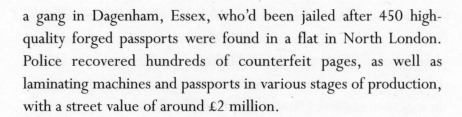

a gang in Dagenham, Essex, who'd been jailed after 450 high-quality forged passports were found in a flat in North London. Police recovered hundreds of counterfeit pages, as well as laminating machines and passports in various stages of production, with a street value of around £2 million.

London's criminal gangs specialising in art are motivated by the fact that most art pieces are worth millions of dollars and usually only weigh a couple of pounds. Transportation is relatively simple, assuming the thief is willing to cut a painting out of the frame and roll it up into a tube carrier. Most major museums have tight security, but there are still many places with high value works that have disproportionately poor security measures, making them susceptible to theft. But the ownership of high profile art is easy to track, so potential buyers are very hard to find. In the summer of 2003 a London gang stole a Leonardo da Vinci painting thought to be worth about £30 million from a Scottish castle. Nothing has been heard of the picture since but art experts believe the gang who stole it was from London and may be sitting on it until a suitable buyer is found.

Although this book has already highlighted many of the older, more traditional foreign gangs operating in London, it is the ever-increasing number of younger criminal gangs that are the new threat to everyday life in the capital. British intelligence service MI5 works completely independently of the Yard's new gang-busting unit but both law enforcement agencies admit they are now witnessing the biggest explosion in street gang warfare seen since Victorian times.

It's worth looking geographically at this new phenomenon to get a real grasp of the sheer scale and numbers involved. On the streets just north of the Thames is The Lock City Crew, usually foreign-born, either African or Jamaican, whilst their nearby rival, Much Love Crew, are north London born and bred.

Then there are the Turkish and Kurdish street gangs who're closely linked to older, more powerful overlords at the forefront of heroin importation throughout the UK. They include the Bombers in Hackney, the Tottenham Boys, and the Kurdish Bulldogs. Most of these so-called street gangsters are in their teens or early twenties.

Over in Wembley, northwest London, rival Sri Lankan gangs have waged a vicious turf war, while the Southall Sikhs (formerly known as the Holy Smokes or Tooti Nung) are active in the heroin trade in West London. In the early 1980s the Holy Smokes consisted of only members from inside the Sikh community but the rules changed following a vicious street battle in 1983. Soon rivalry and violence between local Asian gangs had escalated to include fire bombings, kidnappings, shootings and stabbings. Eventually, in the early 1990s, disputes over leadership caused the Sikhs to break away and form their own gang, the 'Tooti Nungs'. They're now estimated to have 1,000 members nationwide in London, Birmingham, Leicester and Wolverhampton.

In July 2006 the Met launched a day-long operation codenamed 'Enver 2' in the boroughs of Brent, Croydon, Harrow, Newham, Redbridge and Waltham Forest specifically to try and crack down on Sri Lankan Tamil gangs. Alleged offences included theft, possession of offensive weapons, money laundering and drug peddling. Cocaine, weapons, cash and valuables were eventually seized and 29 alleged gang members arrested.

Tensions between Tamil communities across London are constantly rising. In one fight in 2005, Walthamstow and East Ham Tamils fought with swords and other deadly weapons in the middle

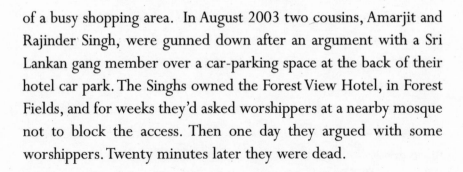

of a busy shopping area. In August 2003 two cousins, Amarjit and Rajinder Singh, were gunned down after an argument with a Sri Lankan gang member over a car-parking space at the back of their hotel car park. The Singhs owned the Forest View Hotel, in Forest Fields, and for weeks they'd asked worshippers at a nearby mosque not to block the access. Then one day they argued with some worshippers. Twenty minutes later they were dead.

In the past decade, murders involving South Asians have risen by 300 per cent. Kidnappings and drug-related crimes are also rocketing. However, there are clear differences between London's black, white and South Asian criminal gangs, who tend to operate within families and clans. They also often flee abroad to other family members after committing crimes in order to launder proceeds and avoid the police.

The early South Asian gangs emerged in the late 1970s when vigilante groups of second generation Asians took to the streets to help protect the Asian communities from white racist gangs, such as the National Front. The Asian gangs were formed to protect their community and local businesses. Asian gangs in the East End were – and still are – territorial and mark their boundaries with graffiti.

One such gang is the self-named Paki Panthers, who have been known to the Met Police since 2001. The gang is a collection of Asian street robbers but it has no defined turf, although it operates mainly in the borough of Waltham Forest. In East London there are at least 26 groups of loosely associated Bangladeshi gangs. They include the Shadwell Crew, Stepney Thug Passion, Poplar Massive and the East Boys of Tower Hamlets and Bethnal Green. In Camden, North London, there is an Asian gang calling themselves the DSB who are direct rivals of those East End Bangladeshi gangs. In early 2005 three members of the DSB were sentenced to 400

hours of community punishment orders after a gang fight in
Shoreditch, with the East Boys of Tower Hamlets. More than a
dozen people used weapons ranging from samurai swords to metal
bars to hockey sticks.

Gun crime is spreading ominously within the Tamil, Sikh, Indian,
Pakistani and Bangladeshi communities and the murder rate within
those groups has tripled over the past decade.

The rise in violence among the Tamil communities first gained
serious concern in the late 1990s following a spate of stabbings and
pavement fights with rival Sri Lankan street gangs across London.
Many disputes involve family or inter-village disputes originating
from Sri Lanka. London is home to around 100,000 Tamils. The
first homicide attributed to the Tamil gangs and given media
attention was in 2002, when a young Tamil was murdered and left
to burn in Roe Green Park, Kingsbury, northwest London.

In 2003 a group of Tamils calling themselves the 'Snake Gang'
shot dead a young man in a feud sparked by a previous incident in
Kingsbury. Another victim was shot dead in his home in Lyon Park
Avenue, Wembley. One of the killers had also tried to execute his
father-in-law. The gang later also attempted to kill the dead man's
brother-in-law in a drive-by shooting. Later that same year a 23-
year-old Sri Lankan was attacked in Wembley and one hour later an
18-year-old Sri Lankan was involved in a dispute between rival
Tamil gangs in Ilford. Both men died in hospital from their injuries.

In early 2004 a teenager was attacked by Tamil criminals from
the 'Ari Ala Gang' brandishing samurai swords, hammers and axes.
The 18-year-old-youth died in his car at traffic lights in Wembley.

In 2005 Scotland Yard created a specialist squad nicknamed 'The
Tamil Taskforce' to deal solely with the rising gangland violence in

Sri Lankan Tamil communities following more than a dozen gang-related murders centred round the Tamil areas of Ilford, Walthamstow and Wembley. The taskforce – acting on inside information – rounded up 13 suspects after 500 officers searched homes in Newham, Waltham Forest, Redbridge, Harrow, Brent and Croydon. During those raids police seized a pistol, ammunition, swords, axes, baseball bats and pickaxe handles. In Newham, credit card cloning equipment was found and five men were arrested on suspicion of deception. Police also seized a £30,000 Mercedes in Waltham Forest.

There are also an increasing numbers of violent Asian gangs in Southall, West London, including the Bhatts and the Kanaks. The Bhatts are heavily influenced by a leading Asian family, with reputable businesses in West London. As one local police officer explained: 'It's a bit like a throwback to the Krays in one sense but this lot are much more cold-blooded. At least the Krays helped little old ladies across the road and donated money to charity.'

Hostilities between the Bhatts and the Kanaks literally exploded in October 2001 when a Bhatt member walked into a known Kanaks hangout – the Lady Margaret Pub in Southall – and wrestled a Bhatt to the ground, confiscated his gun and beat him. The victim left the pub vowing revenge. Two weeks later a shotgun was fired at a senior Kanak member as he walked down Cranleigh Gardens, in Southall. He wasn't hit but an hour later the Lady Margaret Pub was shaken by a huge explosion and fingers were soon pointed in the direction of the rival gang.

On another occasion two Bhatt gang members were imprisoned for killing an innocent Asian car salesman in a case of mistaken identity. Today, the two gangs are still fighting although it is believed the Kanaks now have the upper hand. The Kanaks have strong links with Afro-Caribbean gangs, and whilst the cross-culture alliance is unusual, the Kanaks have been known to hire black criminals to carry out violent attacks for them.

One London man, whose nephew was held against his will and killed by an Asian gang, told journalists their behaviour had been 'inhuman'. Speaking anonymously in fear of his own life, he told BBC News: 'After beating my nephew, they could've just left him or taken him to the hospital, but they set him alight.'

British intelligence believes that many of the Sri Lankan gang members in London are acting as a 'front' for the Tamil guerrilla group, the LTTE. They are trying to take control of numerous Tamil business ventures in London – from temples to schools – and then use them to raise funds illegally for the LTTE. Because of the fears of money-laundering, banks in London have tightened up their procedures for Sri Lankans opening bank accounts.

The authorities are so worried about the terrorist links to the Tamils and other organised criminal gangs from London's growing ethnic minority communities that they have extended Operation Trident – the Met unit which specialises in gun crime in London's black communities – to cover these gang-linked activities. Detectives have identified almost 200 crime networks, including some among the Sri Lankan community. The Met genuinely fears that 'crime-ridden ghettos' will expand throughout the capital if police can't crack down more on these gang members and bring them to justice.

South London's 'Muslim Boys' boast of links with global terrorism. They even use Islam and alleged connection to Al Qaeda to strike fear into their enemies. The gang – with more than 100 members

– frequently hold up local drug dealers and it is rumoured that they even force their own members to convert to Islam at gunpoint before praying to Allah ahead of committing crimes.

Members of this particular gang speak in an American rap music-type slang. Guns are an essential part of their lives and their own secret code of conduct is strictly and violently enforced, making them one of the most feared and ruthless of all gangs. Muslim Boys' leaders were often childhood friends, brought up in some of London's poorest areas. Many keep on the move from house-to-house on an almost nightly basis, making it hard for their friends or foes to keep track of them. Many 'hard-core' gang members have already been sent to prison, but many others remain on the streets, together with a vast number of hangers-on. The Muslim Boys also proudly claim to have connections to other gangs in neighbourhoods around Brixton, Peckham, Lambeth, and Streatham, all in South London.

Operating not far from the Muslim Boys in South London are other big name gangs including the Stockwell Crew and the Poverty Driven Children, also from Stockwell. Then there are the Ghetto Boys, in Deptford; the Peckham Boys, primarily active in Peckham, Walworth and Camberwell; and the South Man Syndicate in Tooting, Streatham and Thornton Heath. As many as 20 hard-core members of each of these gangs are in jail at any one time.

There are continual battles between these gangs in so-called cross-border disputes. The gangs are predominately black and police believe many members are involved in robbery, house burglary, drugs and general street crime. There are even so-called 'junior offshoots' of the street gangs which deliberately attract young recruits. One of those offshoots is called the Young Peckham Boys who were at one stage blamed for the death of 10-year-old

Damilola Taylor on a council estate in 2001, which sparked a nationwide protest.

The Met says it's nothing short of a miracle that more people haven't been killed in the gang wars raging on London's streets, especially since so many gangsters are completely inept at handling their deadly weapons. Many of their guns are deactivated weapons shipped in from the Balkans and then reactivated in London. As one Met detective explained: 'One guy let off a machine gun, riddling a car with bullets. One bullet went right through the door and roof of another passing car, narrowly missing the driver. In a lot of incidents, it's amazing nobody died.'

Many of the bigger, older south London street gangs live off the proceeds of crack cocaine and heroin, often stolen from other dealers and sold on. Indeed, the number of shootings in London is said to be directly related to the amount of cocaine available on the streets. When supplies run dry as the result of a major customs bust, dealers steal drugs from rival dealers and confrontations are inevitable.

A spate of shocking incidents in 2004 in London sum up the street gang situation in the capital: three people tied up and killed in a shooting at a flat in Stonebridge, South London; a woman holding a baby shot dead at a christening party in Peckham; a man shot dead and two other people injured after a pub argument in Ilford, in East London; a man shot after his car smashed into railings in Walworth.

In the early summer of 2006, a haunting photo image dominated the London newspapers. Fifteen-year-old Alex Mulumba – the victim of a stabbing in a London street – lay in a hospital bed, a ventilator tube protruding from his mouth. So shocked was Alex's father, Kamondo, at seeing his son in this condition that he decided to release the hospital picture. But then the **Daily Mail** traced another photo of the same 'victim' on a website belonging to a south London gang – this time dressed in a mask, crouching with a pump-action shotgun.

His father may have known nothing of Alex's secret life but far from being innocent, he was another victim of London's destructive street-gang culture. Alex's gang name was Tiny Alien and he was a member of a gang set up 18 months earlier by half a dozen black boys from a south London estate. They each had nicknames and called themselves the Man Dem Crew.

Tooth, Smacks, S-Man, Drowzie, Stemz and Tiny Alien – all under 16 – saw themselves as big, hard, streetwise men. Brought up on an unrelenting diet of gangsta rap music and violent video games, they dressed the part and talked the talk. The gang's website even featured photographs of the boys posing menacingly with a gun, hooded tops and baseball caps worn back to front. They'd become sucked into the terrifying reality of the world they were trying to ape – a world of gangs, guns, drugs, violence and tragically, in this case, death. Alex was stabbed through the heart with a samurai sword. Two brothers, Adu, 18, and Nana Sarpong, 20, were eventually charged with his murder. His death had been preceded by a vicious fight involving up to 40 youths.

Often lacking positive role models at home and adrift in a subculture built around instant gratification through drugs, sex and crime, gang members like Alex and his assailants are being increasingly manipulated by older, more established criminal gangs whose respect they are trying to earn. These youngsters are even used as runners to carry drugs and guns. 'If they're lucky, by the age of 30 they will be in prison,' said one senior detective from Operation Trident, the Scotland Yard unit that targets gun crime in the black community. 'If they're not, they'll be dead.'

Murder victim Alex was facing charges of robbery, theft and violence, and two members of his gang, Falco Moludi and Ipaon Mosengo, both 15, had been convicted of committing, over a three-month period, a staggering 35 offences. They'd targeted school playgrounds dressed in masks and balaclavas and were sentenced to a total of six-and-a-half years in prison.

One 16-year-old boy needed hospital treatment after being punched and kicked by the two young criminals. Another suffered a broken jaw. On one occasion Moludi pulled out an imitation handgun that he'd been hiding in a small Gucci bag. The two teenagers even bragged of their crimes on their website. When they were eventually caught, one school sent an entire minibus-load of pupils to identify them in a police line-up – while the judge who sentenced them for robbery commented that so widespread was their crime spree that their victims thought it 'normal' to have their possessions stolen.

Moludi and Mosengo failed to show even the faintest hint of remorse at their trial. When they were jailed, Mosengo fashioned his fingers into the shape of a gun, pointed at the investigating officer and shouted: 'Two bullets. Bang! Bang! You're dead.' So the Man Dem Crew was not just a testosterone-charged front.

Kate Hoey, the Labour MP for Vauxhall, in whose constituency Alex Mulumba was murdered, says, 'Gang members are no longer just feral kids. Now gangs are extracting kids from stable families who go to school and pass their exams. Then, outside the home and school, there is a real breakdown and they join these dreadful gangs.'

The stark truth is that gang culture has penetrated London to such an extent that many young children now believe that membership offers security: it is better to be in than out. Take for

example the Dark Side Soldiers, a six-strong, Brixton-based gang of youngsters aged 14 to 19. Beef, the gang's ringleader, says they all routinely carry knives because it is the only way to protect one another. Beef once stabbed someone in the leg, but doesn't think it killed him, although he openly admits he doesn't particularly care. He says: 'The streets are a war zone and I do what I do to survive.' The tragedy is that this sort of attitude only perpetuates the cycle of violence.

There were 361 homicides in the boroughs of Lambeth, Brent, Hackney, Southwark and Haringey in the five years between 2000 and 2005. Clearly, the deprived inner city boroughs still lack the attention and investment they desired back in the 1980s when inner city rioting was a fact of life. In Hackney, for example, street gangs can operate in a small area but are affiliated to larger neighbouring gangs, making it virtually impossible to calculate the real potency of such groups. As a result, shootings between gangs often go unnoticed by the police. Also in Hackney there is one such, known in gang circles as the NYC Deportees, which is rumoured to contain deportees from New York City. Its other name is the Hackney Blood, in deference to the notorious 'Bloods' in New York and Los Angeles.

The story of London street gangster Alexander Baker's troubled life reads like the plot of an American urban gangster film. He was born in Hackney and moved to New York with his mother in the early 1980s – growing up surrounded by the violence and drugs that plagued impoverished black ghettos in the Bronx. The 27-year-old fell in with a set of the infamous Bloods 'super gang', which had been engaged in a bloody war with the rival Crips for decades. Baker took up drug dealing as a way to make quick cash and assumed the gang name 'Miller Gunz'.

He shot people and was badly wounded himself and was arrested in Manhattan for drug dealing and burglary and ended up in the notorious Riker's Island prison. However, US authorities soon discovered his British citizenship and, on his release, deported him to a country he hardly knew. Initially he 'went straight' and lectured kids on how to keep away from gangs. But then he was arrested and sent to Brixton Prison amid allegations he had become a 'Fagin' character. East London police believed he was using teenagers to commit street robberies for him. He later pleaded guilty to a lesser charge of handling stolen goods. He was released for time served on remand.

In recent years the price of drugs from traditional sources has tumbled and many of the so-called old-school London criminals have virtually stopped handling them. When London villains like Great Train Robber-turned-drug-baron Charlie Wilson were at their peak 20 years ago, cannabis from North Africa sold for £675 a kilo. Today it's down to an all-time low of £200 a kilo. A £50,000 investment in a shipment of cocaine will be lucky to earn an investor £10,000 profit. Says one UK drug smuggler in Spain: 'Drugs aren't worth the aggro any more. The profits are shit and the risks are high. Ciggies are brilliant and if you're nicked it's not even considered important.'

The demand for tax-free and fake counterfeit cigarettes continues to grow immensely, thanks partly to tobacco companies. A 2001 report from Customs and Excise revealed that over half the cigarettes seized in the UK the previous year were brands manufactured by Imperial Tobacco and Gallagher, who've been exporting billions of cigarettes to countries where almost no one smokes. These cigarettes then entered the black market and were smuggled back into the UK, especially London. Cigarette smuggling now costs the taxpayer £3 billion a year in lost revenue.

The mathematics are pretty simple: a London gangster in Spain can buy thousands of cartons of cigarettes and then sell them for at least three times the price back home in the capital's street markets, which are now awash with cheap packs of 'under the counter' cigarettes. Also, 20 per cent of customs seizures are said to be counterfeit cigarettes and the main brand being faked is Benson and Hedges, made by Gallagher in the UK.

The tobacco in these so-called 'fake ciggies' is very low quality and often mixed with other materials. So not only is it dangerous because of the tobacco, but there is an added risk that you are inhaling other, possibly toxic, fumes from the materials that are mixed with the tobacco. Some counterfeit cigarettes may also contain higher levels of nicotine, making it even more difficult for people to give up. The brand Regal, currently being smuggled in vast quantities, has become an especially popular target for counterfeiters, many of whom are based in Eastern Europe.

Dozens of traders on the internet offer UK buyers cheap cigarettes smuggled from other countries. 'It's a simple operation and that's why a lot of gangs are getting into it,' says smuggler 'Jerry', from South London, who's set up a vast cigarette-selling network from his new home on the Costa del Sol. 'I'm a one-man band and I know one day I'll get a knock on the door from Spanish Customs and then I'll close down and head off to Thailand. It's safer there.'

In May 2006 two out-of-work Irish terrorists were arrested in Malaga, Spain, for allegedly being part of a complex fund-raising network, which included exporting duty-free cigarettes to London. The pair – members of the Real IRA – were partially identified as Thomas Philip C, 32, born in Dublin, and Aaron William J, 42, born in Lisburn, Co Antrim. (It is customary in

Spain for newly arrested suspects not to have their surnames revealed.) Their sophisticated tobacco smuggling operation had been under observation by undercover Spanish police. A Spanish Interior Ministry statement said the men had been under investigation in Spain since 2004. Two lorries transporting 500,000 packs of cigarettes worth more than £1 million were seized, along with documents and £2,900, in a raid that led to the pair's arrest.

The Real IRA is a splinter group of the Provisional IRA. In 1998 it was responsible for the deaths of 29 people, including a woman who was eight months pregnant with twins, in a bombing in the Co Tyrone town of Omagh. This Real IRA has always refused to stand down, and another splinter group, the Continuity IRA, also continues to threaten violence, recruit members and raise funds illegally.

We're now approaching the end of the first decade of this century, and the face of London's ganglands continues to change constantly. In 2005 the Met foiled one of the biggest attempted bank thefts in Britain. The plan had been to steal £220 million ($423 million) from the London offices of the Japanese bank, Sumitomo Mitsui. Computer experts are alleged to have tried to transfer the money electronically after hacking into the bank's systems and getting account numbers. It later emerged the robbers had planned to send the money electronically to ten different other bank accounts around the world.

With wi-fi hotspots all over the capital, the ability of London's gangsters to tap into computers has improved drastically. People using wireless high-speed net connections are being warned about fake hotspots, or access points. Once logged onto such a hotspot, sensitive data can be intercepted. London has more global wi-fi hotspots than virtually any other city in the world, with more than a quarter of a million at the last count.

Earlier in the decade some old-style crimes came back to newspaper headlines in London. In 2002 a gang was found guilty of an £11 million VAT fraud involving computer chips and were sentenced to a total of 31 years in jail. Confiscation orders totalling £7.1 million were also made against many of the nine gang members. The convictions followed a joint Customs and National Crime Squad (NCS) surveillance probe into the criminal activities of Raymond May and Vincent Stapleton. They had established companies in England and France to buy and sell high-value computer chips in what's now known as VAT Missing Trader Fraud, or 'carousel' fraud. It is a clever updated version of what used to be called the 'Long Firm' con of the 1950s and '60s.

Carousel fraud involves importing VAT zero-rated goods into the UK from the EU which are then sold on through a series of companies in the UK, all liable to VAT at the standard rate, before being exported back to the EU, and in this case to the original supplier who would start the whole process all over again.

When an armed gang stole £50 million from a Securitas depot in Kent in February 2006, in the biggest robbery in British history, it seemed to mark a return to the so-called 'bad old days' of the armed robberies of the 1970s and early 1980s. For this was certainly a curiously old-fashioned crime in an age of global terrorism, electronic fraud, people trafficking, identity theft and drugs cartels.

It is also significant that the raid occurred on a warehouse stuffed with cash in Tonbridge in Kent, a neighbourhood where many of the old, white south London criminal families settled

long ago. Some even believe the robbers may have stolen too much cash to cope with – £4 million would be easier to deal with than £40 million.

Another less sophisticated but just as traditional crime is flourishing in the capital – foreign criminal gangs who can strip down a stolen Mercedes car to a shell within three hours. In the summer of 2006 the Met raided a scrap metal yard in Stratford, East London, and uncovered an operation being run by a gang of Nigerians and said to be worth £1 million a year. The car parts 'ring' included thieves who stole the cars which were then delivered to the scrap metal yard where each vehicle was clinically stripped to a shell – often before the owners had even reported the cars stolen. The Met said afterwards that this gang of highly professional experts were carrying out their 'duties' with the speed of a Formula One pit crew. The parts were then transported to taxi repair firms in certain parts of Africa and the Arab states, where demand for second-hand parts to repair pre-1996 Mercedes cars is insatiable.

The so-called 'car crash scam' is another gangster-related crime which has emerged on the streets of London in recent years. This involves gangs using two vehicles to brake hard in front of lorries so they're shunted, and then fraudulently claiming for damaged vehicle and injury payments using dodgy claims companies. These gangs are cleverly exploiting a loophole in the law that says a person's identity does not have to be proved for a payout. London-based criminals are believed to have made millions in fake claims, but because most claims are £600 and under, they slip through the regulatory authority checks. One ex-policeman was targeted in June, 2006, as he drove his van home. He later explained: 'A white car was in front followed by a dark BMW. Nothing seemed out of

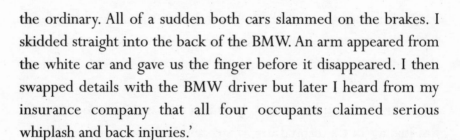

the ordinary. All of a sudden both cars slammed on the brakes. I skidded straight into the back of the BMW. An arm appeared from the white car and gave us the finger before it disappeared. I then swapped details with the BMW driver but later I heard from my insurance company that all four occupants claimed serious whiplash and back injuries.'

Meanwhile, London continues to attract some of the world's most notorious international criminals. In September 2006 suspected mafia gangster Raffaele Caldarelli, 35, was held by armed Met police officers after leaving an East End shoe shop which he owned, following months of undercover police surveillance. The top secret operation had been carried out by officers from the Serious Organised Crime Unit and the Scotland Yard Extradition Unit after a request from Italian police via Interpol. After his arrest, it was revealed that Caldarelli had been living and working in the capital for three years.

In May 2005 another Italian gangster called Francesco Tonicello – one of Italy's most wanted men – was arrested at Vauxhall Tube Station in South London, where he worked, bizarrely, as a newspaper seller. In his other life he was a master forger who used 11 aliases and was a notorious fencer of artworks and antiques. He worked primarily for a godfather from Venice called Felice 'Angelface' Maniero. How the mighty fall.

The funeral of the Kray twins' sidekick Tony Lambrianou in March 2005 brought back memories of the Krays' bloody reign in the East End underworld and of the horrific murders of various other criminals which ultimately saw the end of an era. In many ways it also marked the beginning of the new wave of criminality which has impacted on London in recent years. Lambrianou died

suddenly at the age of only 61. He and his brother Chris had been in their early twenties when they were sent down for 15 years in 1969 for their part in the murder of Jack 'The Hat' McVitie two years earlier.

Lambrianou's funeral, at St Matthew's Church, Bethnal Green, was just a stone's throw from where the Krays all grew up. Three hundred and fifty people showed up to mourn one man, and in the process helped romanticise a way of life and a way of crime that's now slipped into history.

London's ganglands are still thriving but the old-school characters have been replaced by gangsters threatening to bathe the streets in blood. The number of arrests of foreign gangsters has been rapidly rising, even though foreigners still only account for just over 10 per cent of the population and it's going to get a lot worse.

EPILOGUE

GANGLANDS — 25

IN THE EAST END OF LONDON they still reckon that when the Krays were banged up for life the local crime rate doubled overnight, because whatever the twins might have been up to, their presence discouraged the small-timers. Truth is that London's old-style gangsters of the 1950s and 1960s were a very different bunch from today's organised criminals. In those days the big names were outlaws, of course, but they were seen as a stabilising influence within their communities. Their power inspired respect, not just among rival villains but also among petty crooks, who might otherwise have been tempted to prey on people on the manor. Over the river in South London, the Richardson brothers ruled with a similar style of iron hand. 'No one would dare mug an old lady on Charlie Richardson's manor,' one old-timer told me a few years back.

Back then, gangsters were high profile and far less subterranean than the heavy characters around today. The Krays went to first nights, cultivated sporting and West End stars. In their heyday in the early 1960s they were often seen with some of the most glamorous people in London and regularly had their picture in London's newspapers. Today's godfathers prefer to stay in the shadows. Few really know them and, unlike their more colourful predecessors, no one wants to know them.

Maybe after reading the second half of this book, it will be apparent that London is currently in the grip of organised crime. Law-abiding citizens may think that drug dealers are a bunch of seedy, unshaven youths hanging out on street corners flogging crack. But many of them live in detached mansions, drive £50,000 motors and send their children to public schools, while drug turf wars are helping fuel many of the shootings on London's streets.

Back in 2000, a gunman let rip at dozens of innocent people lining up outside Chicago's nightclub in Peckham in the early hours of the morning, injuring nine people, including a 16-year-old kid. The attack was blamed on Yardie gangsters and it didn't even get a mention on the TV news the following day. That says it all.

The statistics speak for themselves. At least 100 murders a year in London can be linked to organised crime. And hundreds more are hurt in shootings like the one in Peckham. Then there are the gangsters who disappear without trace after being chopped into little pieces by their enemies. Even the old-school cockney villains say that in the past ten years the situation has 'got completely out of fuckin' control'. Younger, often foreign, under-40 gangsters are threatening the peace and stability that the older criminal faces will always claim they helped promote.

As one retired London detective explained: 'In the old days, villains kept to their own territory and didn't threaten the main population. But these new, foreign gangs have always got someone waiting in the wings and they don't respect territories or other human beings. It's going to take a hell of a police force to stop them ruling London's streets.'

Crime booms whatever the financial state of a nation. There will always be young men out there happy enough to pull triggers for money or grudges. It's as flash as playing for Chelsea or being a big-time fighter. It's showbiz. And as Legs Diamond said in the musical named after him: 'I'm in showbiz, only a critic can kill me.'

So where does all this blood-letting leave us? There'll always be the Ganglands of London, the Met knows that and merely wonder how to stop its tentacles spreading. These days the police are more reluctant than ever to get in amongst the criminals like they used to back in the old days. Budgets, politics and so-called ethics have all played their role in changing the rules of the game.

The emphasis today is on trying to understand the habits of the criminal, and that is what, to a certain extent, I've attempted in this book. Are these characters really 'born criminal' or did they develop those instincts from the circumstances in which they were brought up as children? Many have attempted to prove that criminal characteristics are inherited. Others will argue, on almost Marxist terms, that 'society has the criminals it deserves'. In other words, society causes crime.

But then crime is undoubtedly a mental activity. The old time criminal legends such as Mad Frankie Fraser and Freddie Foreman made a choice, which doesn't necessarily mean they could do anything to stop it. Those early days of abject hunger sparked within them a need to get out of control and led to antisocial behaviour, which manifested itself in many different forms, from sexual to financial. But a gangster's most significant role has always been the hunger for recognition, for admiration, to be respected. All of us have that innate need, but within the underworld it looms abnormally large.

That hunger for recognition is in some ways a psychic need. Fromm, in his *Anatomy of Human Destructiveness*, called it: 'The need to make a dent.' These characters want the world to know they exist. That demand for more life is all-consuming and

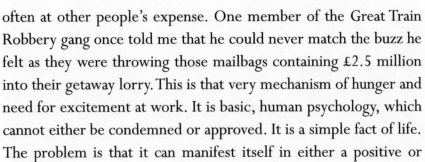

often at other people's expense. One member of the Great Train Robbery gang once told me that he could never match the buzz he felt as they were throwing those mailbags containing £2.5 million into their getaway lorry. This is that very mechanism of hunger and need for excitement at work. It is basic, human psychology, which cannot either be condemned or approved. It is a simple fact of life. The problem is that it can manifest itself in either a positive or negative fashion. In its positive form it leads to entrepreneurs, captains of industry. But in other forms it can end in the ultimate risk-taking enterprise – crime.

In simple terms, gangsters – whatever their race, colour or creed – refuse to accept life as they find it. They don't just want to steal an apple from a tree, they want to burn down the orchard as well. Criminals are the archetypal scavengers, always on the lookout for an opportunity. They also suffer badly from long bouts of boredom and depression, which can often only be conquered by committing a crime.

Most career criminals feel stifled and trapped, viewing crime and sometimes even violence as the only means of escape from that straightjacket. In many ways their existence is a chain reaction, which can only end in their death or imprisonment for life.

Men and women like this don't need to stub their toe to react. They are constantly on tenterhooks, prepared to hit back at society because they don't feel they owe it anything. They never see themselves as being in the wrong and if they did say 'sorry', it would be an unnatural response in a moment of weakness, which they'd later regret.

For gangsters truly are the strangers among us, never one of us. Many labels have been hung on them over the years but they don't tell half the story. Yes, they are often rebels and psychopaths: two shorthand symbols for a state of mind which is hate. Freud said that if a baby had power it would destroy the world from the frustration of its infantile desires. In some ways, criminals represent that baby, who quite simply never grew up. That's why they feel so superior to everyone around them.

When gangsters are at the height of their criminal prowess, the rules of the game are constantly challenged. Yet young criminals need rules to ensure their lives have some meaning. Their aggressive instincts are undoubtedly born out of sheer frustration with the world. It all seems so meaningless to them. There's that feeling of hopeless drifting. Their crimes bring them previously unimagined wealth. Yet they also commit some offences – like stealing cars or shoplifting – purely for the thrill. But even in this environment there is a criminal structure emerging. Codes and rank within a gang are obeyed to the letter. This is also a classic example of youths seeking a purposeful group identity.

So the young criminals, like so many before and since, react partly against their own feelings of inadequacy. They are basically self destructive because their life has no real purpose, despite often loving their wives and children and remaining married their entire adult life. Throwing them into prison does little to stem the problem. For gangsters are intrinsically lacking in the normal psychological vitamins. Their entire life is an act of hunger. To treat them properly would require a proper examination of their development, which is partly what I've tried to do in this book. Punishment, to a true gangster, is no more worthwhile than caging an animal demented by hunger and expecting it to simply reform. The kind of hunger these characters often suffered simply breeds a terrible hatred that feeds on itself.

Many of the old-time gangsters would rather take with them to their graves the secrets of their biggest crimes. Some cash-in through biographical films and books, but the really powerful ones don't usually give much away. Its all part of a deeply rooted criminal philosophy developed while many of them were youths on the streets of London. 'Never tell the police a thing. Never give an inch.'

Whatever the full extent of their power and influence over London life, these old-school criminals revel in their image as participants in 'romantic' crimes. They want to prove that crime really does pay. The big-time gangsters of today work more like a business syndicate, although most of them are perfectly willing to squeeze the trigger if required.

The old-timers used to love pitting their wits against Scotland Yard and its worldwide reputation for skill and dogged determination. They always knew they had one big advantage over the long arm of the law: the police have to work within certain rules and regulations. Criminals, on the other hand, can do whatever they want. For these legendary characters, violence was their raison d'être. They'd grown up in gangs where a fight was the natural means to settle a dispute, and they could never truly appreciate the middle class's abhorrence of violence.

Since the Great Train Robbery in 1963, many Met officers have been thrown out of the force for corruption, having fabricated evidence or dropped charges in exchange for cash. A lot of this overt corruption convinced many London criminals back then that their own crimes weren't so bad. Yet throughout their lives these old-time villains showed total repugnance for the rules and formalities of the modern state – driving licences, permits, paying taxes, passports, car insurance, even National Insurance Stamps.

In some ways the new crop of London street gangsters from all over the world see themselves as the shock troops of the militant poor. That's why they often fall out with their own parents, who, quite simply, do not understand where their children are coming

from. Young and old criminals see obedience to the law and collaboration with the police as a betrayal of their own people, which would mean losing all self-respect. Their obsession with money is fuelled by a desire for the better things in life: freedom, comfort, cleanliness, light, privacy and respect. But the good life that they so desperately crave is never going to be paved with gold.

Violence is explained away as being 'part of the game' or it's 'what has to be done'. Yet the evil that so many thought is endemic in gangsters can be found in any of us and has little to do with the law of the land. There has always been a tendency to look back at a 'golden era' of crime, as if there was once a magical time when no one got hurt, crooks only attacked other crooks, and a strict code of honour ruled.

But times have changed and the extent of crime in today's London suggests that at some time in the future it will explode like an uncontrollable timebomb.

FURTHER READING

My own books, which have provided endless details, include *Moody*, *Public Enemy Number One*, *Killing Charlie*, *Gangsters*, *Hit 'Em Hard* and *Bindon*.

Other books that have proved invaluable include:

Gangland (1992) by J. Morton, Warner

That was Business, This is Personal (1990) by D. Campbell, Secker and Warburg

Making Crime Pay (1945) by P. Cheyney, Faber and Faber

Boss of Bosses (1955) by W. Hill, Naldrett Press

Our Story (1988) by Ron and Reg Kray, Pan

Inside The Firm (1991) by Tony Lambrianou, John Blake Publishing

Mammoth Book of True Crime (1996) by C. Wilson, Robinson

Essex Boys (2001) by B. O'Mahoney, Mainstream

Inside the CID (1957) by P. Beveridge, Evans Brothers

Cherrill of the Yard (1953) by F. Cherrill, Harrap

London after Dark (1954) by R. Fabian, Naldrett Pres

War on the Underworld (1960) by E. Greeno, John Long

Jack Spot, Man of a Thousand Cuts (1959) by H. Janson, Alexander Moring

Soho (1956) by A. Tietjen, Allan Wingate

Deadline for Crime (1955) by D. Webb, Muller

Crime Reporter (1956) by D. Webb, Fleetway

Mad Frankie (1994) by F. Fraser with J. Morton, Warner

The Underworld (1953) by J. Phelan. Harrap

Cloak without Dagger (1956) by P. Sillitoe, Pan Books
Nipper by L. Read with J. Morton
Born Fighter (1990) by R. Kray, Arrow
Smash 'n' Grab (1993) by R. Murphy, Faber and Faber
The Profession of Violence (1972) by J. Pearson, HarperCollins
Mad Frank's Diary (2000) by F. Fraser and J. Morton, Virgin
Elephant Boys (2000) by B. McDonald, Mainstream
Tough Guys Don't Cry (1983) by J. Cannon, Magnus Books

NOW YOU CAN BUY ANY OF THESE OTHER BOOKS BY WENSLEY CLARKSON FROM YOUR BOOKSHOP OR DIRECT FROM THE PUBLISHER.

Free P+P and UK Delivery (Abroad £3.00 per book)

Gangs of Britain
ISBN 978-1-84454-518-6   PB   £7.99

Kenny Noye – Public Enemy Number 1
ISBN 978-1-84454-193-5   PB   £6.99

The Railway Killer
ISBN 978-1-84454-323-6   PB   £6.99

Devil Woman
ISBN 978-1-84454-023-5   PB   £6.99

Romeo Killer
ISBN 978-1-84454-041-9   PB   £6.99

The Devil's Work
ISBN 978-1-90403-493-3   PB   £6.99

Evil Beyond Belief
ISBN 978-1-90403-446-9   PB   £6.99

Wolf Man
ISNM 978-1-84454-504-9   PB   £7.99

Mel Gibson – Man on a Mission
ISBN 978-1-85782-577-0   PB   £7.99

The Boss
ISBN 978-1-85782-550-3   PB   £5.99

Gang Wars on the Costa
ISBN 978-1-84454-808-8   PB   £11.99

Little Survivors
ISBN 978-1-84454-853-8   PB   £6.99

TO ORDER SIMPLY CALL THIS NUMBER
+ 44 (0) 207 381 0666

Or visit our website www.johnblakepublishing.co.uk

Prices and availability subject to change without notice

HELL HATH NO FURY LIKE A WOMAN SCORNED

Wensley Clarkson

Investigative reporter Wensley Clarkson has spent years researching the most extreme and intriguing cases of women who commit murder. His books on the subject have sold across the world in there tens of thousands. *Hell Hath No Fury Like a Woman Scorned* is a gripping collection of twenty of Clarkson's most thrilling true stories.

These are the tales of women who challenge our idea of what we still, mistakenly, often think of as the weaker sex. Their characters and backgrounds are as diverse as they are deadly, and their crimes are every bit as shocking as any of their male counterparts'.

From the case of the beautiful Diana Perry, who suffered years of abuse at the hands of her husband before taking the matter into her own hands, to bobby, a woman whose gruesome interest in blood led to one of the most horrific seduction killings ever seen, this book tells the chilling stories of women who kill, and examines exactly what triggers their murderous intent. The astonishing truth lies within these pages...

ISBN 978-1-84454-847-7

John Blake Publishing Ltd

THE MOTHER
FROM HELL

Wensley Clarkson

'Billy Bob doused his sister with gasoline. His mother watched as he lit a match, dropped it on the pyre and ran back to the car. "If you ever tell anyone about this, you're going to be next," she told him.'

To friends and neighbours, dark-haired Theresa Knorr was a devoted mother struggling to bring up five children on her own. Yet she had secretly become so insanely jealous of her daughters' growing beauty that she arranged terrible deaths for two of them.

The surviving daughter told police Theresa had ordered her own sons to drug, torture and then burn alive one girl. She had also starved the other sister to death. At first the police found the story so grotesque that they refused to believe it was true. But evidence continued to mount and, after some five years, Theresa was finally charged with being the executioner of her own children.

ISBN 978-1-84454-855-9

Blake True Crime Library